FORTY YEARS OF A SPORTSMAN'S LIFE

BY

SIR CLAUDE CHAMPION DE CRESPIGNY

BART

ILLUSTRATED

MILLS & BOON, LIMITED

49 RUPERT STREET

LONDON, W

PREFACE

SOME fourteen years ago I published a volume of memoirs, in the compiling of which I had the kind assistance of the Duke of Beaufort and Mr. G. A. B. Dewar. It having been suggested to me that I have run through a good many experiences since then, I have been tempted to venture into print once more, and the result is the present volume. A portion of the former book, which deals with my earlier experiences, has naturally been retained, but, with the assistance of Mr. Harold Simpson, it has been thoroughly revised and brought up to date, and I have added another fourteen years of sport and adventure by land, sea, and air. If any apology is needed, I offer it here.

C. DE C.

CONTENTS

CONTENTS

FORTY YEARS OF A SPORTSMAN'S LIFE

CHAPTER I

MY SPORTING CAREER BEGINS

THOUGH my early sailoring days can perhaps hardly be said to be part and parcel of my " forty years " of life as a sportsman, I should like to record the fact that I did actually begin my career in the Navy ; and there are a few incidents in connection with those times which may not be without interest to the rising generation of sailors.

My first ship was the now obsolete *Warrior*. I went on board her in 1862, when she made her first trip across the Bay of Biscay, and it is worthy of mention that she was the first ironclad that ever went to sea. Cochrane was the captain of the ship, and Tryon, whose tragic but splendid end on the *Victoria* must long remain fresh in the public memory, the commander. Even at that early period in his career Tryon was thought very highly of, and marked out for certain and speedy promotion.

From the *Warrior* I was presently transferred to the *Edgar*, a two-decker, carrying the flag of Admiral

1

Sir S. C. Dacres. We hung awhile about the West
Indies, then on to Halifax, avoiding Bermuda as we
had yellow fever on board.

Whilst cruising about the North American station,
our headquarters being Halifax, we saw a little, and
heard more, of blockaders and blockade runners.
There were some smart devices practised on more
than one occasion by the runners in order to get their
cargoes in. One of the cleverest tricks I can recollect
took place at Charlestown Harbour. A little runner
wanted to unload the cargo, composed of quinine,
etc., she had on board. To do this she would have
to pass a line of watchful blockaders, an apparently
impossible task. One of the blockaders on her star-
board bow, suspecting mischief, showed a red light,
and the runner at once popped a shot into the same.
At the same time the blockader on her port bow
showed a blue light. She treated that in the same
style, and then steamed between the two blockaders,
leaving them firing at one another.

At another time a runner was desperately anxious
to pass a blockader at, I think, Saint Thomas's.
Now the blockader was not able to tackle the runner
in the harbour, as it was under British protection ;
but directly the runner moved the blockader would
of course pursue, and presently attack her. The
captain of the runner, being in these difficult straits,
asked the captain of one of our ships what he had
better do to evade the blockader. The advice was to
burn some damp hay which was on board the runner,
and so pretend to be getting up steam for a start.
This was done, and the blockader promptly began
to burn coal. Presently her supplies ran short, and

she had to send a boat ashore to get some more. Instantly the runner departed on her way, rejoicing at this completely successful ruse. The blockader gave chase, but had to stop steaming before she was hull down.

The Northerners were very eager to receive efficient seamen gunners, and not a little difficulty was experienced in keeping our men from deserting, as the pay and bonus offered were most tempting. A good many men did succeed in getting away and joining the American naval force.

I allowed my men occasionally to go ashore, on the understanding that they would not overstay the short time allowed them, and would refrain from taking a glass too much. Once one of them came back obviously the worse for drink. I pointed out that he would be the means of getting me into trouble. The other men were furious at his conduct, and asked to be allowed to settle him themselves. I never inquired what course they took, but had a very shrewd suspicion that he got something like four dozen.

The late King Edward, then Prince of Wales, had a narrow escape of being killed when he came on board the *Sultan*, on which ship I was at that time a visitor, to lunch, and to see afterwards the working of a new gun.

With one or two other people I was standing by, a spectator of the incident. The Prince had been watching the working of the gun, and just as he turned round to ask some question of Captain Vansittart concerning the cost of each discharge, the windlass took charge, and the handle flying round with frightful velocity only just missed his Royal Highness's head. If he had been a foot nearer it is not conceivable that he could have escaped. He must have been killed on the spot.

This took place in Portland Harbour. There was a very nasty sea on at the time ; but it did not deter the Prince from going the round of several other vessels lying near by. He was anxious not to hurt the feelings of the other officers, and so put himself to this considerable discomfort. Verily the lines of royalty are not always laid in pleasant places.

I recollect meeting Lord Charles Beresford on this occasion on board the *Sultan*. When he saw me he cried out, what was I doing there ? He thought I had left the Navy for good. I told him I had joined the *Sultan* in the capacity of Chaplain and Naval Instructor. " Good Lord ! " exclaimed Charley, who is always ready with a reply, " why didn't you join as Ship's Cook ? You'd at any rate have got more to eat that way."

Charley Beresford, though full of good nature, is bad to rub up the wrong way. Once he was driving a drag with several ladies in it home from some races —I forget where. Two or three offensive fellows in a dog-cart shot peas at the ladies. Charley bided his time. Presently it came. He managed very skilfully to lock the wheel of his coach in that of the dog-cart. Then, sublimely regardless of remonstrances, he bore doggedly to the right till the dogcart was precipitated with its occupants into a deep ditch. Charley drove on as though nothing had happened.

Beresford and myself, I may explain, had been

fellow cadets a good few years before this incident. We were on the training ship *Britannia* together in the beginning of the Sixties. I cannot say that in those days our now perhaps foremost and certainly widely popular sailor gave any clear indications of the greatness which he was to attain to by-and-by. But I do recollect that he was then, as always, a spirited and plucky fellow. Like Marcus, and myself too, I rather fancy he has been in—well, in two or three " mills " since those days !

It is over forty years since I rode and won my first steeplechase.

Looking back across the vista of years, I really begin to think that I must be getting an old fogey. The fingers of one hand are more than enough to reckon up the cross-country men, amateur and professional, who were riding with me then and who are riding now. Nor is this astonishing when one considers that the steeplechasing careers of most men are compressed into about half a dozen years. Few jockeys, at any rate, either on the flat or across country, beginning like myself at twenty, have ridden after their fortieth year ; and fewer still looked forward in their sixty-fourth year to riding and winning a few more good races on any mount and over any course within the next two or three seasons. Though often taking exception to my luck in various matters, I must say that the fates have been very lenient to me in regard to steeplechasing. Only I wish I had not been denied winning the Grand National. Once or twice I have seemed within measurable distance of success, and each time have been foiled through an unexpected mishap.

Perhaps the first thing which it occurs to any man at all conversant with horse-racing to ask, when he hears that you have been riding for getting on towards half a century, is "How on earth have you done it?" The question has been put to me many scores of times within the last few years. People who are acquainted with my racing career are sometimes more puzzled at the way in which I have continued to ride than those who know little about the noble sport of steeplechasing. They know that I accept mounts which I may never have seen or heard of before, and often at the shortest notice; and also that I am willing, as a rule, to ride in all weathers. That any man can keep up this kind of thing for nearly half a century seems scarcely credible even to those who are perfectly aware that it is being done.

I attribute my success in being able to ride for such a great length of time without getting knocked up, almost entirely to the fact that I have always kept myself at all seasons of the year in condition.

By constantly keeping myself in training, and "hard as nails," I have been enabled not only to ride into my sixty-fourth year, but also to shake off the effects of ugly-looking mishaps in what has appeared a phenomenally short time. In ballooning accidents too I have found the same thing obtains. An ordinary accident on the racecourse or elsewhere is to my mind serious or the reverse in proportion as the body is in perfect condition or otherwise.

How many more lives a jockey may be expected to have than a man out of training seemed to me admirably expressed by a doctor on a racecourse not long since. He had been attending a rider who had just had a nasty-looking spill. Said a spectator, " I suppose he will die ? " " Oh dear, no," was the reply ; " he's a jockey."

My first steeplechase was the South of Ireland Military in the spring of 1867. I was serving at the time with my regiment, the 60th, which was quartered in the south of Ireland, and helping to suppress the Fenian outbreak. These steeplechases were organized by the 12th Lancers, then commanded by that famous old soldier Colonel Oakes, and a rather droll incident in connection with them is worth recalling. I was walking with one of the officers of the 12th shortly before the day of the steeplechasing, when a man came up and thanked us for the pleasure which he had derived from seeing the horses run. " A capital day's sport," was his verdict. My companion was mystified. The steeplechasing, he objected, had not yet taken place. It then transpired that the regimental grooms and servants had taken all the horses of the 12th out on the preceding day, and tried them over the course at the distances they would have to run, and at the weights they would have to carry—a bit of enterprise which has probably never been eclipsed by those who lay themselves out to make money by backing horses. I don't know whether the bookmakers got wind of this extraordinary proceeding ; if they didn't, it is at least conceivable that they had rather a bad time when the actual steeplechasing came off !

The race, however, in which I had a mount, and enjoyed my first triumph, could not have been gauged by the regimental grooms as nicely as one or two of the others. My mount—Maid of the Mist—was not available for these trials, as I was looking after her myself. Maid of the Mist, so called because she was one of three up in a celebrated run in Leicestershire on a misty day, belonged to Major Watts Russell. I was my own trainer, as I have often been since, and the day before the race went carefully over the course. To neglect this precaution is to show oneself deficient in the A B C of riding, whether on the flat or across country. George Fordham used to attach the greatest importance to it, and so do many other leading jockeys of the present time. It is scarcely too much to say, that a rider who thoroughly knows his course enjoys as great an advantage over those who are ignorant of it, as does a billiard-player who knows the table when pitted against one who has never played a hundred up on it before. A jockey should endeavour to sound his course, and find out its strong and weak spots, as a careful batsman or bowler does his pitch. In some of the rougher and more rotten courses I have spent many an hour in searching for a sheep-track, and where the search has been successful, have been materially assisted by sticking to it as much as possible during the race. " A Mad Rider " is the title with which I have been honoured many and many a time. Possibly, if the title be deserved, in this habit of carefully examining my ground lies the method of my madness. It may be added, that in flat racing also it is desirable to avoid rotten places, and this can only be done by examining the course very carefully before the race.

Maid of the Mist started about a hundred to one

"BAY" MIDDLETON.

against, so that my first mount was a decidedly "dark horse." It was not thought that she would negotiate the stone walls, to which she was strange, and moreover, there was no particular reason to feel great confidence in her rider. But I knew my ground and my mount, and so started with high hopes. My most dangerous opponent was none other than "Bay" Middleton, whose death some years back was the cause of such sincere regret to a wide circle of friends and admirers. "Bay" made a fatal mistake in the race, which I pointed out to him afterwards. He took it out of his horse over a bit of nasty boggy ground. Noting this, I let him forge twenty or perhaps thirty lengths ahead till the swamp was passed : then overtook him, and won by a length. Very few people can say that they ever beat "Bay" Middleton through any blunder of his in horsemanship. As all the world knows, he was one of the most accomplished horsemen of his day, specially excelling perhaps in the hunting-field.

"Bay" was a man who rarely threw away a race through carelessness. I recollect an amusing "squeak" which occurred early in his racing career, and which may have proved of after-service to him. He was riding on a course near Macroom, when everything connected with steeplechasing was of course much more roughly done than nowadays. The carriage from which we were watching the race was drawn up by a post some little distance from the judge's box, and when "Bay" passed us, being then about three-quarters of a length to the good, he stopped riding, and Jack Gubbins went on persevering to the winning-post a few lengths further on, but couldn't quite get up. I yelled out to "Bay" to go on, but even as a cornet his hearing was not over-good, and I might as well have shouted to his brow-band. After he had weighed in, and the "All right!" announced, I got him by the arm and said, "Old man, you drew that a bit fine!" "Not a bit of it," replied he; "why, it must have been a good three-quarter length." "Where did you finish?" I queried. "Why *there*, of course," he answered, pointing to where he had stopped riding. "I know you did, but do you see what it is?" "Oh, by Jove!" he cried out, amazed; "why, it's a telegraph post!"

"Bay" had one serious fault as a rider. He almost invariably spurred his horse in the shoulder, being apparently unable to sit his horse without turning his toes out. He ought not to have had any rowels. Many people must have noticed the condition of some of his mounts after a hard race or run, and indeed a friend once remarked to me of a horse that had been spurred in this manner by some rider or other, that it looked as if it had been ridden by "Bay" Middleton.

Watts Russell sold Maid of the Mist after this win for double the sum he had paid for her not long before the race. He himself lost his life some years afterwards in a race at Cawnpore, which a horse of mine named Rockwood won. The South of Ireland Military is the only steeplechase in which I have ever ridden in the distressful country. The fact was, we were in the midst of the Fenian rebellion, and had therefore little time for sport. I left for India moreover shortly afterwards with my regiment.

Cawnpore was a fatal spot for poor Watts Russell. On one occasion he fell in a steeplechase there, and had concussion of the brain, which compelled him to come home to England on sick leave. Then on another occasion he dislocated his knee-cap after he had returned thither from England. Finally, riding far sooner than he ought to have done after this accident, he met by his death on the same course. His horse went sideways, he had no strength to keep it straight, lost all control, and came by his end. I am not particularly superstitious, but an extraordinary fatality does seem to pursue some people in connection with certain places and times.

I have referred to Colonel Oakes as the famous soldier who commanded the 12th in those days. He made it the smartest of cavalry regiments, though, curiously enough, he himself was the shabbiest and most slouching of officers. There never was a tougher old soldier than Oakes, and in my opinion he was far and away, Baker perhaps excepted, the best cavalry officer of his day ; in fact one is sometimes inclined to think that he and Baker have never been equalled. On one occasion Oakes incurred the momentary displeasure of an illustrious Duke, who called him a fool (with an epithet before it) on parade. Afterwards the Duke generously withdrew the words. " Oh," replied Oakes, " I don't mind, sir, your calling me a d—d fool ; only I don't like being called a d—d fool before all those other d—d fools," pointing to the Staff.

At another time the same soldier, coming to see the 12th Lancers at their dinners, found them, to his great surprise, in their shirt-sleeves. He asked for an explanation, and Oakes replied, " You didn't suppose, sir, I was going to tell my men you were coming down to-day! If I had they would have been in a shilly-shallying funk, and would have devoted their time to their accoutrements instead of their horses. Now, sir, you see us as we are every day of our lives."

The Fenians were for the most part cowardly brutes. A favourite Fenian method of attack and defence was to put the women in front and then fling stones at the military over their heads. But they were not a great deal more cowardly than some of the magistrates before whom they were dragged, often enough red-handed. The latter were afraid to do anything in cases where the guilt of the rebels was perfectly manifest. In one instance at Macroom several Fenians came out of court smiling triumphantly over their acquittal. Oakes quite by himself waited outside. The escape of these rebels would have exasperated him at any time, but their insolent mien was altogether too much for the old soldier. So he assisted each of them, as he issued from the court, with a good kick, growling out, " There's something for you to remember old Oakes by ! "

Oakes was a rare campaigner : no sybarite he. Once he growled out in reply to the question, " Have you breakfasted ? " " Yes, I've had my three pipes of shag ; that's my breakfast to-day." It was smoking, I have heard, that had much to do with his fatal illness.

As may be imagined, my short but sweet experience in Ireland greatly whetted my appetite for

steeplechasing, and upon arrival in India I soon
settled down to ride in earnest.   Unfortunately that
" eternal want of pence," which, according to the
poet, " vexes public men," militated a good deal
against me, as I had at the time little more than
my bare pay as an ensign in the Rifles.   Yet I
managed by hook or by crook to get a good many
mounts, and to win a fair number of races.   I never
picked and chose, but rode any mortal thing that
came to hand, and this rule I have followed ever
since.

It is hard to revert to my steeplechasing experiences in India without gleefully calling to mind two
humorous incidents which can scarcely fail to appeal
to people who attend race-meetings regularly in
England, where all the proceedings are transacted
in such a dignified and highly respectable manner.
The judges had not in those days in India the nice
appliances which, even in the case of a very close
finish, make decisions comparatively simple in this
country.   As a consequence, Eastern racing verdicts
used to be at times—well, rather unreliable.   Moreover, the judges themselves were not up to our standard at home, being often selected from purely social
considerations.   It occasionally happened that the
judge would form his decision on the advice of outsiders or even on some faint popular demonstration.
Racing one afternoon at Lucknow in 1869, in a very
bad light, I agreed with my opponent to have a little
fun at the expense of the judge.   I won the race by
half a length, but on retiring to weigh in addressed
my opponent as the winner, which so embarrassed
the judge that he ordered the race to be run off next

day. This was done, and I again won. Imagine such a thing occurring in this country.

There was another occasion at Cawnpore, when the judge was obviously on the point of giving a wrong verdict. Fortunately a friend of the real winner was standing hard by. Quick as thought he realized the position, and shouted out the right name in congratulatory tones. The judge, who had been somewhat confused by conversation with a spectator just as the horses were coming in, heard these words of congratulation, and promptly altered his opinion and decision. Nobody was more puzzled than the winner—myself—when my 'cute friend came up and said, " *I* won that race for you, old man ! "

In India almost anything was deemed good enough for steeplechasing. How the critical crowd at Sandown or Kempton would shake with laughter could they only see a dozen horses, such as we had often to ride in India, turn out on either of these courses. There were five breeds—first the country-bred, secondly the Arab, thirdly the " Walers," fourthly the Cape horses, and fifthly the English-bred. The last-named were few and far between. They were mostly brought over by a few wealthy civilians who were keen on sport. Naturally in handicaps, and weight for age and class races, there was often a great diversity in the weights. The English horses, though they did not as a rule stand the heat so well as any of the other breeds, were when " fit " *facile princeps*, and it was therefore quite common to find them conceding not pounds, but stones, to the Arabs and natives. The " Walers "—so called because they came from New South Wales—were on the whole the most useful horses for Indian steeplechasing. They stood the climate capitally.

I left for India in the autumn of 1867 and returned in the spring of 1870, so that in all—though I commenced riding directly I arrived there, and did not draw rein till it was time to come back—I had only about two seasons of steeplechasing and flat racing. The biggest thing I rode in and won was the Cawnpore Steeplechase on February 27, 1869. It could have been fairly described in those days as the Liverpool of India. The course was a four-mile one, and the jumps on the whole about as stiff as they make them in any part of the world ; there were no regulation fences or ditches then, and we should as soon have looked for a nicely levelled take-off as for a straw-covered course.

To win me this race I bought a mare called Baby Blake for a mere bagatelle. Baby Blake was a superb jumper when she did jump, but she usually fell some time in a race. Indeed so invariable was this habit of Baby Blake's, that even money was laid that she would fall. Her temper was so uncertain, that rumour had it she must always be trained by moonlight. However, I did not take much note of these tales against my purchase, but trained her myself in broad daylight, cantering for miles in the jungle. She started, despite her well-known jumping powers, an outsider. I secured the mare, by the way, by the merest chance, and indeed went to Cawnpore with the idea of riding another horse. It turned out a regular brute, with an action like a dromedary's, and fortunately went lame in its trial. I was then offered Baby Blake.

Amongst many Indian experiences, which, alas! have so long since become "portions and parcels of the dreadful past," recalled not without a wrestle with the memory, this Cawnpore race stands out clear. I can remember with ease every incident of the race. The third fence, composed of a couple of high mud walls as hard as rocks, and in and out of a road, was the stiffest in the course. The whole field with one exception refused. Baby Blake alone cleared the fence, and that gave me a commanding lead which I never lost. She won by half a length, thanks in no small degree to a gallant sowar, who prevented me just in time from getting off the course. In this steeplechase I was fortunate enough to beat several of the best jockeys of the day in India, including a professional rider, who came in second on Happy Boy, and had been backed for a good deal of money.

By a curious chance odds of 100 to 1 were offered against Baby Blake during the race, as they were against Maid of the Mist in the South of Ireland Military before the race. It fell about in this way. One of the jockeys—my friend St. Quentin—was wearing colours very similar to mine. At the second fence his horse fell; whereupon there were bets freely offered of 100 to 1 against Baby Blake. One astute party, by the aid of a particularly good pair of field-glasses, perceived the error which the layers of odds had fallen into. He instantly snapped up the long odds, and made a small fortune out of my win.

The mare, though a very excitable one, was a beautiful fencer when she chose. Whilst I had her, and before I had her, she never lost a race when she did not fall. I recollect once making a "double" like that at Punchestown. She simply flew it. The last I heard of Baby Blake was just before embarking at Bombay for England. She had then very recently won the Lucknow Steeplechase.

A few days after the race at Cawnpore there was a big event at Meerut, and Baby Blake would have probably won that as well had it not been for her queer temper. No one had ever got a spear off her back, and as this was a *sine qua non* in the race in question, she could not qualify for it. As I have already said, I missed no opportunity of riding in India. The majority of the horses I rode, both steeplechasing and on the flat, belonged to friends. Flat racing has never been exactly my *métier*, and, frankly, I consider it a much tamer sport on the whole than steeplechasing. At the same time I have now and then ridden on the flat in England, and frequently did so in India. One of the best horses I owned in India was Rockwood, which I bought from Colonel Robartes. Rockwood was certainly very speedy, far above the Indian average.

The most sensational race I have ever won in my opinion, either at home or abroad, was on Rockwood, the occasion being the First Class Handicap at Lucknow in 1869, the queer ending of which has been referred to. I trained Rockwood, who was, like Baby Blake, a " Waler," on a right-handed course, and had to run him at Lucknow on a left-handed one. As a consequence he went clean out of the course. It was quite a business getting his head straight, and I recollect considering whether it was the slightest good to continue the race. Resolving to have a try, though it seemed quite hopeless, I got

2

Rockwood back, started in pursuit of the rest, and eventually won by half a head. I was top weight—11 st. 7 lbs.—but the time for the mile was 1 minute 57 seconds, a remarkable achievement considering the conduct of my mount.

It is scarcely necessary to say, that none of the jockeys against whom I was pitted in India are riding to-day. One, however, who was riding at that time in India is still well to the fore in the English racing world—Lord Marcus Beresford. The best soldier-rider in India at the end of the Sixties was probably " Ben " Roberts. Most racing men know " Ben " well enough by sight at race meetings near town at the present time, where he attends in his official capacity as an officer of the Metropolitan Police. Many too know him as a good fellow and a first-rate sportsman. In India " Ben " on his favourite mount Tomboy was always dangerous. Good judges never overlaid their book against that pair.

Amongst other prominent riders of the day in India were Jousiffe, Dignum, and Captain Soames. Of these Dignum was quite the foremost, and indeed the best at that time in India on the flat. He was one of the few men who could sit a regular buck-jumper such as occasionally turned up amongst the " Walers." Without bursting the girths some of these animals could slip the saddle off clean over their heads.

In his Indian days Jousiffe could waste to under 9 st. The last time I saw him in England some years back he could scarcely have scaled less than eighteen. He is dead now, poor fellow !

Captain Joy and Lord Marcus Beresford ran a stud between them, and were pretty successful on the flat. To meet Marcus is rightly deemed a pleasure by all save those who are unfortunate enough to come into contact with his fists. But perhaps few people have ever derived such pleasure out of a meeting with him as I did one burning day in 1870. My brother and I had arranged to meet Marcus on that day on the road to Bombay, where his regiment was on the march, and we started by the railway from Allahabad. The line was not at the time quite completed, so we arranged to finish our journey on horseback. But before long my brother's horse dropped from sunstroke, and we were therefore compelled to ride mine in turns. In order to economize time we did it in this way : first I would ride a mile, then tie up my horse and walk on till my brother, now mounted, overtook me ; then I would again ride whilst he followed on foot. In this way we got along at the very respectable rate of about six miles an hour. Marcus saw us coming, and started out to meet us with a flagon of delicious iced drink—an angel he seemed in earthly guise !

In both '68 and '69 we had the cholera with a vengeance in India. Thanks to a good constitution, I was able myself, while others were constantly getting invalided off to the hills, to face the demon with impunity, and both years—without once taking a week's leave—saw the epidemic run its ghastly course. In sticking to my post, however, it may be admitted that I had to a certain extent an eye to business. An officer who managed to see the cholera through in this way might fairly reckon on getting leave later on for racing purposes. In one instance, during the cholera visitation in 1869, I actually had to do duty as chaplain, as the individual who ordinarily filled that post had, in common with most of the officers, made himself scarce for a while. On another occasion I was the acting adjutant and orderly officer. My colonel scolded me severely for coming out during the most deadly hours of the day, and remarked half seriously and half jocularly, "I shall put you under arrest, sir, if you do it again." Whereupon I pointed out as a deterrent, that I was the only officer fit for duty. "Well," said he discreetly, "then I won't do so."

Shortly after this 1869 visitation of the cholera I asked for leave in order to get away from Seetapore, where we were quartered, and take part in the races at Sonepore. I accordingly asked my colonel for a week's extension of my leave; he quite approved, but had not the authority to give it. The general officer in command, namely, General Brooke Taylor, was the person who possessed the requisite authority. As it happened he was away tiger-shooting, and his place filled by a man who evidently burned to make his temporary power felt. The substitute promptly refused the necessary permission. I wired to my colonel to know whether leave had been granted. The reply came that it was refused. Regarding this as very shabby treatment after the way in which I had stuck to my post during the cholera, I felt justified in mistaking the tenor of the telegram, and wired back thanks. I was just beginning to enjoy the leave of absence that had not been granted, when a fresh message arrived couched in a rather peremptory tone, and very reluctantly I had to return. Afterwards, when I mentioned the way in which I had been treated to General Brooke Taylor, he very handsomely expressed his regret, and declared that had he been at his post he would have granted the request himself without a moment's hesitation. Nevertheless the thing made me very sore, and, combined with the infamous terms of my father's will, had a good deal to do with my resolve, carried out a short time afterwards, to quit the service.

My position at Lucknow on my way back from Sonepore was rather humorous in a way when I was in correspondence about my leave of absence. The Brigade Major urged me not to go on the course whatever I did, lest the General should put me under arrest ; and at the very same time an officer high in command sent me the message, " For goodness' sake don't show yourself on the course, for if you do the Brigade Major will put you under arrest ! " As I could not ride a horse of my own at Sonepore I asked a friend to do so, and drove up in a closed conveyance to see him, so I fondly hoped, win the race. Instead I saw my horse bolt off, and disappear at length like a speck on the horizon.

Once I ordered a breakfast against the Lahore Races which cost £6000. So at any rate declared so well-informed an organ as the *Gaulois*. The same paper volunteered the information that I was " worth millions of money," though content to occupy " the modest rank of an officer in the British Army." The breakfast included in the way of drinkables " eighty dozen bottles of champagne, eight hundred bottles of Bordeaux, eight hundred bottles of Burgundy," besides brandy *ad lib.* To cap this extraordinary tale I actually, according to the same authority, paid the bill ! The real facts about the " breakfast " were these. It was a picnic at Seetapore, at which about a dozen friends were present. After we had finished it was the bandsmen's turn. They certainly did themselves handsomely, drinking liqueur out of the finger-glasses. Afterwards the music they played was wild and wandering.

In lieu of big game shooting and pig-sticking, which were rather too costly forms of amusement for me to combine with racing and chasing, I took very kindly to snipe-shooting. " Joe," *alias* Arthur Bagot of ours, was very keen on this sport, and between us we perhaps accounted for as many snipe as most guns in India during the two seasons we were shooting. We got to fancy ourselves so much that we challenged any two officers in the regiment to back their breech- against our muzzle-loaders. But the challenge was not taken up.

Another of my companions out sniping was Captain Thackwell of the 5th Lancers, a very popular soldier in India in those days. Well, I recollect a friendly little bet Thackwell and I once had as to who would make the best bag in the day. We had actually tied when daylight failed ; but on our way home in the dusk Thackwell by a piece of good luck got an unexpected shot, and knocked over his snipe. A kite swooped down and picked it up. Thackwell, who was unloaded, thought he alone had twigged what the bird of prey had done on my behalf. He slyly tried to say very casually, " I say, tickle up that kite, old fellow," but his anxiety was obvious

enough. " Very well," said I, suiting my action to
his word ; " but of course the snipe will go to my
bag," to which he could not very well demur.   Poor
chap, he was killed by a tiger a few days after, or
rather died from the shock of an operation which
had to be performed on him, owing to the terrible
way in which he had been mauled in the jungle.

In the old *Oriental Sporting Magazine* I came across
the following, written evidently by one of his great
friends—" Killed by a Tiger. In a foreign land
far from his own country and his own people, but not
from his friends, for he had many, died yesterday
morning at Baraitch in Oude, from wounds inflicted
by a tiger, Captain F. I. R. Thackwell, H.M.'s 5th
Lancers—one of the finest of soldiers, a true-hearted
English gentleman, and as thorough a sportsman as
ever lived.   The regiment can ill afford to lose such
an officer, and to us that knew him *such a friend.*
There are many far away in the old country who a
very few months ago were sharing with him in the wild
sports of India, who will not be ashamed to find
their eyes wet, when they read the sad account of the
death of one of the many good fellows whose resting-
place is in this distant land, so far from many but
not from all who loved him.   Lucknow, June 25,
1869."

In India too I had occasional opportunities for
pigeon shooting, a sport for which I had acquired
a decided taste in Ireland.   Shooting once in the
distressful country, I was successful in dividing a
good sweepstake with Colonel Chalmer, who then
commanded one of our battalions.   Much later on,
and long after my return to England from India,

I again tried my skill at pigeon shooting, and was rather successful in the Grand International at Brighton in 1886, though I had had no practice. At twenty-five, twenty-seven, and twenty-nine yards I killed all my birds except one. The last pigeon I shot fell just out of bounds, so I had to rest content with third prize ; Vaughan and Blake being respectively first and second. My pigeon shooting, however, has been decidedly spasmodic, and since then I don't think that I have killed a bird over a trap in any important contest.

The period during which I was stationed in India was a very interesting one from a military as well as a sporting point of view. In the end of the Sixties those three superb regiments, Probyn's Horse, Robartes' Horse, and Hodgson's Horse, were still in their prime. There are probably very few soldiers acquainted with those regiments who would declare that their disbandment—for such it practically was —worked wholly for the good of the service. Having seen more than a little of the regiments, and noted their unrivalled smartness and efficiency, I have never doubted that it was sheer folly to do anything but encourage the system. Colonel Robartes never took the trouble to keep exact accounts of what he spent on his regiment. He was a rich man, and his generosity in the patriotic work of making Robartes' Horse the first cavalry force in the world knew no bounds. When he was called upon to render an exact account, he could not do so, and he was therefore never repaid. It was no secret that the Government remained his debtor to an amount not far short of twenty thousand pounds.

Colonel—now Sir Dighton—Probyn was the ideal man for a regiment such as he actually commanded. There was a glamour about his achievements in the Indian Mutiny which appealed irresistibly to every one, and made him in particular the idol of his men. The single-handed combats against the leading mutineers in which he had often engaged, and being a splendid swordsman always successfully, had a spice of old-world romance about them that made him one of the most interesting figures in the military history of the time—quite a modern Bayard. The picture of Lord Cardigan, the " rigid Hussar," as Kinglake has finely called him, leading his men down the valley of death at Balaclava, which we have all drawn in imagination, is scarcely a more stirring one than that of this most distinguished officer coming forth from the ranks as a warrior of old, and challenging to personal combat the foeman most worthy of his steel. This it was that laid the solid foundations of Sir Dighton Probyn's fame.

In recalling these Indian experiences I have found myself at a considerable disadvantage, owing to the fact that my diaries were destroyed some time since, so I may frankly confess that no mention has been made of the particulars of a good many races which I won, simply because they are not obtainable. Before leaving India, however, I ought to say something about two of the most famous story-tellers— in the double sense—of that time. My memory certainly does not fail me in relation to Colonel Bagot —cousin to my friend Joe of that ilk—and Colonel Oakes, who must not be confused with the rough old leader of the 12th Lancers.

Both were in the Indian Army. Bagot was unquestionably a very fine shot at big game, but some
of his accounts of sport seemed a trifle over-coloured
even to the most credulous people. So much fun could
be got out of him that he was often invited to dinners,
etc., simply to amuse the company with his Mun-
chausen tales. Once he was asked to the Government House on the off-chance of his spinning some
exceptionally fine yarns : nor did he disappoint.
After the wine began to circulate Bagot got into great
form, and told one story which perhaps eclipsed
even Oakes' best efforts in the same field. He was
very anxious, he related, to secure a pair of fine
horns, and accordingly went out shooting. As good
luck would have it, he speedily came across two
magnificent stags, and shot them both. " Would
you believe it ? " said Bagot, " at the very moment
I dropped them right and left they shed their horns ! "

A story which has been told in many ways of
many people can be properly related in connection
with Bagot. He once boasted to a friend about an
exploit in snipe shooting, when he killed, so he said,
forty-nine birds in as many shots. " Why not make
it fifty while you are about it ? " inquired a cynical
listener. " Sir," quoth Bagot with befitting gravity,
" do you suppose I would risk my immortal soul for
the sake of a single snipe ? "

Bagot did not hide from the world how very
shabbily he had been treated by the powers that be.
During the Mutiny he had been put in command of
a body of cavalry with instructions to attack certain
villages. " By gad, sir, I carried out my instructions
splendidly," he would say ; " we killed an enormous

number of men, women, and children. Now, what
do you think they did for me after that ? '' His
hearers, usually knowing well enough, would artfully
run through a list of distinctions including the V.C.
As each one was mentioned Bagot would shake
his head vigorously.   Then at length, the guesser
having quite exhausted the list of possible distinctions, Bagot would declare in outraged tones, " Sir,
I give you my word of honour they tried me by
court-martial ! ''

Though a romancist, Bagot was a man of pluck
and resource.   Out tiger shooting, however, one day,
he seems to have made a grave mistake.   In the
company of a friend he followed a wounded tiger
into the jungle.   His friend, the present Lord Downe,
was suddenly attacked by the creature, and Bagot
came to the rescue.   Whereupon the tiger turned
its attention to him, and seizing his leg, snapped it.
Bagot's life, I believe, was saved by the head shikari,
who shot the beast as it mauled its victim.   The
rashness of following a wounded tiger into the jungle
has been commented on by several prominent big-
game shooters.   Captain Doig lost his life in this
manner in 1868, and Sir J. Dormer, Commander-in-
Chief at Madras, also followed a wounded animal,
and received wounds which killed him.   A man to
follow a tiger under such circumstances cannot watch
both front and flanks, which is obviously the work
of three men, and a disaster is therefore very likely
to take place.

Strange and sad was poor Bagot's end.   After
this encounter, and when invalided home, he swore
to return and have his revenge on the tigers.   He

did return, and set out into the jungle, taking with him two kinds of powders—arsenic for preparing the skins of the beasts he might shoot, and baking-powder for bread. He had not been out long before the servant confused the two powders, and the master took arsenic in his food by mistake.

The "hen-coop tale" has been told in connection with various men, but there is reason to believe that Bagot is the real hero of it. As Bagot told the story, he was wrecked in the Indian Ocean, and managed to save himself by clinging to a hen-coop. After a while he became quite at home on the hen-coop, and made for Aden. He met a steamer on the way thither, and the captain offered to take him on board. Bagot asked where the steamer was going to, and the reply was Bombay. "But I am going to Aden, thanks," said Bagot, "so I'm afraid I must decline your kind offer." Thus they parted, Bagot merely accepting the loan of a few biscuits and some ship's rum to keep him going till Aden was reached. Once when Bagot was telling this adventure of his he ended up with, "Good fellow that captain; I have never met him since." A naval man present thought he would take a rise out of him; so he cut in with, "Give me your hand, sir; I was that captain!" Not for a moment at a loss, Bagot said, "Oh yes, old fellow, of course! I had quite forgotten you! I think you have grown your beard since then."

Oakes must have got shockingly muddled about racing when in the early sixties he came home on leave of absence. He spoke to me about Rupee winning the Oaks. I rather fancied I knew something about the subject, so ventured to take exception to this statement. Oakes persisted, and offered to bet me a gold mohur he was right. I took the bet, and we then consulted the authorities. There we found that Rupee had won, not the Oaks, but the Ascot Cup, a vastly different affair. Oakes paid his bet and admitted his error, explaining that he had seen so much racing about that time that he had confounded Epsom with Ascot !

These two inveterate *raconteurs* were, by the way, popularly represented as being rather afraid of one another. Each thoroughly recognized no doubt the other's reputation for wonderful tales. They accordingly avoided meeting as much as possible, and when it was said in the presence of Oakes, " By the way, Bagot's been invited," or, " By the way, shall we invite Bagot ? " he would reply, " Well, between you and me Bagot's the biggest liar in all India." Bagot for his part used to express himself quite as freely about Oakes.

CHAPTER II

I ARRIVED home from India in the spring of 1870, and almost immediately afterwards left the service—to be precise, I retired from the Army on April 27th, 1870, having served with the 60th about four years. Before I had been back many weeks I planned out a little chasing for myself in the waning of the season. It happened that a meeting was being arranged at Childerditch, which is outside Lord Petre's place, Thorndon Park, close to Brentwood. I secured a mare, which, in affectionate memory of my best Indian mount, was named Baby Blake. But she was a poor jade compared with the superb fencer on whom I won the great Cawnpore race, and could not carry my colours nearer victory than third place. My old friend and companion Billy White was riding that day. Billy was my first instructor in riding, and blooded me with the Essex and Suffolk Hounds, at the tender age of seven years.

This Childerditch meeting was remarkable in more ways than one. I was boasting just now of having ridden for over forty years, and into my sixty-fourth year. But there rode at Childerditch, and rode bravely, a man of no less than seventy years of age, namely, Briant, a horse-dealer of repute in that part of the world. A steeplechaser of well over seventy years of age seems to me at least as remarkable in his own province as a Prime Minister like Mr. Gladstone of over eighty. I should think that the case of Briant is almost unique, and have certainly only heard of one other which at all compares with it, namely, that of Lord Buchan. I had it from Lord Buchan himself that he rode and won a race in the Isle of Wight after he had passed his seventieth year. After the race, however, he fell off from utter exhaustion, whereas Briant was comparatively fresh.

But Childerditch was remarkable in another, and much less creditable, respect. It was notorious that some of the most flagrant " ramping " on record took place at that meeting. In one race there were three horses running in the same interest. Now the order had undoubtedly been given to win with one of these horses, and that probably not the favourite. But the horse kept on refusing, and the jockeys on the other two horses didn't know what to do. They dared not come on, and so commenced falling all over the place in a pretty palpable manner. At this point a well-known dresser, who only died very recently, was observed by those who noticed what was proceeding to go down and give them the requisite directions. When he came back he very properly got his head punched for his trouble, though that no doubt he—or at any rate his gang of rascally associates—regarded as a detail. Lord Petre was greatly shocked at these scandalous proceedings, so much so that he actually took the extreme course of abolishing the meeting.

This is one of the worst instances of swindling which has ever come under my notice throughout my racing and chasing career. Probably I have ridden at a good many meetings where foul play has been manifest to many experienced observers; but the seamy side of horse-racing is always more likely to present itself to persons who have considerable financial interests at stake than to those who ride from sheer love of the sport. I have never made it my business to look very closely into these matters, except of course when they have obviously affected my chances of winning, because I have never gambled to any extent on horses. We most of us have an occasional side bet of a sovereign or two on an event which interests us. Even Lord Falmouth himself is recorded to have backed one of his horses on a certain occasion to win him a small silver coin, and I will frankly confess that when I have believed myself to be the possessor of a really good bit of information, I have frequently had a trifle on. But that is all. It is my belief that betting regularly on horse-racing, whether on the course or over the tape, is a very poor game except to the very few who give up all their time and energy to it and can reckon on really good information. Even then a man finds it passing difficult to reckon on making a sure income every year, as the bookmakers now lay far shorter odds than formerly.

Rogues there doubtless are, and to spare, connected with horse-racing. It is inevitable that a sport, so indissolubly connected with gambling, should draw round itself a large crowd of blacklegs and pilferers. Indeed it is perfectly safe to lay it down as a hard-and-fast rule that no sport or game in which betting is a feature can remain utterly incorruptible. Idle is it, therefore, to attempt to whitewash the dark side of horse-racing. I was reading some years ago, in the *Pall Mall Gazette*, the letter of " a regular race-goer," who took up the cudgels on behalf of his favourite sport. Some of his arguments were ingenious, but unsound. He asserted that there were probably not a dozen owners then running racehorses in England who would order them to be " pulled." This may be so, though scarcely owing to the reason given, namely, that such a " pulling " order would place the owner and trainer for ever after in the power of the jockey. A jockey's word is not better than that of an owner or a trainer ; and besides, if the jockey obeyed, he would in his own interests keep his mouth closed. There are other ways of preventing a horse from winning a race besides that of " pulling." A horse can be " stuffed " before the race ; that is probably a much safer, and an equally sure, method of accomplishing the sinister design. I recollect once a well-known cross-country jockey, immediately after dismounting in a race, give the owner the last thing in the world he expected or bargained for. " You —— villain ! " said he ; " you ' stuffed ' that horse. Never you ask me to ride for you again ! " *O si sic omnes !*

" Good things " in racing and betting often turn out to be the worst things. Once I prided myself on having made what I regarded as a really nice little wager with the Duke of Hamilton. We were discussing the weights horses had carried in the Grand National, and referring to Cortolvin,—which had no less than 11 st. 13 lbs. on his back, the heaviest impost ever carried to victory at Liverpool, excepting

3

that of Cloister,—I mentioned the horse as winning in '66. The Duke said no, he won in '67. I was perfectly certain that '66 was the year, and the Duke equally so that '67 was correct. He was so certain that he offered to bet 100 to 1, and I said, " Well, I must take that, Duke." So 100 to 1 in sovereigns was laid twice and taken. We referred to the *Turf Guide,* and found that '67 was the year. The weights used to come out much earlier in those times, and the betting also commenced earlier in consequence, and this it evidently was that had deceived me. The Duke of Hamilton was a very difficult man to catch tripping in a matter of this kind.

Of course it is a fact that a backer who keeps his eyes open and watches his chances carefully, may sometimes get the better of the bookmakers. A remarkable instance of this was given me by Lord ——. He had backed Blue Gown to win him a substantial sum in the Champagne Stakes. Blue Gown won, but was disqualified. Wells was a carelessly inclined jockey, and in this case would not take the trouble to waste. As a result he scaled overweight, and a pile of money on Blue Gown was lost by backers. My friend had arranged to put his Blue Gown winnings—counting his chickens, after the manner of many backers, before they were hatched —on Achievement for the Leger. Unfortunately he had none to put, otherwise he would have been something like ten thousand pounds in pocket. Determined to make up for his Blue Gown disappointment, if possible, he went to two or three hole-in-the-corner meetings in Scotland, whither he knew several of the big bookmakers were pursuing that

plunger of plungers, Lord Hastings. It was a case of
the pursuers pursued! He having good information
at his disposal won no less than six thousand pounds
at these pottering little Scotch meetings.

I would not have any one suppose from these
views, expressed perhaps with " brutal frankness,"
that I am joining in the hue-and-cry of the hysterical
folk who regard horse-racing as the most iniquitous
of sports, and support the ridiculous movement of
the Anti-gambling League initiated some years ago.
On the contrary, I lost no time in setting down
my name for what it was worth on the list of the
Association which very properly commenced what
amounted to a counter-campaign. In the first place,
the attempt to stop people from betting by such
means as the Anti-gambling League adopted—notably
their wild attack on the Jockey Club—has proved to
be utterly fatuous; and, in the second place, the
movement was in reality a thinly veiled one, not only
against gambling, but also against the national sport
of horse-racing into the bargain. It is a monstrous
thing to try and discredit and injure this our noblest
and most national sport, simply because it has the
misfortune to be used as the means of gambling by
those who are more interested in the odds than the
horses or the horsemanship. Fortunately the sporting instinct seems to-day stronger than ever amongst
all classes, and the tide is not likely to be stemmed
by a few faddists whose programme is to carry the
war into the camp of no less a force than human
nature itself, by the aid of grandmotherly legislation
and frivolous actions against a body of gentlemen
who represent the best traditions of the turf, and do

not a little to make horse-racing a pure and honourable pursuit.

Childerditch was the only English meeting in which I rode in the spring of 1870. The season was indeed then practically over, nor had I many opportunities of racing or chasing for some time to come. The summer and autumn of that year were whiled away for the most part in small and miscellaneous sport and pastime. It was in the summer of 1870 that wars and rumours of wars eventually took shape and form in the declaration of hostilities between France and Germany on July 19, 1870. This occurred to me as a capital opportunity to see a little service abroad, and I crossed the Channel with the object of getting, if it were possible, to the front.

Arrived at Amiens *viâ* Ostend and Brussels, I found a fair going on, and mixed freely amongst the crowd. Something in my personal appearance, or in the faultiness of my accent, I suppose, conveyed the impression that I was a German spy. A mob of angry Frenchmen soon began to gather round, and, being quite alone and defenceless save for my fists, it occurred to me that for once in a way a retreat would be discreet. Therefore I retired leisurely to my hotel, followed by the suspicious mob. The Commissaire of Police was sent for, but after talking with me and seeing my passport, he expressed himself as quite satisfied that my business was a legitimate one. He recommended me, however, to get out of Amiens as speedily as possible. I hired a conveyance and left the town with all despatch at midnight. My driver knew the ropes well, and managed most skilfully to get me past all the *francs tireurs*. Eventually, though not without some ugly-looking hitches, Chermont was reached.

Subsequently I walked on to Chantilly, and here I was hospitably received by Colonel McCall, the factor of the Duc d'Aumale. I offered to join the Saxon Uhlans, but they were not in need of any fresh men, and accordingly I had to cast about for some other way of seeing a little active service and of getting to the front. I was given the opening by a young Prussian Lieutenant in the Garde Cuirassiers, named Schwarz, whom I had the pleasure of introducing to Prince Blucher at a little 'Waterloo' dinner I gave about six years ago. They had not met since the Battle of Königgrätz in 1866. Whilst waiting for the bombardment of Paris, he and other officers had been enjoying a little sport in the way of steeplechasing near Chantilly, and this was how I came to know the young lieutenant. One day, when walking in the forest, I met Schwarz with several others in a waggon. He told me that they were going to the front, and asked would I join them. I did so forthwith.

The Saxon Uhlans were a splendid body of cavalry, and more active than the Cuirassiers, owing to the fact that they carried far less weight. They inspired many of the French troops with a very wholesome dread. At least one-third of the cuirasses were struck in the course of the war. At about 300 yards the bullets of the French rifles would penetrate their breastplates, which however were effective against fire at 350 yards and greater distances.

At Chantilly I had left my kit at Colonel McCall's. It was sent for after I had gone to the front with Schwarz, and after passing through a great number of hands came back to me intact. To show how remarkable was the organization in the Prussian Army at this time, I may mention that even the cognac in my flask had not been touched. The most careful inventory had been kept of everything in the kit, down to a novel, the name of which had been copied out on the receipt form which was handed to me for signature.

Very soon I was fortunate enough to get to St. Denis, just outside Paris, and here in company with Prince Wreda saw something in the nature of active service. At night-time both sides would often send out advance guards, so that the combatants tended to get closer and closer to each other. We were within a hundred and fifty yards or so of the French lines on at least one occasion. In the morning these advance guards would retire.

I usually, too, joined one of the parties that were sent out after the balloons which ascended from Paris in numbers for the purpose of disseminating false information about the state of things prevailing in the front. These balloons were of a small size, and as they travelled at no great height, we were sometimes able to riddle them with bullets. We used to fire at them with the French chassepot rifles which had been taken in action or else flung away by fugitives. The chassepot was a better weapon than the Prussian needle-gun. It was perhaps this balloon hunting which first sowed in me an ineradicable passion for aeronautics.

Though I had some good fun with the Prussians, and was hospitably entertained, I scarcely liked to overstay my welcome, especially as there was very little food for very many mouths. So back I started

to Chantilly, and after again receiving hospitality
from McCall, went on to Amiens.   I travelled a great
deal on foot, and was in all arrested three times.
When at length I reached Amiens, I found myself
once more in hot water amongst the townsfolk.   I
was suspected, arrested as a spy, and taken before
the head of the police—not my friend of a prior occasion.   My position looked a very nasty one indeed,
followed as I was by an angry and threatening mob
of Frenchmen.   But again I was treated with much
consideration.   It happened that I had with me—
first, the accounts of the Duc d'Aumale's estate which
Colonel McCall had entrusted to my hands, asking
me to carry them back to England and deposit them
in safe keeping there; and secondly, a number of
cartoons which severely caricatured various things
and people French.   The first packet aroused the
suspicions of the people who arrested me, the second
their fury.   But the head of the Amiens police having
glanced at the seal of the Duc d'Aumale on my first
packet, and learnt my name and nationality, courte-
ously sent me on my way rejoicing.   Shortly afterwards I was crossing the Channel.   The accounts
of the Chantilly estate I sent upon reaching England
to Coutts', where they were safely lodged.

Though I am bound to say that I found the Prussian
soldiers most kind and obliging, it seems that some
of them acted with marked meanness towards Colonel
McCall, who had shown them every hospitality at the
château.   Despite the fact that he had invited some of
the officers to dinner, and stood them the best wine in
his cellar, they sent him an imperious message on the
following day to the effect that they required at once,

I think something like a hundred dozen bottles of champagne. Rather scurvy treatment this after the hospitality they had received. McCall replied that he had not so much in his private cellar.

The Duke of Hamilton had a racing stud at Chantilly at the time hostilities commenced between France and Germany. His horses were sent back to England in the midst of the war, but not, I was told, before one or two attempts had been made to seize them for military purposes. I am not sure both the French and Germans did not meditate annexing the stud. Some German soldiers, at any rate, actually made a raid on the stables, and as luck would have it first entered into the stall of an old horse called the Czar. He was a regular Tartar, and savagely went for the intruders, who promptly showed the white feather. They probably adjudged after this that the stud was one to be avoided, and made no further attempt to annex it for their own purposes.

The Duke of Hamilton, by the way, was, though a thorough Englishman, related rather closely to most influential personages on both sides in this Franco-Prussian War. He was nephew of the Grand Duke of Baden, and cousin of the Emperor of the French. Hence he was called the "International Duke." Under the circumstances, it was rather too bad of the combatants trying to seize his racing stud.

The Duke was known amongst his friends as a capital all-round sportsman. With the gloves he used to be a pretty hard hitter some years ago. Once he was sparring with a mutual friend W——. W—— tapped the Duke several times in a very short space of time, and a professional who was witnessing the

bout criticized the latter's method of defence. " Put
on the gloves yourself then and try him," was the
retort. The professional did, and was speedily
floored no less than three times by the amateur, who
was undoubtedly a very clever boxer.

Chantilly was the scene of the Duke's famous
match in the Sixties with Baron Malortie. This
match was to ride from Paris to Chantilly and back.
The Duke just outside Chantilly galloped clean into
a heavily-laden market cart, and fairly spread-
eagled its contents ; so he never got over the second
half of the course at all. Malortie was a duellist of
renown in those days.

Baron Malortie, Bismarck's nephew, whom I used
at one time to see a good deal of, had been engaged
in many affairs of honour. Several of his duels have
become famous. Once when the ground had been
paced, and it only remained to give the word to fire,
a sergeant sprung out of the bushes hard by, and
ordered the combatants to lower their pistols. Malortie recognized in the unwelcome intruder a comrade
who had fought with him all through the Mexican
War. He reproached him bitterly for the interfer-
ence. The sergeant was touched by Malortie's re-
proach, and expressed his regret that the combatants
had not chosen their ground on the other side of the
road, for if the duel had only taken place there he
would not have felt it necessary to interfere, as it
would have been beyond his limits. Next morning
the duellists met again, and fought out their quarrel
uninterrupted. Malortie fired too hastily, missed
his aim, and was thus placed at the mercy of his
antagonist. He crossed his arms, exclaiming that

he would be shot like a man and not like a dog. He
was hurt, but not mortally wounded. Lying on
the ground, Malortie was too proud to allow his foe
to see how badly he was hurt, and so requested his
second to give him a cigar. Malortie was constantly
engaged at one period of his life in fighting men who
abused his beloved Hanover.

The Baron was a pleasant *raconteur* in matters
other than duelling. He would tell how, when on
the Staff of Maximilian's General, and dining a party
of four, the Emperor, the General, and their two
aides-de-camp, he had the honour to give the former
a glass of particularly good Madeira. The Emperor
had expressed a desire for some Madeira, and the
General reminded Malortie of a very fine sample
which he possessed. The wine was produced, and
Maximilian praised it greatly. He naturally asked
where it came from. With a respectful request that
the information might not go any further, Malortie
informed the astonished Emperor that it came from
his own caterer.

The ducal stud at Chantilly was under the well-
known trainer, Mr. Planner. I met him there for
the first time, and had some interesting conversation
with him concerning matters equine. The next
time we met was under very different circumstances,
on Lambourne Downs, when I was tramping through
peaceful England from Oxford to Southampton.

The few years following my dash into the midst of
the Franco-Prussian War offered comparatively few
opportunities for sport and adventure. My riding
was chiefly confined to the hunting field, though I
occasionally turned up where practicable at a cross-

country meeting, and put in from time to time a good deal of miscellaneous sport of lesser kinds. In the summer of 1871, for instance, I did much canoeing, chiefly in the Thames and its tributaries. I had acquired a little knowledge and taste for this pleasant form of aquatics in Nova Scotia, where I was stationed for some time when a lad and serving in the Royal Navy, and accordingly, in lieu of more stirring forms of amusement and exercise, took to it again during that summer. Frequently I used to go well out to sea in my Rob Roy or single-sculling boat, and spend nearly the whole day on the water. There are adventures to be got even out of what seems rather a tame kind of amusement to many who prefer sterner modes of sport. I recollect one aquatic adventure in particular. I was out between Ryde and Southsea one evening when a blinding mist came on, and soon completely hid the dim outline of the land. There chanced to be a wind blowing which I knew would take me right into Southsea. Eventually I reached the shore, which I subsequently hugged, about half a mile to the west of the Gilkicker Fort. The mist was as impenetrable to the eye as a dense London fog.

About this period of my life I was compelled to spend a good deal of time in London, being engaged in legal proceedings. People outside my immediate circle of friends and relatives can scarcely be expected to take much interest in a matter of purely private import like this, and I should not mention the matter were it not for the fact that the press has at various times commented on the legal results of a particularly cruel Will, which has hampered me throughout my life, and brought me into contact with the cumbrous and costly machinery of the English law. The law is one of the few things which, I have now come to the conclusion, it behoves every sensible man to flee from. But no man can tamely submit to great injustices.

Exercise is as daily bread to me, so that a little London life goes a long way. But besides walking, I sometimes found in London a form of exercise which entailed a vigorous use of the arms. About three- or four-and-thirty years ago it was a quite common thing to meet at night-time a band of half a dozen or more young men—probably for the most part they were composed of shop assistants—walking the streets with linked arms, with the object of driving unoffending foot passengers off the pavement. They marched along in much the same way as the undergrads at Oxford used to do in days of town and gown rows. Once crossing Hungerford Bridge with a companion I was confronted with such a body of amateur bullies, and naturally made up my mind to go through them. This was done. Several of the young heroes then turned round and threatened to give us a hiding. As it turned out, instead of receiving hidings we gave some ourselves, and there were soon several black eyes and bruised faces at the south side of Hungerford Bridge. Before long a policeman appeared on the scene, and one of the injured innocents at once proposed to give us in charge for assault. Several others were ready to follow suit, and with so many witnesses arrayed against us, the prospect was distinctly ominous, especially as we had not a scratch and several of our aggressors were knocked about. Besides, we had to outward appearance first commenced undeniable hostilities by breaking through their line. Under the circumstances we compromised, and agreed to pay £50 to one of our opponents who had come very badly out of the fray. In an age of *chantage*, this is the only instance I can recollect of having yielded to a risky, and as a rule an ineffectual, method of extricating oneself from an awkward dilemma.

On another occasion I was invited to square matters by "a trifle down," under very different circumstances. This was also in London, but at a much later date. It arose from an altercation with a hansom-cab driver, who was incensed at my only paying him sixpence over his fare. He got off his box, and followed me into a confectioner's shop in Victoria Street. He would not accept, so he said, a farthing under two shillings, and in order to enforce his claim laid his hand upon my coat collar. I warned him once and warned him twice, that this would lead to complications, but being a big blustering bully, he persisted, and seemed ready to shake the extra sixpence out of me. I then freed myself, and my patience being quite exhausted, returned the assault with interest. He did not fall down, but spun half round. I failed to resist the temptation after this to thrust him out of the shop by means of my foot with just the amount of necessary force for such an operation. A constable appeared on the scene, and next day cabby and I met at the Westminster Police Court. It had occurred to me directly after the fracas in the confectioner's, that if I gave my full name the man might bring up relays of witnesses with the idea of getting a handsome sum of money out of me ; so I refrained from doing so. The prosecutor, with a black eye, saw me waiting outside the court, and offered to drop his case against me if I would pay for the damage I had done. " No," said I, " it is too late for that. If you had made that proposal yesterday I might have listened to it. Now we'll see it out." The man upon appearing before the magistrate proceeded to give a nicely prepared version of the affair. I had offered him a shilling, he had declined, and upon his dismounting I had offered him one-and-six with one hand and knocked him down with the other, all this taking place outside the confectioner's. Then I was called upon to give my version. I related the affair as it had occurred inside the shop. " You said it took place outside ? " remarked the magistrate to the plaintiff. " Oh yes," admitted he, " I forgot ; it was inside." " The case is dismissed," said Mr. D'Eyncourt curtly, which was blow number three for cabby.

This incident reminds me of an escapade which happened in what may be called my salad days— about which I have been writing—assuming that I ever really had any. Supping, or rather preparing to sup, one night at a West End restaurant with a friend, there was set down before me a lobster in almost a state of putrefaction. The waiter after serving up this horrible dish whisked out of the room. I went down and remonstrated with him. He deemed my manner, I suppose, very threatening, and accordingly dashed a pepper-pot which he held in his hand full at me ; the top came off, and the contents covered

my clothes, fortunately not getting into my eyes.
I proceeded to chastise him, and had to answer next
day to a charge of assault at Marlborough Street
Police Station, before, so far as I recollect, Mr. Knox.
I had no witness on my behalf, as my friend had
not actually seen the affair take place, and it seemed
likely that I should get the worst of the case. But
the careful suppression on the part of the waiter of
the facts about the pepper-pot, which came out when
my friend was sworn and referred to my condition
after the affair, was noted by the watchful magistrate. He reminded the prosecutor that he had
not mentioned this incident, which put a different
aspect on affairs, and in the end I had to submit to
a small fine. For long afterwards friends were fond
of exclaiming when they met me what a *strong smell
of pepper* was about !

That lobster cost me rather over five pounds in
all. The affair reminds me of a bill I saw with my
own eyes at the Black Swan, York. It was made
out to the late Lord Glasgow, a notoriously short-
tempered man. The items of the bill were : Chop
a shilling, champagne ten shillings, and for breaking
waiter's arm five pounds. There is a much better-
known story of Lord Glasgow and a ticket clerk at
a railway station. His lordship needed change, so
handed a ten-pound note to the clerk, who told him
that he must endorse it. He therefore wrote " Glasgow " on the back, which made the clerk say, " I
want your name and not where you are going
to, *silly mon !* " The last two words were scarcely out of the clerk's mouth, before the irate peer
had dashed his fist through the booking-office win-

dow, accompanying the blow with some forcible epithet.

Writing of Lord Glasgow reminds me of a nice ruse which was once resorted to in order to prevent his exercising the right to blackball a candidate for membership at his club.   The late Lord X—— being, like Glasgow, rather a peppery fellow, was not very acceptable amongst a certain circle of racing folk. His name was down for the Jockey Club, where two blackballs were sufficient to pill a candidate.   Now it was well known amongst his Lordship's friends who were trying to secure his election that two members—General Peel and Lord Glasgow—had resolved to blackball him.   Accordingly they had to devise a scheme to get these two out of the way. On the day of election both General Peel and Lord Glasgow were suddenly summoned away—one of them, I fancy, so far as Newmarket—on urgent business.   The trick was done by two bogus telegrams and was completely successful.   There was no opposition to Lord X——, and he was elected.

In the early Seventies Mrs. Frederick Thistlewayte was living in town, and often entertaining illustrious visitors.   I recollect not a few interesting conversations with prominent public men at the dinner-table. Mrs. Thistlewayte herself was a distinctly well-informed woman and a clever hostess.   Lord Shaftesbury used often to visit her : no doubt she helped him materially in his many philanthropic schemes.   A particularly fascinating woman too was Mrs. Thistlewayte, as may be gathered from the following perfectly true tale.   Once Lord Shaftesbury called when an extremely well-known statesman was in the lady's drawing-room. She skilfully managed to bring this statesman to his bended knees in an attitude of unspeakable devotion at the very moment when the door was opened and his lordship announced. A certain photograph of Bismarck and a renowned singer sent a scream of laughter through Europe, though it was speedily explained away. But conceive the sensation which this extraordinary incident would have caused had Lord Shaftesbury babbled! He kept his lips closed, however, nor, to do her justice, did Mrs. Thistlewayte proclaim her triumph from the house-tops. It will scarcely be denied that this tale may be fairly included in a book of sporting reminiscences.

We were not above practical jokes in those days, and in the *sturm und drang* of youth. The very friend who was so useful in my pepper-pot case strove to play me off at Evans's one night very neatly. A nice joke was to put the yolk of an egg in a friend's hat. I managed to get one in W——'s hat all right at Evans's on this occasion, but he appears to have seen what was up and to have transferred it to mine. It was a gay party, and between us we made so much noise that old Paddy Green sent the chucker-out to quiet us. This fellow came at me; I clapped my opera hat over his eyes, and to our delight the yolk trickled down his face. Finding that we were showing fight Paddy came up with plenty of " saft sawder," addressing us as " Dear Boys," and the affair passed off amicably.

But for a baulked practical joke, commend me to one which was to have been played by three officers in the 4th Hussars, amongst whom was my friend

4

Wilson T——. The trio conceived the brilliant idea of posting down to the west of England, and visiting the house of a certain gentleman well disguised as bum-bailiffs. Their scheme need not have miscarried had it not been disclosed to a fourth party, who wired down to the intended victim warning him that three notorious London cracksmen were shortly going to visit his house. The police were put on their guard, and directly the conspirators appeared they were "run in," despite all remonstrances and show of indignation. In durance vile too were they kept for several hours, until they were able to prove themselves three cavalry officers.

The useful art of self-defence is one in which I tried to instruct myself early in life. Even the most peaceably inclined people admit that it is often a really desirable one ; and especially is this the case at times in the rough-and-tumble of the racecourse. Every man ought to have some idea of how to defend himself with his bare fists, and above all of how to defend ladies who may be in his company, and for whose safety he is therefore responsible.

Unfortunately I was too young at the time to see the Sayers and Heenan fight, though I had a good description of it from a friend, who was only eleven years old at the time, but was lucky enough to be present. With an enterprise beyond his years he managed to smuggle himself into the vehicle in which his father drove from Aldershot to see the great fight, and, arrived at the scene of action, a kind word from a gentleman who admired his spirit got him in. The Sayers and Heenan fight, so far as I know, is the only record of a man fighting with a broken arm. It can certainly be done with a broken finger. When I was cramming at Lendy's, I had a fight lasting for an hour and a half with a waterman. My second was General —then Captain—Sir Owen Lanyon, who was at that time cramming for the Staff College. After ten minutes or thereabouts my finger got broken, and for an hour and twenty minutes I had to fight on with this disablement. Odds of three and four to one on me were being offered when the police stopped the fight. A professional prize-fighter said to me afterwards, " When your finger was broken you ought to have hit him with the wrist end of the flat of your hand."

At the time of this fight I was in my teens. I am not conscious of having been the aggressor in many of the encounters in which it has been my lot to be a principal since then, though frequently enough the first actual blow has come from me ; but there is certainly no denying the fact that I have been in the wars a great number of times since that bout at Sunbury. In a number of instances hostilities have been initiated by a heartily expressed desire and intention on the part of various persons who have fancied themselves as fighters to give me a sound hiding ; and people who talk in this vein are often the easiest to subdue, as they are inclined as a rule to quite over-rate their own powers and under-rate their adversaries'.

One of the soundest thrashings I ever recollect, administered by ordinarily a non-fighting man, was on Oare Hill, the scene in past years of a review of the troops. The pugilists were a burly tramp and St. M——, a fellow Green Jacket of mine who now sports the Strawberry Leaves. The tramp was leathering his wife, and my friend bade him desist. Whereupon the man turned upon the intruder. St. M——, who was a man of great stature and strength, proceeded to administer the wife-beater a tremendous thrashing.

St. M—— was perhaps one of the biggest men in the Service in those days, and he had several tall brothers. It used to be a common joke in the regiment to say, "Here come thirty-one feet of St. M——." I suppose the strongest man in the Army in recent times, not even excluding two or three gigantic troopers who engaged in Homeric hand-to-hand conflicts at Balaclava and Inkerman, was the present Lord Methuen's father. At one time he could, it used to be said, hold out Sir Watkin Wynne, himself a heavy man, at arm's length like a dumb-bell. Lord Methuen, however, seems to have tried this feat once too often. On a certain occasion he attempted to repeat it in barracks, and as a result the seats of three pairs of overalls went ! The peer had no doubt forgotten that he was getting an older man and Sir Watkin Wynne a heavier one.

I was married in the autumn of 1872, and for a season or two my wife and I lived in the west of Ireland. On the Shannon there was some capital punt shooting. Wild fowl were numerous, and the shooting was particularly good, chiefly because there were only a very few guns at work. Since then I believe sport has much deteriorated, owing to the great increase in the number of sportsmen who repair thither every season. Though I have done a great deal of ordinary English covert shooting in

my time, I have always preferred the mixed and
rougher kind of sport one gets in wilder districts.
The shooting in Ireland at this period was good all
round, and I enjoyed some particularly good woodcock shooting at Lord Inchequin's fine place, Dromo-
land in County Clare.   What the bags averaged
I am scarcely prepared to say, not having made
any notes about them at the time, but I don't think
Bagot and myself did better in the course of a season's
shooting in the Mediterranean, to which reference
will be made later.

In the winter of 1873–4, from our house in the
wilds of Clare, we did a certain amount of fox-
hunting.   When the fox took to the hills one had
often to get off one's horse and lead it, or hunt on
foot—a form of sport which little recommends itself
to heavy weights.   On one occasion when out with
Reeves' hounds, I performed what the field was
pleased to regard as a sensational exploit.   In order
to save the life of a deer, which was close upon its
death struggle, I had to gallop across a narrow
arched brick footway over a stream which separated
us from the hounds.   Nobody else could have followed, even had they meditated doing so, as my
horse distributed the loose bricks right and left, and
practically demolished a good portion of the footway.
I was just in time to save the deer.   The scene of
the incident was close to Newmarket-on-Fergus.

A feat in horsemanship such as this usually implies
quite as much intelligence and skill in the animal
as in the rider.   It is extraordinary indeed what
cleverness a good horse whose blood is up will display
when he is called upon to make an awkward jump.

Out one day with the East Essex, I rode my chestnut mare Cartridge—rather a famous animal in the county—at a stile on the other side of which was a narrow footbridge across the lock at Springfield. She took it without hesitation. There was a second stile a few yards on at the other end of the bridge ; two short strides brought her to this, and over she went like a bird. No one else except my son tried to follow me, and his pony refused. It was certainly an awkward thing getting over these two stiles on either side of the narrow lock footbridge. Most of us ride for a fall now and then. What on earth is the use of going out hunting if one is going to ride only at obstacles which one is certain to surmount ? Better to jog along the high-road, or better still walk.

The most tremendous leap I ever knew a horse take was out with the Cheshire hounds at Marbury in 1870. A fine mare I was riding cleared a five-foot fence with a bound that covered over thirty-one feet. We measured it directly afterwards, and it was stated at the time to be the second best jump in point of length on record, the best being thirty-three feet. This latter jump, however, which was performed by Chandler at Warwick, is open to much doubt. After the horse had made it, his rider had to finish the race, weigh in, and dress before taking any measurements. Meanwhile several spectators on horseback had ridden over the course. It is worthy of remark, that the best long jumps of horses are little better than those of men. Mr. C. B. Fry, in his Oxford days, would have been a good match against some fair equine performers in the hunting field and racecourse. There is this difference of course—that a horse usually takes off from comparatively rough ground, and moreover can clear height and length in the same jump. Good jumps are often achieved by horses over hurdles. Harold, for instance, schooling over low hurdles once at Epsom, cleared twenty-seven feet. Clean jumps of twenty-four and twenty-five feet are frequent.

In the summer of 1876 I was again in Ireland, this time bent on soldiering as well as sport. I joined the Limerick Artillery Militia for its annual training, and managed whilst engaged in this occupation to be concerned in several aquatic adventures. On one occasion, when my battery was practising at flags erected on floating wooden frames beyond Tarbet Lighthouse, I paddled out in my canoe to secure a trophy in one of the flags which had been hit. When I arrived, however, at the target I found that I could not get near enough to grasp the flag, the sea being far too rough. After several fruitless attempts I got out of my canoe, and swam up to the buoy. I then got the flag, but, turning towards the shore, found that the canoe had drifted away, and was quite out of reach. It looked as though I must abandon the flag, and get back to shore a beaten man. But being in good swimming form at the time I resolved to try and swim in, holding the flag and knife in my teeth.

Eventually, after a hard struggle with the waves, I reached my canoe and got in again. Those on shore saw the empty canoe, and feared some disaster. So alarmed was Colonel Vereker that he started at a run down a steep incline in order to get a boat and a rescue party. He was a corpulent man, and having

once started at this rate was quite unable to pull
himself up, and ended at a tearing pace, which sent
the whole company into explosions of laughter. Some
averred that he was only stopped from going clean
into the water through a collision with the lighthouse.

On November 15, 1876, in accordance with the instructions of the Duke of Cambridge, the bronze medal
of the Royal Humane Society was presented to me
at a full-dress parade of troops at Winchester. I
cannot deny that the occasion was a proud and happy
one to me, though of course I was well aware that I
did nothing more than any man worthy the name
would do when I went into the sea at Limerick after
a drowning man. These things, in a slang phrase,
are " all in the day's work " : only heartily I wish I
had had more opportunities of the kind, as my West
Indian experiences have given me great confidence
in the water.

The facts in connection with this presentation
were as follows :—On July 17, 1876, I was in charge
of the regimental bathing parade at Tarbet, where
I was stationed with the Artillery Militia. Information was brought to me that a man was drowning,
having been caught in an overmastering current by
the lighthouse known by the name of Tarbet Race.
I repaired to the spot, and found that the man was
the best part of a quarter of a mile from the shore
and very much exhausted. My brother was making
preparations to go to his rescue, but my position
being more advantageous I was able to reach the
poor chap first. He was then, though a fair swimmer, fairly beat. I got him by the left upper arm,
and sustained him till the lifeboat from the Coast-

guard station came at last to the rescue. They had launched her so hurriedly that she got stove in, and when she reached us was full of water. The man behaved very well in the water, and obeyed my directions, which greatly facilitated the task of holding him up till the boat came. Thus the force of discipline evidenced itself in a very serviceable manner.

At the Winchester presentation Colonel Newdegate said some uncommonly pleasant things about personal bravery, and so forth, and there was a good deal of cheering. This was the more gratifying to me in that it came from my old regiment the Rifles.

The last opportunity I had of putting my swimming powers to practical service in saving life—or in this case unfortunately in endeavouring to save it— was when bathing near Maldon in the Blackwater. My attention was drawn to some cries for help on the south side of the river, and being in mid-stream I rowed across and dived in as near as I could ascertain to the spot where a boy had disappeared a few minutes before. The water was very thick and I could see nothing, so came up for breath, and then went under again. I repeated the operation several times, but in vain, and eventually left, feeling assured that life must be extinct. The body was recovered some little time after at low tide. At the inquest I felt it only right to talk very straight about the conduct of one or two people who were on the spot as the lad disappeared, and made no attempt to save him. The jury in returning a verdict of accidental death by drowning were good enough to declare formally that " credit was due to Sir Claude

de Crespigny for his unflagging energy and prompti-
tude in attempting to rescue the lad."

When a lad of fifteen I had the good fortune to
save a man's life at " The Hard " in Alresford parish.
We had been sailing in the Colne, when I jumped
overboard for the purpose of swimming ashore. My
companion could not swim a stroke, but he followed
me promptly, apparently quite unaware that he would
find himself out of his depth. It was rather a difficult
business to lug him ashore, but I eventually succeeded in doing so. A fisherman saw our critical
position and tried to come to the rescue, but we were
safe before he arrived.

CHAPTER III

FOX-HUNTING AND OTHER DELIGHTS

WHEN not in Ireland with the Limerick Artillery Militia in 1876, I was for the most part hunting in the south of England. During this and the next few years I put in an enormous lot of riding to hounds. I hunted in 1876, '77, '78, and '79 with the following packs : Tedworth, Luttrell, South and West Wilts, Essex, Chiddingfold, Lord Leaconfield's, Lord Radnor's, New Forest, Lord Portman's, Vine, H. H. and Hursley ; and also with two packs of stag-hounds, namely, the Devon and Somerset, and the New Forest, the master of which was Sir Reginald Graham, the son of that fine old sportsman Sir Bellingham Graham, and father of Malise Graham, of the 16th Lancers, who represented England only the other day in the International jumping contests in America. In addition I was sometimes out with beagles and with Lord Pembroke's and Mr. Raikes's harriers. That keen sportsman, the Reverend W. Awdry of Ludgershall, kept a small pack of beagles during these years. I used to go out with them, and occasionally too with the Hawking Club at Everley. This meant hunting at times four, five, and even six days a week, and it entailed some very long rides to meets. There was a tradition popular amongst my friends that I once rode sixty-six miles to a meet. As a matter of fact, I rode down to the New Forest from my place in Wiltshire with the object of exercising my right of voting in the Verderers election, and by way of killing two birds at one throw put in a day's hunting. This, however, was quite eclipsed by a performance of Lord Queensberry's. After hunting all day with Lord Wemys's hounds he started off across the Cheviots for Kinmount on the Solway, *a distance of one hundred and two miles*, riding most of the way on the sorriest of posters, and finally, having arrived home at 2 a.m., hunted his hounds the same day.

The severest fall that I ever experienced from off a horse was in the hunting field. On February 23, 1878, I came a tremendous cropper, when out with the Tedworth, and near Penton Lodge, then the property of Sir William Humphrey. I rode at a gate which I thought was closed all right. The gate, however, turned out to be open. Down we came, an awful crash, on the other side, and right on some vile cobble stones which were covered with treacherous moss. My arm was broken very badly at the elbow, and it has never been quite straight since. To make things worse, some over-solicitous spectators tried to drag me by the smashed limb into Lady Humphrey's carriage, which happened to be near. It was currently reported, and several newspapers have persisted in the statement, that I knew the gate to be on the swing. That was not so ; nor was I aware that there were cobble stones on the other side.

Head-quarters during the fox-hunting period were at Durrington in Wiltshire, and the Tedworth was the pack most easily reached from that point. The praises of this famous pack, hunted of old by the immortal sportsman Assheton Smith, have been sounded so often that they need scarcely be repeated here. It is impossible, however, to revert to those Durrington days without saying something of a few of the men who then formed the Tedworth Hunt. First and foremost to the mind of every one who regularly rode with the Tedworth in those times comes Jack Fricker. Old Jack was quite an ideal huntsman. I take it there was no man in England of that day who more thoroughly understood foxhounds than he. He could distinguish by tongue most of the hounds in the pack. Certainly he knew the tongue of any hound likely to be in the van. Jack lived and almost died in his breeches. He was very uncomfortable in any other attire, and equally out of his element on the very rare occasions when he was compelled to drive instead of ride. It is said, however, that he was surpassed in knowledge of hound life by his predecessor Carter, of whom Parson Gale gave one or two remarkable reminiscences in a little book he published some years since. " Sir Claude de Crespigny," he wrote, " had resided at Durrington Manor House for some few seasons, and whilst there had hunted regularly with the Tedworth hounds. Some time after he had left I received a letter from him, asking me if I could find out from old George Carter anything respecting a certain hound which was in the Duke of Grafton's pack at the time he was acting as his huntsman, and might possibly have come with him to Tedworth. Sir Claude was, I believe, tracing out some pedigrees ; at all events he wanted to know how the hound in question was bred. I took an early opportunity of mentioning this to my old friend, and he said at once—

" ' Remember him ?—of course I do. He were a very good hound, and came with me from the Duke of Grafton's to Mr. Smith's.'

" ' Can you tell me, old friend,' I continued, ' how he was bred ? '

" ' Yes,' replied the huntsman, ' he was by —— out of ——' (I cannot myself remember the names of his father and mother) ; and calling to his daughter, he told her to look into his bureau where he kept his old papers, etc., and see if she could find the hound list of the Grafton of such and such a year. The girl looked for the list and found it, and sure enough the pedigree old Carter had given was perfectly accurate."

But an even more remarkable instance of Carter's knowledge of hound life is supplied by the following. Parson Gale was looking after a hound named Matchless which very often would run down to the old huntsman's cottage. On one occasion a hound came into the garden and commenced baying under the window of the bedroom in which Carter was lying shortly before his death. He bade his daughter —herself "a rare good girl for a hound "—to go see what hound it was baying. She looked out of the window, and then said, " Oh, 'tis Matchless, father, Mr. Gale's puppy." " I tell you 'tis a dog hound," rejoined the old fellow, " for I know the note." He was as usual in such matters correct. It was a brother of Matchless, called Monitor, the two being so exactly alike that the girl had mistaken one for the other.

Several other tales about this huntsman have been told often enough in the hunting field, originating without doubt from Parson Gale, who was quite the Boswell of Carter. On one occasion a young fellow, very anxious to show his prowess, came cantering up to Carter, taking one or two fences on his way with great nonchalance, his mount being a very good one. "Nice fencer, isn't he?" said Poppinjay to Carter. "Ahem, hope you won't want it by and by, sir," was the stern reply. But the best tale of all is told by Parson Gale, who accidentally heard Carter remark in an undertone concerning one of Mrs. Gale's little girls, whom the loving mother had been introducing to him, "Nice pup: pity she weren't born a hound." He was horrified when he discovered that he had been over-heard, and proceeded to offer many sincere apologies.

It was always Assheton Smith's ambition to hunt in his eightieth year. Carter, though he resigned the office of huntsman to the Tedworth at the age of seventy-three—not without a kind of protest—did actually hunt after he had turned eighty, so that he beat his master in this respect. Carter's admiration for Assheton Smith does not appear to have been absolutely unqualified. On several occasions he found himself unable to approve of the master's active and peremptory orders, and after his death thought the Tedworth would still survive and greatly flourish, which it certainly did. Carter was an ab-stemious man, and a God-fearing one too, we have been told. There resided at one time in the Tedworth country a man who was well endowed with this world's goods, and had great advantages in the matter of position and family connections. But he was avoided by the county people, and had few friends. Once he tried to find a companion in Carter, who felt compelled to cut short his advances with these words—" I don't drink, I don't smoke, and I don't tell lies. So I'm no use to you, sir."

Two of the keenest fox-hunters I ever met were clergymen, one this Parson Gale, and the other the Rev. W. Awdry. Both hunted regularly with the Tedworth, as did one or two other gentlemen of the cloth. With Awdry, who was a good all-round sportsman, always went Mrs. Awdry, herself far better versed in fox-hunting than most men who ride to hounds. Awdry could really distinguish by tongue the leading hounds of the Tedworth almost as well as Jack Fricker or even Carter. " How we all used to love hunting," he wrote once in recalling those Tedworth times, " when we knew the names, breeding, and principal peculiarities of every hound in the pack."

Parson Gale could of course well recollect Assheton Smith. Hard by Fosbury, in the Tedworth country, there is a very steep and sudden descent into farmland. The parson once seeing me ride rather furiously, as it appeared to him, down this place, complimented me upon the achievement. He declared that in all his days he had only seen one man do it, and do it with a loose rein, and that was Assheton Smith. As a matter of fact I could not claim to have emulated or rivalled Assheton Smith in this matter, because my horse took me down before I had time to realize the position ; once started it was in any case impossible to draw up till the bottom of the hill was reached. I am told, by the way, that a Welsh pony belonging to Mr. A. W. Dewar—the owner of Doles Wood—would alone amongst the Tedworth Hunt take this and other neighbouring hills without the slightest hesitation, and at the steepest point.

The question of whether or no a clergyman ought to hunt has long been hotly disputed. For my part I should be content, if amongst my various vocations I had ever donned the cloth, to abide by the view of a parson who does not hunt himself, but is none the less perfectly tolerant of it in his brethren—Mr. Baring Gould. He writes concerning this matter, " Why not ? Why should not the parson go with the hounds ? A more fresh and invigorating pursuit is not to be found, nor one in which he is brought more in contact with his fellow men. There was a breezy goodness about many a hunting parson of old times that was in itself a sermon, and was one on the topic that healthy amusement and Christianity go excellently well together. "

Occasionally the hunting parson, it must be admitted, is rather handicapped in the pursuit of sport by the obligations of his profession. Two instances of this occur to me relating to clergymen I have often hunted with. " How's X—— doing now ? " inquired a friend of a hunting parson during a check. " Oh, well enough," was the reply. " On Monday, Wednesday and Thursday we had capital sport. To-day too he will be having good sport no doubt with the C——. Then as to to-morrow— well, I haven't heard what his arrangements are for that day." " Oh," observed an attentive and rather shocked listener, " but surely he will have his duties

5

to attend to to-morrow. He has a burial." "Well,"
replied the parson, gallantly sticking up for his
brother clergyman, "he can get a curate out of A——
to do that, you know, easily enough, for a sovereign
or so."

On one occasion the hounds I was out with had
a clinking run hard by a churchyard where a well-
known sporting parson was conducting a burial
service. Afterwards I tried to describe the run to
my clerical friend, but cutting me short he painted
it himself in glowing colours. He was ready with
the name of every spinney we touched, and could tell
which was the leading hound at every portion of the
run. Whilst performing his duties at the open
grave he had heard the hounds running, and knowing
every yard of the country was able to diagnose the
sport—as the hounds ran in a semicircle—at least
as accurately as I who had been there from start to
finish. Imagine the restraint which he must have
exercised over himself whilst reading the service!
—the wonder was that he didn't rush off after the
hounds before his duties were completed.

There was not much fencing with the Tedworth
out of the Pewsey Vale district, but we often got
grand runs ; whilst as for the hounds, they were in
the time of Jack Fricker's huntsmanship probably as
fine as any in the country. Often enough in the case
of a meet in an out-of-the-way spot, the field was
limited to about half-a-dozen of us or even less in
the afternoon. The late Duke of Wellington was
a well-known figure of the Tedworth Hunt in those
good times, and some time since his Grace was
affectionately recalling to me the sport we used to

enjoy. Sir William Humphrey was another familiar figure during these years, and before she came by a very nasty accident Lady Humphrey was known as one of the most excellent horsewomen of the hunt. Penton Lodge was Sir William's Hampshire residence. It afterwards passed into the hands of a Mr. Moon, who was a regular " Jubilee," getting through his thousands in an incredibly short space of time.

It is curious how entirely undeveloped is the bump of locality in some people. Once when out with the Tedworth we came upon Penton Lodge, which everybody recognized save the owner thereof. " Now that's a nice place, and how well situated," said Sir William ; " what's the name of that place ? " He had evidently never viewed Penton from that particular aspect before.

I have already referred to a bad fall I had out with the Tedworth through riding at a gate which was more or less on the swing. I was driven to it by the behaviour of my horse, who had gone through instead of over a gate a short while previously. My brother and I were both riding greys, and I recollect being much tickled when, after I was bandaged up, he told me that in his agitation and hurry he had ridden off on my horse to enlist the services of a doctor, and had not noticed the mistake till he had gone some distance.

A tremendous run we once had with the Tedworth from Sir John Astley's place at Everley to Marlborough—the fox was killed close to the London road just outside the town—may still be remembered by some members of the hunt. One gentleman had the use of three horses, but was not in at

the death. Sir William Humphrey returned home
before the bitter or rather glorious end, so, intending
to do him a good turn, I wired to Penton Lodge,
"Killed our fox." Lady Humphrey opened this
telegram before Sir William had got home, and
directly she saw the first word in it rushed to the
conclusion that it must refer to her husband, and
sustained a severe shock. "Killed" is certainly an
indiscreet word to begin a telegram with.

A remarkable character in the Tedworth country,
and a most dogged old customer, was Caleb Simonds,
the Savernake Forest keeper. A fox went to earth
during the cubbing season in Savernake, and Simonds
started to dig. But the ground was very sandy, and
at length Jack retired with his hounds. It was
eight o'clock in the morning when Simonds began
to dig. He declared he would not budge from that
earth until he had dislodged the fox. As good as
his word, he dug on till ten o'clock at night, when
at length he came upon his quarry.

Simonds was as fearless as he was dogged. Hearing shots fired near his cottage at Bedwin Brails on
a winter's night he went out in shirt and trousers with
only a flail in his hand. Soon he came across three
armed poachers, and informed them that they
would have to come along with him. At first they
were inclined to surrender, believing that the keeper
who thus, though unarmed, boldly accosted them
had a force behind him. But finding out that he
was alone one of them made a murderous assault on
him. Simonds with a blow of his flail killed one of
his assailants on the spot. The other two then
surrendered, and were marched off by the old keeper.

One of the most awkward spots, by the way, for hounds to get at I ever saw a fox resort to in extremity was a culvert at Savernake. The careful huntsman hesitated to let his hounds go after the fox, lest they should be unable to turn when fairly in this drain. Whilst we were waiting and wondering what could be done, a sweep with his bundle of implements came up. He asked whether it was a fox we wanted to dislodge. " What else do you think it could be ? " inquired Jack with scorn. The sweep said he would have the fox out, and fitted together his rods. He then inserted them, with a dexterous twist caught Reynard in the jacket, and dragged him out in no time. That is probably the single instance of a sweep's rods being used in fox-hunting.

A more unusual resort of a hunted fox, however, was witnessed by those out with the East Essex some years ago. The fox was found in a covert north-west of my Essex house, Champion Lodge, and running under our window made for Goldhanger Creek on the Blackwater—a real good point. There I espied him crouching on a small salting two hundred and fifty yards or thereabouts from the river wall. Of course the hounds could neither view nor wind him. I accordingly swam out to his coign of vantage with the whole pack after me. Finder, a big black and white stallion hound I had from Jack Fricker, was first up, and the two leading hounds drowned poor Charlie. I at once proceeded to dive, and after some rather exhausting struggles recovered his carcass, which the hounds broke up on the salting.

Another incident with the East Essex pack may perhaps be of some little interest to hunting men.

Once when the hounds were running I deemed it well to follow for a while along the line of the Great Eastern Railway, being afraid of losing them unless I took this course. Before very long I saw a train coming, and called out to an official who was near to open the gate. He refused, as it was, he declared, contrary to rules. There was no time to stop and argue with the man, so I managed to coax my horse over the signalling wires, and then dashed him over some posts and rails alongside the gate. Glancing round when these were successfully negotiated, I saw that we had got over not a moment too soon. It had been rather a ticklish position, though I was speedily out of it.

Everleigh was Sir John Astley's Wiltshire seat, though in my time he never hunted with the Tedworth. By the death of Sir John, or to give him his far more familiar name the " Mate," I lost one of my oldest and best friends. Very fond of his practical joke, he once, at one of his " sing-song nights," played rather a severe one on me. I got very sleepy after the dinner, and the fumes of smoke finally sent me off into a profound slumber. The Mate could not resist the temptation of painting me a moustache with a burnt champagne cork. My son and a friend who were present permitted it with perhaps some misgivings. They would certainly have allowed no other man but Sir John Astley to take the liberty. Of course I was made to look distinctly ridiculous, and to add to the absurdity some one tried to wake me up, saying, " De Crespigny, do you know you have a moustache now ? " I only half woke up, and murmured, " Proper thing

SIR JOHN ASTLEY.

too for a cavalry officer." Afterwards I had to retire, and wash off the burnt cork—quite a long business. But it was impossible to take umbrage at anything the old Mate did in the way of a practical joke. He could have played any number on me with impunity.

All the years I knew Sir John intimately, I never but once saw him " down on his luck." That was at Stockbridge Races many years ago. He was frightfully depressed for a day or so on that occasion —I knew not why—but the cloud soon passed completely by. The Mate did undoubtedly bet at times in large sums of money. Once I recollect having a modest fiver with him at Stockbridge over some event or other. I lost. Meeting him on the course the next day I at once proposed to settle. Not having the exact sum I asked for change. He put his hand in his breast-coat pocket and drew out an enormous packet of bank-notes—thousands of pounds worth, it struck me.

It was owing to Whyte Melville that I changed the venue for a little while from Hampshire and Wiltshire packs to the North Devon and Somerset. I never saw so much of that accomplished writer as I should have wished, but what I did confirmed me in my opinion, derived from his books, that he was a perfect gentleman and a true sportsman. Many people consider that his glowing panegyrics of the sport to be obtained in hunting the wild deer in Devon and Somerset were altogether overdone. Certainly some of the runs described in one or two of his works—notably that run in *Katerfelto*, when the stag was finally brought to bay at Watersmeet—seem incredible. The opportunity occurring, I put the question to Whyte Melville whether such runs actually took place in the hunting of the red deer. " Make no mistake," said he, " they sometimes are undeniably good." So, soon after that I set out on horseback to the West.

The Devon and Somerset yielded me fair but not exceptional sport. One adventure not connected with hunting, though resultant therefrom, I have often thought over since ; it was of the kind that are not easily forgotten. Leading my mare home one evening into the town of Dunster, my attention was attracted by a woman who came rushing out of a house hard by, and collided with me in her wild flight. A man came across the road in pursuit, and struck the fugitive with violence. I called upon him to instantly desist, whereupon he turned upon me with much savagery. I had scarcely let go my mare, who, being fatigued, stood still, before he assailed me. So sudden was the onslaught that I did not think of dropping my hunting crop, which I held in my right hand as I encountered his blows. I was not conscious of being particularly flustered, or of defending myself unskilfully, but for all that I soon found that I was getting all the worst of it. He seemed to get with ease through my guard, and to be raining in terrific blows. It was too dark to see properly the exact method of his attack, but when I found blood flowing freely from several cuts on the head I concluded—not a moment too soon— that there was foul play somewhere. I therefore landed him a blow on the side of the head with my crop, and he dropped like a stone in the road. I then discovered his secret power, and the instrument with which these strange and telling blows had been administered. He held in his hand a big leather trace with a buckle that had cut me like a knife. How effectively the author of *Lorna Doone*, who has so picturesquely described the encounters of John Ridd and other west countrymen, could have dealt with this incident ! There was something distinctly out of the common in this short and sharp struggle— the place, the fast-waning light, and above all the mysterious blows combining to impart to it a weird element. When afterwards the facts of the case were brought to the notice of the police sergeant, he told me I had had a narrow shave. The man, who, by the way, was in liquor, possessed immense strength, being a match for any two in the district. " If he had closed with you, sir," quoth the sergeant, " nothing could have saved you." He added the information, that when not driving the coach to Ilfracombe, the fellow was leathering his wife's lovers. " We constantly have to lock him up," said the sergeant, " but it takes me and two of my men to do it."

Whilst living at Durrington—which I often used to find from twenty to twenty-five miles distant at the end of a long day with the Tedworth !—I would sometimes pay more than flying visits to the New Forest, where there was excellent shooting with nice mixed bags, and hunting. Captain Frank Lovell, a fine horseman, was out two days a week with his fifteen couple or so of hounds, and some of the runs with that pack have not inaptly been compared with hard bursts with the Devon and Somerset. A nice horsewoman was Miss Alma ——, then a well-known figure in New Forest fox-hunting circles. Smart too and supercilious with Cockney sportsmen was Miss Alma. Such a sportsman one day when the hounds were at fault imagined he had found the slot of the buck. He held up his hat to Miss Alma, who rode up. Now what he had really seen was the slot of a pig, which to the uninitiated eye closely resembles that of a buck. "Pig!" exclaimed the young lady, looking hard at him, and instantly rode off.

Occasionally I used to go out with the Hawking Club, though in no respect proficient in the art of falconry. The old Hawking Club came into existence in the year 1864. In the previous year the Hon. Charles Duncombe had done a good deal of rook hawking on the Wiltshire downs, with Barr as his falconer. The sport became so popular amongst some of the residents in the district, that it was found quite practicable to form a club, which took over the management of the hawks. Amongst the original members of the club were Lord Lilford, one of the greatest authorities on British birds, and author of the monumental work thereon, and the Maharajah Dhuleep Singh. But in after-years the club flourished chiefly owing to the exertions of the Hon. Gerald Lascelles, who was known as one of the foremost, if not the foremost authority on Hawking in the country. His work on the subject is of course indispensable to those who desire to devote themselves to this decidedly interesting, if not intensely exciting, form of sport. Mr. Lascelles succeeded Mr. Duncombe in the Seventies as secretary and manager of the old Hawking Club.

Mr. Lascelles has given us some particulars concerning the number of head of quarry killed during recent seasons by the club. The first of these records is contained in his own work on the subject in the Badminton Library. In 1887 the total bag was 576 head, out of which the greatest number was composed of rooks ; but there were also over a hundred partridges, together with a sprinkling of other birds, and over a hundred rabbits killed. The club being a travelling one, is able to include on its list upwards of a hundred grouse killed in Scotland. Subsequently it did not go in for any game hawking in Scotland, and moreover, as it has not kept a goshawk of late, the returns are not quite so large as formerly. " I think," wrote Mr. Lascelles some years ago, " that more people take up hawking than formerly, but it can never become universally popular, because the greater part of the country is enclosed, and but few people can follow the sport at their own homes, whereas at one time most people could do so. It is perhaps the most scientific and difficult of all sports." Hawking has this advantage—it can be followed all the year round, which is the case with so very few of our sports and games.

During this hunting period with the Tedworth, New Forest, and other packs, I was rarely present at steeplechases, save in the capacity of a spectator. I took part in one rather memorable meeting, however, on April 5, 1877. This was the Beaufort Hunt at Dauntsey, near Chippenham. Though not quite so bad as Hurst Park course, round which two 'Varsity Blues double-sculled during the great flood of 1894, the scene of the Duke's annual meeting was so much under water that we could not have aspired to get round without swimming our horses, so the course had to be altered on the very morning of the races. I rode a mare called Countess, with whom I hunted with the Tedworth. But she was not much good in deep ground, and fell with me when about half way round.

The racing, as the name of the meeting implies, was confined to hunters, and I cannot say that it was of a very sensational character. But there were some excellent riders taking part in the meeting; amongst them Archie Miles, a really good man to hounds. My mare Countess, by the way, came from that favourite sportsman, Fog Rowlands, about whom many of us have pleasant recollections.

The Durrington district was very handy for Stockbridge; I attended the pleasant meetings there pretty regularly, and a little later on sometimes had a mount, though flat racing has been even less my *métier* in England than it was in India. Proposed by that grand old sailor, the late Admiral Rous, and seconded by the late Lord Portsmouth, I was elected a member of the Bibury Club, and enjoyed excellent sport and conviviality there.

At times there used to be some rough company at Stockbridge. Once, with several members of the Bibury Club, amongst them Lord Marcus Beresford and Sir John Astley, I was dining in the coffee-room of the Grosvenor. Suddenly a most detestable odour arose, which quite put us off our dinner. What on earth could it be? Whilst we were wondering a raid was made on the door leading from the street to the entrance-hall by a handful of roughs, who evidently came to lay their hands on every article they could find worth carrying away. Marcus and I rushed to the door and managed to keep these fellows at bay. They could not do very much against us, as the passage was narrow and we quite filled between us the doorway. Great sport we had, both of us managing to work a good deal of havoc amongst the intruders. How it all comes back to me! At length the roughs, getting better than they gave, retired, several of them with more or less broken heads. I had just got rid of one of my aggressors, and was rearranging my collar and tie, which had got misplaced, when old Peter Crawshaw of all men in the world came up, and intimated that the man on the ground was a particular friend of his. It looked as though I should now have to do battle with Peter, but taking a second look he discovered that he had made a mistake, and the matter ended in laughter.

The appalling odour which had put us off our dinner was now accounted for. It seemed that one of these would-be looters had managed to pass the porter and waiters and to find his way into our room. There he proceeded to break a bottle of assafœtida, in the vain hope that its smell would clear the room, and so enable him and his fellows to make a clean sweep of any valuables therein. The disappointed rogues tried on the same game again higher up the street. They ended up the day in Andover Gaol.

The Bibury Club has always been a very exclusive one. I recollect a candidate against whom no word seems to have been breathed, being " pilled " in a really extraordinary fashion. This candidate was

Lord ——, grandson of a great and rather notorious
lawyer. It happened that when his name came up
neither proposer nor seconder was present. Lord
—— was not a regular racing man, and nobody in
the room seems to have known anything at all about
him. His name was received with ominous silence,
and he was rejected. I was completely mystified,
and whispered to the Duke of Hamilton, the President,
" Why has Lord —— been pilled ? " " Must have
been mistaken for his grandfather ! " was the reply.
Had either proposer or seconder been present, Lord
—— would surely have been elected, for there was
nothing against him.

The late Lord Portsmouth was to be seen regularly
at Stockbridge meetings at this period. He was a
rare good fox-hunter, and indeed a rare good fellow
generally. Horse-racing was not his favourite pursuit, and it was therefore not very extraordinary
perhaps to find him once at Stockbridge taking
evident interest in an animal which looked quite out
of its element in the company of thoroughbreds. I
remarked on the poor quality of this beast, and was
tickled by his reply, " Yes ; but it would do very
nicely for my second whip." It is not often you
find a man engaged in spotting hunters at a race
meeting like Stockbridge.

It was just about the time when I settled at
Durrington that Sandown Park was started, and I
did not miss many of the first meetings. It is only
fair to say that the credit of starting this most
popular course belongs largely to Lord Charles Ker,
though no doubt plenty of credit also attaches to those
who, since his connection with Sandown ceased, have

taken a great part in the work of making it one of the most successful and paying racing institutions in the country. The site was, I believe, originally pointed out to Ker by the late Mr. J. Milward. He felt so satisfied that it was an excellent one that he purchased it, and forthwith proceeded to make a racecourse. He also planned the stands himself, originated the club, and got the first seven hundred members together. As stewards for the first year Ker got three excellent men in Admiral Rous, Lord Alington, and the late Mr. George Payne. Finally, he drew up the programme and the arrangements for the first meeting. He had long had a great ambition to improve suburban meetings, and to do this partly through an increase in the gate money, and by having nothing under £100 added to races. Afterwards, as all the racing world knows, General Owen Williams, Hwfa Williams, and Sir Wilfrid Brett became connected with the course. Sandown was the first race meeting of the kind in England where gate money was made a feature. Now there are a number of courses conducted on pretty much the same lines.

A man I used to see a good deal of about this time or a little later was John Chambers, one of the best pedestrians and oarsmen Cambridge ever turned out. He it was, it may be recollected, who started the Lillie Bridge grounds, where the 'Varsity sports used to be held, and revived the Leander Club. I gave a trophy for the Amateur Athletic Association High Jump, in which he was so much interested, and it is still competed for. Chambers was a fine swimmer, and may be said to have brought out Webb. As a pedestrian too he was at his best, and forty years ago or so was the first winner of the seven-mile champion race of the Amateur Athletic Club. He once offered to back himself, with George Payne, to walk twenty-one miles in three hours, which would have been a remarkable record had it come off. But the project fell through. He told me he was pretty confident that he would do it, and was sure of his first fourteen miles in two hours.

Chambers was a close friend of Lord Queensberry's at Cambridge, and though not very handy with the gloves himself, he thoroughly understood boxing. Indeed, Lord Queensberry assured me that he, practically speaking, drew up the Queensberry rules. They were of course passed by Queensberry, but scarcely edited at all, save in one or two matters respecting weights, etc. That he did his work well is shown by the fact that the rules have undergone no substantial change since they were adopted.

I trained for the Light Weight Amateur Boxing Championship, but in doing so put on no less than eight pounds, and not seeing the fun of wasting this additional weight flung it up.

That Queensberry himself was no mean runner at one time will be readily conceded by those who can recall the incidents of a memorable and very sporting race he ran many years since against Fred Cotton, the author and composer of *The Meynell Hunt*. This race was a four-mile one over Bogside (Eglinton Hunt) Steeplechase course, and several stiffish obstacles had to be jumped. Cotton won, though only by six yards, after a magnificent race. The time was twenty-four minutes and fifteen seconds,

THE MARQUIS OF QUEENSBERRY.

and the feat, under the circumstances, does not compare by any means badly with some of the best records of the day over a cinder track. Cotton was in those times a first-class runner and also walker. On one occasion he backed himself for a thousand to one to walk from Ashbourne in Derbyshire to a certain point in Perthshire, a distance of 347 miles, in seven consecutive days. His feet went all to pieces so early as the second day, and he actually fainted twice. He struggled on gamely, however, and won with three and a half hours in hand. Another remarkable performance of his at Christ Church, New Zealand, deserves to be placed on record : he walked for a wager one hundred miles in twenty-two hours.

There are very few subjects in which Mr. Gladstone was not interested. About horses, I have been told, he neither knew nor cared anything : but he used to be not a little interested in pedestrianism. Nearly forty years since I often met him at the house of a friend, and talked with him more than once on the subject. He was much concerned to know what a walker could accomplish without thoroughly exhausting himself.

6

CHAPTER IV

SHORTLY after the Wiltshire period, I was enabled to return once again to my old love, steeplechasing, and ever since 1880 have been almost continuously riding in meetings all over the country. In the early Eighties I got a good many mounts on my own and other horses—chiefly the former—though I was also addressing myself about this period to the pursuit of ballooning.

Upon settling down in Essex, one of the first matters to which I turned my attention was, of all things in the world, party politics! This was the first (and I hope it may be the last) time in my life that I took any share in the dull game of politics. Now-a-days, at any rate, it seems to be pretty generally agreed, even amongst the combatants, that party warfare is so much "sound and fury signifying nothing." Sir William Abdy was standing for the division in which my house is situated, and I helped to canvass the district for him. However, insufferably dull as party politics are as a rule, it chanced that there was a certain amount of sport in this particular election.

82

There was much fear that the factory hands—
mostly confirmed Radicals—would not allow the
freemen—most confirmed Tories—to come up to
the poll, keeping them away by threats and by actual
deeds of violence. I told the people who feared
intimidation on the part of the factory folk, " What
you want is a handful of fighting men to keep those
fellows in order, and to get your free men to the poll."
They took up the idea, but gave me rather a large
order. I was to draft down to Maldon three or four
hundred fighting men. It was necessary to explain
that there were not so many in England. However,
we did get some men down who understood their
business, and the freemen were able to record their
votes all right. To make assurance doubly sure, a
nice little gang of three score of coal-heavers, in
addition to the trained pugilists, were drafted down
from Colchester. I marshalled and commanded this
force myself, but grieve to say that certain of the
party officials, when they saw how thoroughly I had
carried out the work, shunned me religiously on the
day of the election !

Whilst on this subject of latter day electioneering,
it may not be out of place to turn back to the time
of my grandfather, the late Sir John Tyrell. He
was in Essex politics for not less than half a century,
making his *début* in 1826. In that year Sir John
stood on the hustings to second the nomination of
the Hon. G. Winn. It was a great contest, very
protracted, very bitter, frightfully costly. It was
said indeed that Mr. Winn's dearly-purchased victory
on that occasion cost him the greater part of £50,000.
But that contest was not half so eventful as one

which took place four years later for the county of
Essex, when my grandfather was the Tory candidate
against Mr. Collis, afterwards Lord Western, a Whig
politician of considerable note, and Mr. Long Wellesley, a nephew of the Duke of Wellington. Mr. Wellesley went so far in his virulent abuse of Sir John
Tyrell that he had to be called to account. He
disclaimed, however, somewhat after the usual custom
of politicians at the present time when heaping
terms of abuse on each other, any intention of assail-
ing his opponent's personal honour. My grandfather
accepted this disclaimer, but took the opportunity
of intimating that he was " to be found at Boreham
House," if wanted at any time. Good old days those
were, with all their corrupt electioneering ! A
politician then was deemed not a madman nor a
criminal, but an upright gentleman, because he held
his life not more valuable than his honour. Sir John
eventually headed the poll, Mr. Western and Mr.
Wellesley coming second and third respectively.

Rather curiously, though this Mr. Wellesley, who
afterwards became Lord Mornington, did not see
his way to take on my grandfather, Sir John Tyrell,
he was actually engaged in a duel later on with my
great-uncle—the Rev. Heaton de Crespigny—who
prior to being a parson fought in the celebrated action
between the *Amelia* and *L'Aréthuse*. Wellesley had
insulted Sir William de Crespigny, his father, who
was paralyzed, and my great-uncle accordingly had
him out. " You think I have only got a black coat,"
he said to Wellesley ; "you are wrong : I've a
shooting one as well."

This engagement between the *Amelia* and

L'Aréthuse is quite one of the most interesting incidents in the naval history of the century, and it is curious that it should be so little known in comparison with the contest between the *Shannon* and *Chesapeake*, or between Sir Richard Grenville's *Revenge* and the Spanish fleet. Tennyson has made the latter immortal in his ballad, but it has been questioned whether the melting away of Lord Howard into the "silent summer heaven" on that occasion with five ships of war, was altogether a creditable affair, though the post did his best to exonerate his discreet lordship. In the duel between the *Amelia* and *L'Aréthuse*, on the other hand, there is nought that reflects anything save glory on all concerned on the British side.

The incident took place early in Feb. 1813, during the great war with France. Captain Irby, whose family, by the way, intermarried with mine, was just thinking of leaving Sierra Leone, where his ship, the *Amelia*, had been stationed for a while, when a Lieutenant Pascoe came in hot haste to the Sierra Leone river with the crew of the gun-brig *Daring*, which he had been obliged to run ashore and blow up in consequence of having been pursued by a French frigate backed up by two other ships. A reconnoitring party was at once despatched by Captain Irby, who soon found a force consisting of two frigates, of the largest and most powerful class, named *L'Aréthuse* and *Le Rubis*, together with a Portuguese ship that they had captured. Captain Irby left Sierra Leone and worked up to the Islands of de Loss. He speedily fell in with *L'Aréthuse*, and endeavoured, not unsuccessfully, to draw her off her consort, as he was naturally not anxious to engage both these powerful vessels at the same time if he could help it. When the last vestige of *Le Rubis* had disappeared, the captain of the *Amelia* shortened sail, and stood towards his threatening and probably overweeningly confident foe. The French ship was far stronger in guns and complement than the British, and eagerly availed herself of the invitation to battle. She carried on her deck some heavy French twenty-four-pounders in addition to other guns.

At about seven in the evening the French ship ran up her colours, and three-quarters of an hour later, the two vessels being then within pistol-shot of one another, a great duel commenced. Both fired the shots at about the same time, and both preserved throughout the encounter pretty well the same position. For over three hours and a half they poured shot into each other. All the onslaughts of *L'Aréthuse* were repulsed by the brave men of the *Amelia*, who, like the men of the *Revenge*, shook off the Frenchmen—

> "as a dog that shakes his ears
> When he leaps from the water to the land."

Then at length *L'Aréthuse* bore away. She went with many dead and wounded on board and not uninjured as to her hull, and made no further attempt then or afterwards to tackle the *Amelia*. The British ship, when the duel was ended, was found to be in a quite ungovernable condition. Her sails and rigging were all cut to pieces, and her masts lay in ruins about the decks. Captain Irby was himself wounded when on the quarter-deck, and his list of killed and wounded numbered 141. The *Amelia*, it should be mentioned, had, like the little *Revenge*, a number of sick men on board, and she had barely her full complement fit for duty when she dared the French ship. Some may feel inclined to ask, like little Casper, what good came of it at last; but few will deny that it is a splendid incident in the history of our Navy.

The affair above mentioned between Heaton de Crespigny and Wellesley took place in the year 1828, and is thus described in a newspaper of that time: " On Thursday, a duel was fought on the sands at Calais between Mr. Long Wellesley and Mr. De Crespigny. The dispute originated in a remark made by Mr. Wellesley respecting some parts of the conduct of Mr. De Crespigny's father. He was requested to retract it ; and on his refusal a challenge was sent to him by the two Mr. De Crespignys, when all the parties started at full speed from Dover to Calais. Colonel John Freemantle of the Guards was second to Mr. Wellesley, and Captain Brooke, also of the Guards, attended his antagonist. The duel was fought on the sands immediately after the arrival of the seconds. Both parties fired together on a given signal at the distance of ten paces, and neither of them happening to be wounded, the seconds immediately interfered. A question here arose with respect to the second challenge, as to how far it was or was not to be accepted, when Captain Brooke decided that Mr. Long Wellesley had done as much as he was required to do. The parties then separated and returned from Calais on Friday morning to

Dover, where *Mrs. Bligh* at the York Hotel was waiting with great anxiety the arrival of Mr. Wellesley, and accompanied by him and Colonel Freemantle, she has since left Dover for London." The final paragraph has more than a spice of the new and personal journalism about it.

My own views on duelling were freely expressed some years since in the press, and they have undergone no change since then. The duel, when it generally prevailed in this country, was not without its grave attendant evils, but the same may be said of many desirable institutions. The code of honour which regulated the acts of the Iron Duke is surely good enough for most of us, and we all know that he was not inclined to shirk a duel when his personal honour was concerned.

Most men who have reached the meridian of life can recall some fracas or episode in which insulting expressions have been made use of by those supposed to be of the *crème de la crème* in the world of society, when an appeal to mortal combat has been suggested as the only method of settling the difficulty; and why the trusty steel of these fire-eating but degenerate descendants of gallant gentlemen has remained unsheathed has always been a mystery to me. Of course—though challenges are perhaps more frequently flying about amongst English gentlemen than the world seems to be aware of—it would be an act of folly to go out in this country, law and custom both prohibiting it. But, across the water, duelling is practically winked at. I would not go so far as to say that the injured party is compelled to parade the wrong-doer, but I do maintain that should the latter be challenged, he is bound, if a gentleman, to go out.

One of the last duels fought in this country was between Colonel H—— and Lord M——. The former, whom I knew well for many years, but whose full name I refrain from giving in order not to cause pain to his family, was a wonderfully fine pistol-shot. But in this instance, owing probably to the sun being in his face as he fired, his ball only grazed his opponent's face. Lord M—— discharged his weapon in the air.

Before quitting the subject, I may refer to a curious memento which used to be worn by Baron Malortie, whom I have already alluded to as a duellist. This was a bullet made into a scarf-pin. It had struck him on a rib over the heart, and been cut out near the spine. He wore this, believing that it would bring him luck in future combats.

This duelling digression has taken me a good way from the subject of steeplechasing, with which the chapter commenced. I had for some time before settling down in Essex had it in my mind to have one day a cross-country meeting of my own. At that time Lord Guildford, so far as I am aware, was about the only man who had carried out such an idea. His meetings at Waldershare were a decided success, though I do not speak from personal experience, never having ridden there myself. More recently Mr. Harry McCalmont has established a course on his own estate, though naturally on a more princely scale than that at either Waldershare or Champion Lodge. Moreover, the Waldershare and Champion Lodge steeplechasing meetings were started with the idea of catering principally for local hunts, which was not, I take it, Mr. McCalmont's object. I had already had experience in making a steeplechase course, having been engaged in the work in India. In the autumn of 1876 I made a course for my regiment at Seetapore. I tried Baby Blake over some of the jumps, and, when the meeting came off, won a good race. Few cross-country riders have had the chance perhaps of winning about the first race over a course they have themselves made.

The task of making a steeplechase course in India in those days was not a hard one to a man with any knowledge of the sport. There were no regulations as regards the jumps, and native labour was cheap. My Seetapore course was a mile round, and the jumps consisted of a stiffish double, a mud-wall, and bush fences. I superintended, and set two or three riflemen to keep an eye on the natives employed. In March 1881 we set to work to make a course at Champion Lodge, and in less than a week had it ship-shape. The expenses were inconsiderable, as the work was performed by men in my own employ. There were several suitable fields round my house, and practically all we had to do was to make the necessary jumps, and erect a stand or two. It was necessary later on, but not at the time of the first meeting, to comply with the regulations as regards fences, etc., laid down by the stewards of the National Hunt, as the meetings were to be held under the ægis of that body ; but this proved an easy enough task. As regards stands, I found a man ready enough to put up one for nothing on the condition that he should be allowed to erect a second one on his own

CHAMPION LODGE : THE HALL.

account, and charge those who use it a small sum.
We decided not to go on the gate-money principle.
It would not have tended to make the meetings popular in the district, and the object of the Champion
Lodge private course has always been to afford sport
and amusement to Essex folk, as well as to our own
immediate circle of friends.

The posts and rails, as every one knows, have
been abolished in steeplechasing ; and we never had
them at our little meeting. Some people think
that the change was not for the best. The last time
I rode over posts and rails was at Ipswich. They
certainly had this drawback, that horses occasionally
got into a habit of chancing them, as they chance
hurdles, with evil results. A stickler for timber
jumps persisted on having posts and rails once at
Aldershot. General Byrne was one of the stewards.
" Very well," said he ; " what height will you have
them ? " The reply was " three feet six inches."
They were put up, and on the day of the meeting
the only man who came to grief was the stickler himself. He broke his collar-bone over this particular
jump.

At Ipswich the posts and rails were substituted
one year for the big double fence—which was properly
a couple of fences with a space of a yard or so between
—but found a failure, and once more abandoned.
There was a certain feeling against this big fence, and
I was approached by the malcontents and asked to
get up an indignation meeting in the matter. I
declined, not regarding the jump with disfavour.

The abolition of the posts and rails may to a
certain degree have lessened the danger of steeple-

chasing. In a blinding storm, for instance, the jump was sometimes a difficult one to see properly. Does the lessening of danger in this, and other respects, tend to emasculate the cross-country sport? People are constantly asking me whether I consider that steeplechasing has degenerated since I first donned colours. On the whole, I am not prepared to say that it has. The horses are far finer creatures than they were a quarter of a century ago : no "cock-tail," such as often used to win in those days, would have a chance in a big race now. Then the courses are far more numerous, as are also the riders. Last, but not least, the pace is greater and the jumping more perfect. At the same time, though it will be seen I am not indiscriminately in this matter a *laudator temporis acti*, I am bound to admit that to a certain degree steeplechasing to-day is rather inclined to become, in certain respects, a kid-glove kind of business compared with what it was of yore. Many of the best and biggest courses are attended to almost like tennis-lawns or cricket-pitches. The "take-off" and landing in particular are looked after with the greatest care. When a frost threatens, straw is usually put down to keep the ground from becoming too hard, and one even hears of the whole course being in some instances treated with the same tenderness. Then all the jumps are strictly in accordance with regulation. In short, there is an undoubted tendency now-a-days to, as it were, "cut and dry" our steeplechasing.

A similar tendency evinces itself in various other sports. We become more scientific and more methodical. Compare, for instance, the hunting of big game as practised to-day with the same sport as practised a quarter of a century ago. We face big game now with weapons which make the clumsy old rifle seem a thing only fit to be put in the hands of a savage ; and in proportion as our weapons become more perfect our method of big-game shooting must become more of the kid-glove kind. When I first entered the steeplechasing world, we had often on quite important courses to face in bad weather the most frightful ground. To ride over heavy ploughed land was quite the rule rather than the exception, and the jumps were often of the rudest character. It is when I contrast this state of things with existing conditions that I feel inclined to use the expression kid-glove style in reference to steeplechasing at the present time. On the other hand, the vast improvement in horses makes great amends for the falling off in these respects. The steeplechase is to-day, as ever, a magnificent form of sport.

I doubt, however, whether it would long remain so if the safety-at-any-price party had their way. I have admitted candidly that the posts and rails had drawbacks, but really there are people calling themselves sportsmen, well nigh ready to put an end to jumping altogether. There is the open-ditch scare, which periodically arises. Drawing-room sportsmen take exception to the open ditch because, so they declare, no horse can manage it with safety unless regularly educated over a wholly artificial jump ; and it has even been described as a death-trap. When Sly came to grief over the open ditch —as we all must expect to do more or less from time to time—the Grand National Hunt were adjured to

do away with it. Lord Queensberry proved con-
clusively some years ago that the agitation against
the open ditch was a most unreasonable one, in-
stancing the number of times it was negotiated in the
Grand National without any casualty.

According to my experience, the open ditch is
right enough provided a horse has been properly
schooled, for naturally out hunting one finds as many
ditches on the take-off side as on the landing ; whilst
with guard-rails, which most steeplechase courses have,
the take-off is much more distinct to the horses.   Of
course it happens now and then that a most perfect
fencer will slip in taking-off. Lord Chancellor, the
best of fencers, went wrong thus, and old Champion
more recently, at the mature age of twelve years,
slipped into the open ditch at Plumpton, where I
have on one occasion found myself, and alongside
of which poor Billy Sensier was killed. Some say
that this ditch at Plumpton is the most formidable
in the south of England.

But the bulk of " the grief " is simply owing to
a lot of half-schooled four-year-olds bringing down
other horses. Sly's accident, I was informed by
reliable eye-witnesses, was attributable to the severity
of the pace, which had exhausted the horse, so that
a sheep-hurdle would have been as likely to have
caused the mischief as the open ditch which actually
did so.

Before quitting this subject, a few words may be
said about the agitation against steeplechasing on
the ground that it entails frequent cruelty to animals.
Almost as much has been said on this score at various
times as on that of damage to the riders.   It is moon-

shine. The number of accidents fatal to man and beast on the steeplechase course are remarkably few, and the sufferings of the latter are, on the whole, as nothing compared to those endured by many a London cab-horse. No pains are spared to get steeplechasers into the most perfect condition. They live in the best stables, and on carefully selected oats and hay, in return for which they are expected to make an effort lasting for a few seconds about a dozen times in the year, and to negotiate fences over which they are constantly schooled. Moreover, the pain suffered by horses that do come to grief would seem to have been, except in the case of breakdowns, altogether exaggerated. At all events, I have myself observed a horse with a broken back calmly grazing, though necessarily unable to move its hind-quarters. A broken leg is comparatively painless until stiffness sets in, and before that, as a rule, a friendly bullet has done its work.

The opening meeting of the Champion Lodge Hunt and Military Steeplechases took place about a fortnight after the course was got into final order, namely, on March 30, 1881. The programme consisted of six events, namely, Farmers' Cup, Ladies' Cup, Hunt Cup, Military Cup, Consolation Steeplechase, and a match. The course was about a mile in length, and there were about half-a-dozen jumps. The fences were regarded as rather stiff ones, the in and out being the most ticklish to negotiate. There was no serious accident, but a fair number of tumbles, and one horse looked as if it were done for, though it ultimately turned out that it was not injured at all. The most popular win was probably that of Billy

White, who steered his horse Tommy Dodd to victory in the Hunt Cup. Billy at the time was between fifty and sixty years of age, yet he romped in as he was wont to do at Middlewick. The Ladies' Cup fell to Lady de Crespigny's Wild Georgie, which I rode myself. Cartridge got beaten in the match by Mr. Laurence's Sam, ridden by owner.

Previous to this meeting at Champion Lodge, I had been getting my hand in a little over a few local courses. For instance, on September 18, 1880, Wild Georgie carried me to victory in the Officers' Challenge Cup, in the Regimental Races, got up by the Loyal Suffolk Hussars at Bury. We all rode this cup race twice over, owing to an odd mistake made by Colonel Blake, who was leading, and took us the wrong course. The mistake discovered, we had to return, and re-ride the race.

It does sometimes happen that in a mist or a bad light a jockey goes round the wrong post by accident. But once at Bury St. Edmunds, in a race I was riding in, I could not bring myself to believe that an opponent who did so was quite unaware of his mistake. In this instance the leading horse went wrong, and whilst the other jockeys in front of me were turning their heads to chaff their friend, they missed a post themselves. Being second, I lodged an objection against one of these jockeys who beat me, and with several witnesses in my favour, including the rider who first went wrong, the decision went against him. Still he swore thick and thin that he had not done anything of the kind. I accordingly went down the course with him, and pointed out where the thing had taken place. As it happened, I was able to show

SIR CLAUDE CHAMPION DE CRESPIGNY.

p. 96]

his horse's footmarks on the wrong side of the post. This seemed conclusive, but still he persevered in his well-played part of injured innocence. "Those are the footmarks, Sir Claude," he exclaimed, as a last resort, " of a cantering, not a galloping horse ! " He afterwards got warned off, and eventually took to driving a hansom cab.

Many a jockey has lost a good race, more especially no doubt in bad weather, through being deceived by a post. These little things happen much more often than many onlookers may suppose in both racing and steeplechasing, and help to increase the glorious uncertainty of the sport. Billy Bevill once pointed me out a post at a Bibury meeting which he described as one that had been the means of losing more races in its time than any other in England. "Do you see the one I mean ? " he asked, pointing it out to me. "Perfectly," I replied. We advanced a few yards. "Do you see it now ? " he asked, and I found that I had quite lost sight of it. Curiously enough, this post won Bevill a race on that very day a few hours later. Jewitt, whilst leading, was deceived by it, and took the favourite, who was following him, out of the course. That gave Bevill a good lead, which he maintained, winning easily.

Earlier in 1881 my mare Cartridge, whom I had purchased in the New Forest from an officer quartered at Christchurch, and brought with me to Essex, won a jumping competition in some sports got up by Major Yeldham at Yeldham. She cleared the hurdles very clean, and so won the prize, though pitted against a decidedly brilliant jumper, who only a short time before was first at the Agricultural Hall

7

with a jump of six feet three inches. On this occasion my opponent " chanced " the hurdles, and so got beaten by Cartridge.

I must not omit to mention a remarkable accident to a horse which I witnessed early in the same year, when out with the East Essex near Braxted Park. Huzzar, a horse belonging to my brother, which a friend was riding, got pierced in the stomach by a stake, and died in two minutes, owing doubtless to the severance of an artery. Colonel Holroyd, an old Master of Hounds in my part of the world, was near when the strange accident occurred, and called me back just in time to see the horse fall over, with a stream of blood pouring out of the wound. The injury was inflicted by a pointed stake, which had evidently been removed from its place in the hedge in order to make a gap. Both ends were pointed, and after removal from the hedge one stuck in the ground, whilst the other was tilted up at an angle of forty-five or so, by the horse's fore-foot, just right for spearing a horse in the stomach. As luck would have it, the horse had been sold only the same day at Brighton.

We have happily never had any fatal accident, though now and then a few unimportant ones, on the Champion Lodge course. In 1882, however, I came very near killing Mr. Bruen in a way not altogether dissimilar to that recorded above. In finishing the race for the United Service Cup, my horse, Twelfth Cake, trod on, and struck upwards, the spike of the flag. Bruen was coming up immediately behind me, and the stake grazed his horse's shoulder, actually removing some of the hair without drawing blood. Seeing what had happened, Bruen instantly loosened his grip of the saddle and allowed the lance to pass between his thigh and the saddle-flap. He carried the thing a few paces, and then opened his thigh and let it drop—a very narrow escape for both horse and rider.

A trip to Aldershot in April 1881 was not productive of much sport. I did not take part in the Point-to-Point Steeplechase on the 13th, which was ridden along the Hog's Back, and finished on a farm of Mr. Shrubb, a late Master of the Tedworth; whilst a week later Wild Georgie refused, and spoilt any chance I had of winning the steeplechase open to officers of the Auxiliary Cavalry.

The next entry in my diary is May 9, 1881. Marcus Beresford and myself repaired to Epsom, I to ride Twelfth Cake. The horse was purchased from Marcus, and won some fair races in this and following years. On May 12 Twelfth Cake, with myself up, got first past the post in the Military Steeplechases at Ipswich. In this race Wilson Todd, on Punchbowl, came down at the fence opposite the Stand, and the crowd rushed in apparently ignorant of the fact that there were other horses to come up. I was last up, and to stop was out of the question. Twelfth Cake went in amongst the mob pell-mell, and bade fair to make some human mincemeat. There seemed to be eight or ten of them down at the same time. I know that it occurred to me that about the next place I should find myself in would be a coroner's court instead of a racecourse; but no serious damage seems to have been done, and Twelfth Cake, despite this incident, won the race. On the same day I was successful with Wild Georgie, in a match against Silvertail, who was ridden by the owner.

On the following day there was more chasing, and Twelfth Cake was entered for one race. Finding, however, I could not ride the weight, I put up a boy, who rode well enough, but got beaten. On the 14th there was pigeon-shooting, and I won the Regimental Cup and double rise. Indeed, I was in good cup form at this meeting, winning three in all, namely, Swordsmanship, Pigeon-shooting, and Regimental. It was at Ipswich that the Duke of Hamilton made a present of Pudding to Wenty Hope Johnstone. Many people thought that the horse was an utter crock, but after he had passed out of the Duke's hands he won a heap of races. As a six-year-old this horse—who was by Brown Bread out of Claretto, and was a half-brother of Twelfth Cake—won no less than eleven races, giving on one occasion as much as 10lbs. to Johnnie Longtail.

Four days later came the Suffolk Yeomanry Cavalry Races, when for the second time running I won on Wild Georgie the Challenge Cup, and was therefore entitled to keep it. This mare was an undeniably useful one. She was by Rosicrucian out of Bel Esperanza. The former, all racing men know, was one of Sir Joseph Hawley's very best. Walking early in the Seventies from Oxford to Southampton, I looked up Porter at Kingsclere, and he told me that the world had no idea of what a superb horse Rosicrucian really was. He said he wanted to bring him out once more, to let people see how good he was, and then put him to stud. Rosicrucian was brought out after this at Ascot, and won the Ascot Stakes

carrying 9 stone, and the Alexandra Plate carrying
9 stone 7 lbs. He made hacks of all his opponents.
Bel Esperanza does not appear to have been a particular flier. Wild Georgie was purchased from old
John Tubb, the Winchester dealer, quite a character in his line. Once a horse let out for the day
by Tubb bolted with the carriage and its unhappy
occupants the best part of the way back from
Cranberry Park to Winchester. Arrived home, the
hirer remonstrated with the worthy dealer, saying
that this was about the hottest specimen of a nag
he had ever had, which was saying a good deal, from
those stables. Thereupon Tubb quietly called his
irate customer's attention to the extreme originality
displayed in the fixing of the reins, which had been
buckled to the rings of the collar.

On another occasion Tubb found it more difficult
to defend himself. An officer had entrusted a horse
to the dealer, with injunctions to give him a nice
loose box, as he needed rest. He returned from
leave to the stables before Tubb expected him, and
could not see his horse until a team from Hambledon
Races came in. In that team was his animal. De-
nunciation ensued : " Well," exclaimed the aggrieved
dealer, " if this isn't hard on me, sir! I never can
do anything wrong without being found out ! "

This meeting of the Suffolk Yeomanry Cavalry
was in one respect unfortunate for those taking part
therein. All the horses were disqualified for ever
afterwards. The event had been sent in a few hours
too late to appear in the *Calendar*. This being so, the
best thing for Wild Georgie was to go and try her
fortune in a race or two abroad. I saw her off at

St. Catherine's Wharf next month, having lent her to a gunner friend, who was keen on winning a race at Spa. He only managed, however, to be placed second.

A little incident in connection with an old acquaintance of mine, Baker, which took place about this time, will perhaps not be read without interest by the many admirers of that most gallant and excellent soldier. On June 25, 1881, I came to town for the purpose of giving my vote at the " Rag " in the matter of his candidature for re-election. I rather fancy that Baker is the one instance of a member of the " Rag " being re-elected after his resignation. There was rather a strong contingent against him, and as a result the balloting was a close thing. I was with my brother during the balloting, and when his turn came observed that he had selected a light-coloured ball, and was about to flip it carelessly into either pocket. Now, though a light-coloured ball, it would if it had gone into the wrong pocket have been counted as a black ball. Fortunately I just warned him in time, and he sent his ball into the right pocket. On a balance there was only a very narrow margin, two or three in favour of Baker, so that if my brother had sent the ball into the wrong pocket it would actually have been a case of rejection. No doubt Baker felt his practical banishment from England acutely, but in a way it was the making of him. I mean it is likely that had it not been for this he would never have had the splendid opportunities which actually presented themselves to him in the Russo-Turkish war and in Egypt. Surely the proudest moment of his life must have been when the Colonel of his old regiment requested Baker to place himself at its head for a brief while. It is difficult to conceive a greater triumph for an officer than this.

Less serious perhaps was the attempt made at the same club some years later by a small clique to get rid of me, because I went to Carlisle to see that no hitch occurred in connection with the execution of three murderers there. An ex-High Sheriff having informed me my name was likely to be pricked for the office of sheriff, I considered that I was not exceeding my duty in seeing to a matter of this kind. The attempt to remove my name from the list of members of the club proved an utter failure. Two V. C. men led the opposition in my favour, and an overwhelming majority voted against my expulsion.

In my diary for the summer and early autumn of 1881 were entries concerning cricket matches, of which I rather fancy I was not always *magna pars* in either batting or bowling—lawn-tennis, and—haymaking ! In the autumn and winter of the same year I devoted myself more to fox-hunting and shooting than to chasing ; but on one occasion I won a race or two at a meeting at Galleywood Common in October. Cartridge in a match turned the tables on Sam, and Wild Georgie won the Hack Race. The meeting was of a decidedly hole-and-corner character, and was not held under National Hunt Rules. We never got paid our stakes, and perhaps it served us right for taking part in such a bogus meeting. I recollect amongst other things that the muddled starter asked me how many horses there were at the post ! In those days they were not so mightily particular, and probably experiences similar to my Galleywood Common one have fallen to the lot of a good many men who rode much at that time, and were ready to ride anywhere if there was a chance of sport.

In its palmy days, though, Galleywood had amongst its patrons some very prominent sportsmen, such as Admiral Rous, General Wood, Caledon Alexander, and Prince Soltykoff, all of whom have now, alas! joined the great majority.

Riding through the heavens rather than on the earth took my fancy in the following year. But as my ballooning expeditions have been invariably made in the summer time, aeronautics did not greatly militate against steeplechasing. Before 1882 was very old, I had been in the saddle more than once at Epsom, riding Twelfth Cake, Ethiopian, and other horses in Jones's stables. My visits indeed to Epsom all through the Eighties were neither few nor far between, and one and all were directed to the stables of my old mentor Jack Jones. The two best cross-country jockeys at the time when I first seriously addressed myself to steeplechasing in England were, in my opinion, Jack Jones and Bob I'Anson. The former taught me much of what I know about riding. For nine years he was top of the tree amongst cross-country jockeys—a brilliant record. Bewicke and Nightingall were worthy successors of Jones and I'Anson.

At one time and another a good many criticisms, some complimentary, some the reverse, have been passed on my riding, and some years ago the *Sportsman* was discoursing on what is not inaptly called

the " free cant back," which has been identified with
my style of horsemanship. This so-called " cant
back," one of the great and obvious advantages of
which is the removal of the weight in jumping from
off the horse's shoulder, was eminently characteristic
of Jones's style of horsemanship, and I suppose I
fell into the same style myself from riding so much
with him at the time. That superb rider Billy
Morris, like Jack Jones, was certainly a believer
in the " cant back," and I have noticed the same
in Arthur Nightingall, and other amateur and professional riders.

Here is the reference in the *Sportsman*—a very
friendly one : " Do not let any one think that I am
holding Sir Claude de Crespigny up as a model steeplechase rider, though I will say this for him—none
sits better over his fences than he does. I allude
specially to the *free cant back* on landing, which so
few ever master. Arthur Nightingall is one of those
few, and I have often thought on seeing him landing
over a fence with his horse's croup nearly touching
his back, what a lot he must save his mount as compared with the crouched-up images who are never off
their horses' shoulders."

A sly fellow, when he chose, was Jack Jones. One
day, discussing with him the merits of various
jockeys, I remarked on the admirable riding of men
like Billy Morris and Greville Nugent. " I suppose,
Jack," I said, " you don't expect to see many more
soldier riders as good as those two ? " " Ah, indeed,
no," he replied ; " let's see, sir ; Mr. Greville
Nugent—ah, yes, I knew the gentleman, and, if I
recollect aright, he was killed at Sandown." This

was pretty cool, coming from one who not a great while before had admitted before a coroner's jury that he had himself jumped on Nugent, and been the cause of his death.

To return to chasing in 1882. On March 13, 1882, we had our Champion Lodge Steeplechases, then becoming a regular annual fixture in the East Anglian sporting world. This year the whole country side turned out to see the sport, and Maldon was quite a howling wilderness. Some thousands of spectators favoured us with their presence, and the vehicles were most remarkable for their variety. "Every sort of vehicle," said a report, "that would run on wheels was there, from the well-appointed barouche and fast drag to the humble cart drawn by the ' poor man's Arabian.' " The course was almost the same as in the preceding year, but the events limited to four. Mr. Bruen on his two mounts, Bunny and Cronstadt, and my brother and myself were fortunate enough to share between us the spoils on this occasion. The Hunt Cup produced the best race ; Jimmy, ridden by my brother, beating Twelfth Cake, the favourite, ridden by myself, by a head, after a sharp set-to.

At Galleywood, a fortnight later, I won the Baddow Steeplechase on Twelfth Cake, and recollect that I beat Mr. Tippler's Lizabeth, which was placed second, owing, to some extent at any rate, to the kind coaching of the late Major Bringhurst, who knew the course far better than most of us. Bringhurst was a good sportsman in very truth, and it is interesting to record the fact that it was he who gave George Fordham his first winning mount on

Hampton, a two-year-old, in the Brighton Stakes, fifty-eight years ago. I sent a picture of the jockey and the horse to the Duke of Beaufort, who was naturally much interested in all relating to Fordham, and it is hung in the smoking-room at Badminton.

A lesser event was a match between Wild Georgie and Jimmy, a horse belonging to, and ridden by, my brother. They laid 2 to 1 on my mount, and two hundred yards or so from home Jimmy was done for, and I was suffered to win anyhow. Twelfth Cake came out again in a hurdle race the same day, but was well beaten by Mr. J. Goodwin's Gold Finder.

The hardest race I ever rode in and won, was over this course at Galleywood. Part of the course was across a field which had been very recently ploughed up by the Derby Digger. It was so heavy that we all had to slack into a slow trot, and when the horses did get on to turf again they were one and all utterly done. I had never dreamt of such heavy going as that in all my steeplechasing philosophy, and hope never to experience anything like it again. The ordinary ploughed field was nothing compared to it.

A note concerning the late Major Bringhurst. Though essentially regarded as an Essex sportsman, his residence being near Chelmsford, where he passed away at the age of seventy-three, the Major graduated in horse-training and racing at Brighton. After retiring from the 90th Foot, with whom he had served in South Africa and India, he settled down in Sussex, and devoted his attention to thoroughbreds. Then later he migrated to us in Essex, where he speedily became a general favourite. After a while he came to be regarded as quite the Nestor of horse-racing in East Anglia, and was in great demand as steward at Essex meetings, as also at others outside the county. He stuck to the saddle as a fox-hunter till late in life. There were other things besides horse-racing and training at which the Major was an expert. He was particularly clever as a turner and carver, and in many Essex houses are treasured up as mementoes little specimens of his handiwork.

At Harlow, on April 12, 1882, I could only manage second honours in the Open Steeplechase, but did better at the Suffolk Yeomanry Cavalry, on May 13, in the last races I was destined to ride that year owing to the ballooning accident at Maldon. Twelfth Cake carried me to victory in the Hunt Cup, in which Mr. Rodwell's Cronstadt, ridden by Mr. Bruen, was second, whilst on the same mount I was second in another event—the open race. Lyndon, however, was disqualified, so I secured this race also.

Though fully recovered, save for a limp, from the injuries sustained in the ballooning mishap in June 1882, recorded elsewhere, I was not sorry of an opportunity of a complete change of air, scenery, and sport, which a shooting and yachting expedition to the Mediterranean offered. Early in November I started for Corfu, to join Joe Bagot of the 60th, my frequent sniping companion in India days, and Lord Churston. They had gone out to the scene of action by P. and O., having made arrangements to meet their yacht on the other side of the Bay. Our prime object was the shooting of woodcock and pig in Albania. The cock shooting in this part of the world is some of the best in Europe, but we knew before-hand that it varied very much from year to year.

One season you may bag sixty, seventy, or even a
hundred couple of cock a day ; while the next, perhaps not more than fifteen couple may be killed.
The latter bag, however, is, or was a dozen years ago,
decidedly, I should say, below the average.

Bagot, who is great in the practical art of equipment
and outfit for sportsmen, recommends for sport in
Albania and adjacent lands one or two guns and a
good service revolver.   A rifle he is inclined to regard
as a superfluous weapon, because for pig or deer an
ordinary smooth-bore No. 12 is usually more effective
than the best Express bullet manufactured.   As a
proof of this he gives an instance of where he once
put two bullets from an Express rifle through a boar
at about twenty yards' distance, the only apparent
result being an acceleration of the brute's pace.   A
little later the boar fell to a shot from a 12-bore
handled by a member of the party, and when examined, it turned out that both Express bullets had
passed clean through without touching any vital
part.   The ammunition difficulty, as I once found
when on a shooting expedition in Spain, is not
very   easy   of   solution.   Cartridges   and   powder
should be sent out in the yacht, as there are great
difficulties experienced in getting them through the
Continent.   Three or four thousand cartridges, with a
supply of bullets, slugs, etc., should suffice for a shoot
of a few weeks' duration.   Stout clothes are needed,
as the cover in Albania is of a very thorny character.
Some strongly advocate taking out English dogs,
either cockers or spaniels, but it is a moot point
whether it is not better to leave the native beaters
to provide them.   A beater is paid from £12 to £14

a month, and for this he is expected to supply dogs both for cock and pig shooting. A small medicine chest may be useful, and a supply of quinine.

Our yacht, the *Eva*, which Bagot found for the trip, was 130 tons, with a crew of eight, besides two stewards and a cook. Bagot was rather afraid that my game leg might seriously hamper my movements over the rough ground we were about to shoot, but when I reached Corfu, where I had agreed to meet him, I scouted such an idea. Our first beats were at Butrinto and Vrarna, and resulted in moderate bags of cock, widgeon, and snipe, with an odd quail or two. It was very pretty mixed shooting, with plenty of diversity and incident.

One incident in which Churston played a prominent part afforded us much amusement, though it might have had a serious ending. A shot from the top of a green ivy-covered bush attracted the attention of Bagot. He repaired to the spot to find Churston perched in the bush, and surrounded by a pack of savage Albanian dogs. They were speedily driven off, and then Churston told how he had been suddenly, and for no earthly reason, attacked by one dog, which he managed to beat off. It retired only to bring up a strong reinforcement. Churston was then pressed so hard that he was compelled to back to the nearest tree, keeping the furious brutes off as well as he could with the muzzle of his gun. When he reached the tree he returned the onslaught with interest, and then made a dash up into the lowest branch, one dog actually taking a piece out of his coat as he whisked out of reach. These Albanian dogs are of a most vicious breed, but their masters set great store by them, and have no scruple about knifing any stranger who kills one.

Waterfowl shooting we found an interesting form of sport at Butrinto, our first bag consisting of twenty-two ducks, besides teal and divers, with a few snipe. At Pagania we had our first boar drive. Nine or ten Albanians, all armed to the teeth as though they were going into battle, were employed as beaters, and these men brought a dog or so apiece. The head beater decided on the place of action, and stationed us at various points. Then, all being ready, at a given signal the drive commenced, and wild shouts, varied by the occasional discharge of a pistol, marked the progress of the beaters. Suddenly the dogs would give tongue, the beaters raise a greater uproar than ever, and one or perhaps several black objects dart through the underwood at such a rate as to be scarcely distinguishable. A boar will carry a good deal of lead, and two or three shots would be sometimes needed to bring one to book. It is a stirring sight to see the wounded animal dart out of its retreat with great flakes of foam flying from its tusks, and its eyes gleaming like fire-balls. Unless speedily found by the gunners, a wounded one will attract a crowd of hungry vultures and jackals. A few days after our first hunt, the head beater discovered a couple of tusks, which were about all that remained of a pig we had hit several times, but had not successfully followed up.

Nor was the sport confined to the game already mentioned. Besides boar, cock, snipe, and waterfowl, one of the party went eagle-shooting with success. Near Dragomastre there was some very pretty shooting at pigeons. At a cave we waited for the birds to come in after feeding. In point of numbers our sport was very far behind that once enjoyed by Lord Londesborough on the Nile, when he killed hundreds of birds with his ordinary 12-bore in a single day; but none the less it was excellent fun bringing down these wild blue rock, which were as quick as lightning. The country, by the way, in this district was, and very likely is now, rather barbarous, the populace being of a distinctly cut-throat disposition, and by no means above a little brigandage on occasions. It is advisable to go about well armed, and if possible in a party.

The first chases in which I engaged after returning from this shooting expedition in the East, were at Chelmsford on April 5, 1883. I won the Steeplechase Plate that day, beating Chance—P. Tippler up—my mount being Twelfth Cake, whom shortly before the race I had made a present of to my brother. I also was victorious in the Military Steeplechase on Pictus, a horse belonging to Percy Coke of the 15th. Bohemia, ridden by the owner, George Hayhurst, was second; and Mr. Chaston's Wild Irishman, ridden by Mr. Beever, third in this race.

As a rule when your horse makes a mistake in steeplechasing it is all over so far as that particular race is concerned, unless your opponents also blunder. This fact has been borne in upon me again and again in the course of nearly forty years' experience of racing. But exceptions there are now and then that prove the rule. This race at Chelmsford was one of these, for Pictus came down as we were jumping in and out of the course. I was just picking myself up when another horse jumped right into my saddle, and struck me clear of my horse, at the same time coming down itself. Whereupon my horse trotted away down the course. I gave chase, caught him up, remounted, and went in pursuit of the other horses that had passed us. I came up with them in a few hundred yards, and just beating Bohemia, who was trained in the same stable as Pictus, won the race. That was a field-day, by the bye, for our stable, which was in the hands of Jack Jones. Between us we managed to win four out of five races, not entering in the fifth. I won two, " Billy " Morris a third, and George Hayhurst of the Fusiliers the fourth.

The owner of Pictus was so pleased at the result of this race, that he presented me with a pair of silver candlesticks, which recall not the least pleasant memories among my various sporting trophies.

Percy Coke is a rare driver, and when put on his mettle pretty reckless of consequences. I hope he will not be offended if I illustrate this by a story which certainly does him no discredit. Driving to Aldershot station, he found the road, which was being repaired, blocked by a pole stretched across it. He asked a navvy, who was on guard, to remove the impediment to allow of his getting to the station. The man flatly refused. Percy therefore, remarking that his horse was " good at timber," drove him at it. There was an upset, followed by a general set-to, as this headlong intrusion was resented by the road-menders. The navvy went for Percy : Percy gave him a *coup de pied*, as he stooped to pick up a brick-bat, which sent him flying head foremost into his

8

own heap of mortar. Another time he was driving to the same station after some steeplechases. As we whirled round a corner, more on one wheel than two, we passed Billy Morris. His face was a treat ; " Poor Claude ! " it seemed to say, " he's survived the steeplechases only to be killed by Percy Coke's mad driving. "

Twelfth Cake continued to flourish after passing out of my hands, and won the Aldershot Cup with my brother up a week after the Chelmsford Chases. My new love was Shepardess, a mare my brother and I purchased from Jones. Shepardess began pretty well, winning for me Brassey's Cup at Sevenoaks in May 1883, when she started 7 to 4 on, and won by twenty lengths. My chief opponents were so dead beat on this occasion, the going being heavy, that both horse and rider appeared to run their heads clean into a clover rick just off the course.

In the summer of this year I rode on the flat at the Bibury meeting, Shepardess being matched against Morning Star, the property of Fred Beauclerk. I walked over, and this was the only win—if it can be so called—that the mare scored after Brassey's Cup. She was a roarer, and turned out quite a failure, never doing anything afterwards.

" Give a dog a bad name and hang him." The downward grade, swift and sure, of the late Marquess of Ailesbury, afforded, I think, an excellent object-lesson in the truth of this old saw. Ailesbury, as a matter of fact, never had a chance of retrieving himself. He began to go wrong, and at once everybody's voice was raised against him. Yet to start with he was an excellent good fellow, and a thorough gentleman. Knowing this full well, I ventured to make a stand for him when he was going downhill so awfully quick. I worked hard to get him elected a member of the Bibury Club, and elected he actually was. Unfortunately it came too late. He had sunk too deep in the slough of evil companionship, and nothing could save him. The public have never seen any save the dark side of Ailesbury, and they formed their estimate of him on that alone. But there was plenty of good in the fellow at one time, and I shall always believe that the hue and cry was responsible for his ultimate utter degradation. It is only fair to say that what influence his wife had over him when he began going altogether wrong was salutary. A few words from her could, and often did, stop a volley of oaths.

No doubt the Jockey Club knew what they were doing when they warned Ailesbury off, and had more evidence against his past career on the turf than was actually divulged. But I must say that he was overtly condemned for directions which are, as a matter of fact, used again and again by owners to jockeys without getting them into trouble. " Cut it fine " is often the injunction given to a perfectly straight jockey by an equally straight owner. It has been given to me on at least one occasion when I have been riding for another man. At Galleywood I can recollect being asked by the owner of the horse I was riding not to come away till over the last fence. I carried the injunction out faithfully, and won without taking it too much out of my mount. It was rather amusing to see the glowing accounts of my horsemanship in the papers, which declared that I just managed to win with fine judgment, etc.

Sporran, by Grouse out of a half-bred mare, proved at least a better investment than the jade Shepardess. The first race he won me was the Steeplechase Plate at Chelmsford in March 1884. I found I could not ride the weight myself, so put up a gunner, who won the race for me.

The Champion Lodge Steeplechases were on April 1 of that year. We had as usual a goodly concourse of Essex folk, with more than a sprinkling of people from beyond our own neighbourhood. Sir Charles Staveley was amongst our guests. His relations with Gordon are familiar to many people, and it may be worth noticing that one of the very last communications through the post ever received by an Englishman from the General in beleaguered Khartoum, came into the hands of Sir Charles on the Champion Lodge Course during the annual steeplechases. It came in the shape of a postcard, and caused a considerable sensation, everybody's mind at the time being full of Gordon.

The Stewards included the Duke of Hamilton, the Marquess of Queensberry, and Colonel Byrne; Charley Page Wood acted as both starter and clerk of the scales; whilst Holroyd was judge. As usual we had glorious weather—our steeplechases have always been most fortunate in this respect—and some fair sport. There were eight events on the card, including a match between Wild Georgie and Rizpah, which did not however come off, as the latter went lame. The first race was the Point to Point, over which there was some brisk speculation, the book-making fraternity being present in force. Sporran, with myself up, started a pretty hot favourite—6 to 4 on—after his recent victory at Chelmsford. It turned out anything but a hollow thing, however, as Waggoner, the third favourite, ridden by Mr. Fellowes, the brother of the owner, Mrs. Coope, was beaten by no more than a neck. The Coopes' stable was more fortunate in the Hunt Cup and the Consolation, both of which they secured, the first with Pat, steered by Billy Morris, and the second with Jack, steered by Mr. Rodwell.

Lady de Crespigny's Zante started favourite for the Ladies' Cup, but I did not succeed in getting placed, the event falling to Mrs. Reid's Lady Alice, ridden by Mr. Fellowes. Sporran had a walk over for the Loyal Suffolk Hussars' Cup, and Mr. Rust's Architect won the Farmers' Cup, starting second favourite.

April 3, 1884, Ipswich.—Here I won the Sudbourne Plate Hurdle Race on a recent purchase of my brother's, Elmina. Jack Jones was present, and there had been some talk as to whether he or I should ride the mare. I gave him his choice, acknowledging the superiority of his horsemanship by pointing out that if he rode she would start 2 to 1 on, and if I rode then the odds would probably be 3 to 1 against. This reasoning appeared to Jones to be sound, and he voted in favour of my having the mount. The only dangerous horse came to grief at the first flight of hurdles, and after that there was not much doubt, in my own mind at any rate, as to the result, though there appeared to have been some in others. The mare won easily enough.

Possibly had it not been for a mistake made by Grayson in this race, Elmina might have been pressed a little bit more, though I do not think, bar accidents, she could have lost. At the last flight Grayson rode at the outside hurdle, and was carried over the rope. Personally, I have always made a rule on Ipswich racecourse, when there were no wings at the hurdles, of riding at about the centre hurdle.

A change of scene next found me on April 1, 1884, at the Vale of White Horse Steeplechases, where I could not do better than get third place in the open chases on Mytton's Maid, who was a bit thick in the wind. The following month, however, I won on Captain Barkley's Hurdy Gurdy in the Regimental Races at Ipswich, and so wound up the spring chasing season of 1884 with a measure of success. This race was on May 23, and on the following day Simmons and myself made an ascent in the " Colonel," and after a voyage of four hours and seven minutes came down, not without a narrow escape, between St. Ives and Huntingdon. Thus I made three eventful balloon voyages in three successive years, 1882, 1883, and 1884. Perhaps I may boast of having achieved a world's record in winning a race and making a balloon ascent well within the space of twenty-four hours.

Though attending at Stockbridge in the summer of 1884, I did not ride on the flat, but contented myself with being a spectator of the sport, and in taking part in the Bibury Ballot. The next entry in my diary is as follows :—" Wye. Won Selling Hurdle Race on Baron Hill : to London for Balloon Cen-

tenary afterwards." This Baron Hill was bred by
Sir Richard Bulkeley at Baron Hill. He was an
own brother of the mare Elmina. Jones and I
differed a good deal in relation to this horse, I
believing him to be honest, and Jones being equally
positive that he was a rogue. I took him as I found
him, and with me the horse always behaved well
enough. However, nothing would dissuade Jones,
who still viewed Baron Hill with disapproval after
he had been entered in this Wye Selling Race and
had won it. A short time before Jones had ridden
him at Chandler's Ford, a course near Winchester
and just outside Cranberry Park, which has since
been abolished. I gave him ten sovereigns to put
on the horse, but saw none of it back, as he got
badly beaten. After the Wye race Baron Hill passed
into the hands of Arthur Yates, and, beyond winning
one small race for him, seems to have done very little
good. Curiously enough, a brother officer was riding
to hounds somewhere in the Midlands on a horse
lent, I suppose, by a friend. It behaved anything
save well, and the thought suddenly flashed across
him, "Why, this must be Baron Hill!" When he
looked into the matter, he felt convinced that he had
stumbled on the truth, and told me so the next time
we met. He had known the animal in its chasing
career, and when it belonged to me.

As mentioned in an earlier chapter, I usually make
a rule, like many other jockeys, of critically examining a course before riding. But on this occasion at Wye I had not time to do so. I therefore
followed in the wake of Sensier the first time round,
when his horse broke down. By that time I had

learnt all I need know about the course, and was enabled to win my race.

I repaired to this Wye meeting with Arthur Yates, who was running a horse there in the first race against mine, and rather fancied him too. The trains, we found, ran so unkindly that I deemed it to be practically impossible for me to be in time to ride Baron Hill myself, and therefore wired to Billy Morris, asking him to do so. But there were professional jockeys riding in the race, and had Morris complied with my request, he would have lost his weight allowance in Irish steeplechases. As a matter of fact, though it was a great rush, I did arrive on the course at Wye just in the nick of time to ride. Jack Jones, hearing of the incident afterwards, remarked that I was luckier than he and his friends were on one occasion, when, having missed the train, they had a special, put three hundred on their horse, and got beaten a head.

At Wye once I recollect being assaulted in rather a curious way, though perfectly unconscious of having injured or offended anybody. As the crowd rushed over the course at the end of a race, a fellow struck my horse with considerable force; I charged right into the crowd after him, and in so doing got a tremendous cut across the thigh from another man, probably his pal. I suppose they were wild at my not having won the race in which they may have backed me.

A first-class rider, and the straightest of jockeys, was poor Sensier. On a good horse he had scarcely a superior in the steeplechasing world, though on a bad one there were one or two rivals, notably Dollery, who were generally admitted to be stronger.

An item concerning Yates :—Once at a meeting at Somerleyton, Sir Savile Crossley's place near Lowestoft, I did not miss a single race. I rode eight out of eight, winning two and being placed second in several others. This record pales, as probably do all others, before that of Arthur Yates, who once at Kingsbury rode seven races in the day and won them all !

CHAPTER V

SOME BALLOONING EXPERIENCES

IT was not until the year 1882, some time after I had finally settled down in my Essex home, that I first began to seriously turn my attention to ballooning, and resolved to engage in this most fascinating and exciting pursuit. I had seen, however, something of ballooning many years before, during the Franco-Prussian War, when, as I have already stated, we used to ride after, and shoot at, the bold aeronauts who ascended from Paris during the siege.

Altogether sixty-six of these balloons were sent up from Paris, and they held 168 persons. Fifty-two fell in France, five in Belgium, four in Holland, two in Prussia, whilst two came down into the sea. The number which fell into the hands of the Prussians was eighteen, some of which were more or less riddled by our bullets. Gambetta, it may be recollected, ventured to ascend from Paris in one of these balloons, and, for what I know, he may have been shot at. One balloon, named " Ville d'Orléans," actually crossed the water safely, and came down on November 25, 1870, in Norway. The aeronaut in this case was a Monsieur Rollin. He made his descent close to Christiania, after having travelled no less than 750 leagues—a remarkable voyage, which he accomplished in rather less than fifteen hours. The remains of a balloon were, a long while after the last of these ascents, discovered in Iceland. It was supposed that it had come thither from Paris. The balloon sent up by the besieged Parisians contained upwards of ten and a half million letters, etc., some of which were duly answered by the aid of carrier pigeons.

Colonel Burnaby had more than once dilated to me on the pleasures to be derived from ballooning, and this, combined with what I saw during the siege of Paris, had much to do with my resolve to become an aeronaut., Burnaby, like most other aeronauts, has been often accused of recklessness and utter disregard of danger, but it cannot be denied that he applied himself to the scientific side of ballooning. It is more than thirty-five years since he made a notable ascent in the company of an enthusiastic fellow-officer in the Guards, from the Crystal Palace. Burnaby on that occasion tried a machine which he had himself devised with the idea of ascertaining the course of the wind above the clouds, when the earth was concealed. I cannot say that the machine was ever used to my knowledge by such skilled aeronauts as Dale and Simmons, but the trial in question was described at the time as a decidedly satisfactory one.

So great is the dread entertained by many people of exposing themselves to the slightest danger of accident—though the same persons often think nothing of leading the most unhealthy lives, of destroying the digestion, and shattering the whole nervous system by almost every means in their power —that it is easy to understand the abhorrence and even contempt with which ballooning used to be regarded in some quarters—though now the remarkable strides made by the science of aviation are beginning to open people's eyes a bit.

Every person who ventured off the solid earth in those days had to be prepared to hear of himself being described as a madman. In the same way the boldest mountaineers lay themselves open to the charge of being crazy, and Arctic explorers are often placed in the same category. Of old we were accustomed to regard the pleasures and perils of exploration on land and sea, as well as in the sky, in a very different spirit. It is not too much to say, that many of the greatest discoveries of modern times, which have increased the resources and the wealth of mankind, would not have been made, except for a dauntless spirit of adventure. Had Columbus entertained the exaggerated dread of exposing himself to unknown danger, which is too noticeable a feature of to-day, he would not have paved the way for the opening up of continents. It can certainly not be said that he undertook the discovery of the New World from commercial objects or for purely scientific purposes. The spirit of adventure and of daring and suffering all things moved him, as, according to the delightful old Greek tradition, it moved Ulysses, even in his extreme old age, to leave sceptre and isle, and " sail beyand the sunset " in search of a newer world.

It is possible, however, that if some of the least

adventurous people could only realize the unspeakable splendour which so swiftly opens out to the gaze of the aerial traveller, they would admit that ballooning has great and natural attractions. The sensations the aeronaut experiences in the ascent, and during his voyage through the skies, are pleasurable beyond description. The motion of the balloon is perfectly smooth and easy, no matter how quickly the wind is travelling, which is to be accounted for by the fact that the balloon goes with the wind. There is not the slightest resistance to the air, and consequently no disagreeable motion. On the perfect tranquillity that prevails in the heavens I have dwelt elsewhere. In the descent a jarring is sometimes experienced, and of course both before the balloon has got fairly away from the earth, and also after it has in coming down been impeded by the grapnel or by unwelcome obstacles, sensations may be experienced the reverse of agreeable. Indeed, the great majority of the accidents occur in the ascent and descent.

So remarkable is this tranquil and easy motion through the air, that the aeronaut is scarcely aware of the rate at which he is travelling. Mr. Green, the well-known balloonist, was once carried away at lightning speed by a furious whirlwind, and yet knew nothing about it. He was even unaware that he was moving at exceptional speed ! Not till he approached the earth, and marked there the fury of the wind, which threatened to tear the grapnel from its hold, did he realize the situation.

As to the scenery which the aeronaut enjoys, it is often beautiful beyond compare. The rising and the setting sun as seen by the balloonist are more brilliant and thousand-hued than even the mind of Turner conceived. Mr. Glaisher saw both spectacles. He witnessed the sun rising on an autumnal morning. Ascending slowly above the clouds, the aeronaut saw the sun rise, flooding with light the whole extent of cloudland beyond, which glistened under its beams like a lake of pure gold. "Grouped around the car," he said, "both above and below, there were clouds of alpine character sloping to their bases in glistening light, or towering upwards in sheets of shining vapour, which added the charm of contrast to the splendid tints of sunrise." Then suddenly the clouds spread round ocean-like, and continually changing their forms, "suddenly gathered themselves into mountain heaps and closed all round, hiding the sun in neutral-tinted gloom." Quite as dazzling in its splendour was a sunset once seen by Tissandier when ballooning over France; but perhaps Mr. Glaisher was most fortunate of all aerial voyagers, when he once viewed London at night. The air was perfectly clear, and the great city, with its millions of lights, looked a very Milky Way of the earth. So free from mist and fog was the atmosphere, that he was able to distinctly see persons moving along Oxford Street, with their very shadows cast upon the pavements.

General Brine's unsuccessful attempt to reach the French coast in 1882, and Burnaby's successful one in March of the same year, made me impatient to cross the water myself, either the Channel or the North Sea. Brine in the company of Simmons made an ascent from Canterbury early in 1882, with the object of crossing over to the French coast, but owing to a sudden and quite unlooked-for change in the wind—a danger which the aeronaut of course cannot guard against—drifted out to the North Sea. The aeronauts therefore had to take to the water, where fortunately they were picked up by the *Foam*.

Burnaby cherished the belief that under certain conditions the aeronaut might be able to overcome a difficulty such as Brine and Simmons experienced when the wind suddenly began to change and blow them out toward the German Ocean. He said he believed that when the wind was blowing in one direction at a certain height in the atmosphere it would very likely be blowing in a directly contrary direction at another one. Thus, his idea was, that the aeronaut might in many cases, finding the wind against him, ascend to a much greater height, and try his luck there. Unfortunately this cannot always be done with safety, as Messrs. Coxwell and Glaisher found out. It would be a rash experiment to make when placed as Brine and Simmons were, for supposing they had ascended to a great height, and still found the wind in the same direction, the delay of a few minutes might have cost both of them their lives.

Early in June 1882 my own arrangements were complete for a trip across the water. Simmons, the brave and skilful aeronaut, with whom I made my later ascents, arrived at Maldon on June 10, 1882, with his balloon, and next day the process of inflation was commenced. My sister Agnes, not to be deterred by the experiences of Madame Durouf, fully intended to accompany us, but Simmons decided that it would be advisable to take as much ballast as possible, and our plan had accordingly to be modified in this respect. As the morning wore on Simmons began to entertain serious doubts as to quite a different matter. The wind, though in the right direction, blowing towards Calais, was very boisterous, and under these circumstances the aeronaut thought it his duty to warn me through Mr. Waller, who was managing the preparations, against making the ascent at all. I could not think, however, of putting off the expedition, and resolved, come what might, to brave the breeze. So between twelve and one o'clock, in the presence of a great concourse of people, including Lady de Crespigny and several members of my family, we got into the car, and at once attempted the ascent. Everything would have no doubt gone off right enough had the men who were holding down the balloon released her at the right moment, just when Simmons gave the order. They delayed ; and as a consequence the car was dragged across the field, and dashed with great violence against a brick wall.

All this occurred in considerably less time than it takes to write it. Directly I perceived that a dangerous collision was inevitable, unless it could be averted by a great effort of strength at the critical moment, I took up as firm a position as possible, and sitting on the side of the car endeavoured with my left leg to push off from the wall. The task was probably beyond human strength, and, as it was, my leg was crushed between the car and the balloon. Curiously enough, I was not fully conscious of the injury I had sustained till I felt the bones grating, and glancing down, saw that my foot was at right angles to its natural position. A friend was standing close by amongst the spectators, and I remarked to him, " My leg's broken." He leant over the side of the balloon, and took hold of the right leg. I said, " No, not the right, the left one." There now seemed to be every prospect of the balloon getting away, and I did not like the idea of a trip across the Channel with a broken leg. To say nothing of the discomfort of a journey under such circumstances, there would probably be danger in the descent, which often entails a good deal of jarring. I therefore managed to raise myself by means of the ropes on to the side of the car, and was then assisted out backwards. An examination showed that my leg was broken in two places just above the ankle, and that the fracture was of the compound order.

Unfortunately I was not the only person who was injured by the mishap. There were several men clinging to the car at the time it dragged across the field, and one man was crushed as by the wheels of Juggernaut against the wall. Two of his ribs were broken, and he was in a very bad way until attended to by Dr. Gutteridge, who also treated me very skilfully. One or two other persons were slightly damaged, nor did Simmons himself escape scot-free. His arm was hurt, and, to use his own words, his side " seemed to be caved in." Apparently not recognizing exactly what had happened to me in the confusion and excitement which took place when the car struck against the wall, Simmons called out, " Tell Sir Claude to get in." Learning what had happened, he none the less resolved, and in my opinion rightly so, to make the ascent alone. My sudden removal from the car had left him in a somewhat

9

awkward position. But he managed to replace my weight with some ballast at hand, and then in a lull effected a capital ascent. I was lying down in the field with my head propped up, and with great interest, and greater disappointment at my own inability to take part in the voyage, saw him dart up into the sky.

From the short account which Simmons supplied of his trans-Channel trip, it seems that his chief difficulty was to keep sufficiently high to clear all impediments, and yet be able to see where he was going. The clouds were exceedingly low, so that it was not at all easy to do this. He heard the sound of the breakers soon after the start,—the balloon travelled at a tremendous pace,—and this satisfied him that the wind was a true one from the earth's surface to a great altitude. Upon dipping below the clouds he ventured down to have a look at the sea. The sound of the breakers had then ceased, but presently it was repeated. He could just dimly perceive a sandy coast-line in front, and concluded that he must be right for France. Presently the balloon dipped again below the clouds, and the aeronaut found that he was over land. He guessed it to be Kent, and in a few minutes more was able to distinguish Deal, which lay a little to the east. It was next to impossible to keep low enough to be under the clouds, so as to see the coast-line around, and at the same time be high enough to be sure of getting a good sweep over it.

At 1.45 Simmons was right over the Calais-Douvres steamer, and could see the passengers waving excitedly to him, as people always will to an aeronaut.

Twelve minutes after passing over the English chalk cliffs he was over the French coast. He was then so near Calais as to be able to distinguish all its streets and public bulidings. The water safely crossed, he took off his cork jacket—without which no balloonist who knows his business makes an ascent near the sea—and meditated a trip inland. But suddenly recollecting that my accident and removal from the balloon had left him with very scanty pecuniary resources, he decided to come to anchor as soon as possible. He looked out for a landing place, but for some time could see no hedge or ditch on his track suitable for the purpose. Nothing was passed save fields divided by different crops of corn. After Simmons had gone as he supposed about a hundred miles into France a large city was reached. The inhabitants rushed out into the principal square to witness the strange sight. Floating over them at a height of about six hundred feet, he asked in French, " What's the name of this place ? " and the reply came " Arras." A few miles outside the city he descended, and after dragging a long distance over some level ground, and damaging the crops, he crippled the balloon, and managed to get out of the car in safety. He had traversed one hundred and seventy miles in slightly over an hour and a half.

The incidents of this ascent supplied the news-papers with some excellent " copy " at a not over-exciting period, and one or two of them—rather ungratefully, it has occurred to me !—censured us severely for what they were pleased to regard as our foolhardiness. The fact is, there was a kind of anti-balloon scare just about this time. To General

Brine's misadventure allusion has been made. Then some years previously two French aeronauts had perished in the higher atmospheric regions whilst directing the balloon " Zenith." But far fresher in the mind of the public than any other aeronautic disaster was the fatal ascent of Mr. Walter Powell at Bath. With regard to this particular disaster, it has always seemed to me that Mr. Powell and his two colleagues, Major Templar—who was afterwards in charge of the ballooning in the war in Egypt— and Mr. Gardner, made mistakes of a kind which the least experienced aeronaut ought to avoid. It was said that they intended crossing the water. If so it was little short of madness to start as they did late in the afternoon, light, as every one can understand, being a *sine qua non* to the safety of the balloonist. Then to deliberately endeavour to leave the car as it dragged along the ground, as was done in this case, was to invite a catastrophe. It appears that the aeronauts, finding themselves going out to sea, resolved to leave the car, if needs be, whilst the balloon was still in motion.

The balloon was accordingly brought to earth close to Bridport. There was nothing to make the grapnel fast to, so the balloon dragged or skimmed along the ground. To leave the balloon whilst it was so moving was something like getting out of a train going at a good pace. Mr. Gardner in leaping out fractured his leg, but Major Templar with great good fortune managed to reach the ground without injuring himself. The balloon, relieved of the weight of the two men, shot up again, and Mr. Powell had not time to join his companions. It passed over the cliffs and floated away to sea. Mr. Powell when last seen by his companions was clinging on outside the car. In a minute or two he disappeared altogether from view, and never more was seen by mortal eye. His precise fate must therefore remain for all time uncertain. What the party clearly ought to have done when they found themselves going over the cliffs was to come down in the sea, and then with their cork jackets on swim to shore.

The injury I sustained in the Maldon ascent left me *hors de combat* for many a weary week. From Saturday, June 10, to Saturday, July 29, my diary is a dismal blank. On the latter day I went downstairs, and drove to Witham. Two days afterwards I went up to town, visited the theatre, and luxuriated in a Turkish bath. But swift retribution followed this too swift return to the joys of life. My bones had not perfectly mended. In a few days I was down again, and invalided till almost the middle of September. The various accidents I have sustained chasing and hunting, all combined perhaps, punished me less severely than this balloon disaster.

With that happy knack, rare amongst princes as amongst their subjects, of always doing and saying the right thing at the right time, the late King Edward, then Prince of Wales, sent me a kind little message through my brother after this ballooning disaster. " Tell your brother," he said, " that I am very sorry to hear of his mishap ; but also say that I cannot approve altogether of his trying to make the ascent under the circumstances."

Before concluding this account of the first ascent from Maldon, I may note that the rate at which

Simmons crossed to France was, with one exception, the fastest on aeronautic record. That exception was Simmons's trip from Peekskill to Bedford in New York county, a distance of twenty-five miles, which was accomplished at a perfectly phenomenal rate.

By the time I had fully recovered from the injury sustained in this first Maldon ascent, the time of year was too far advanced to make, with any great chance of success, another attempt to cross the Channel. But in the following year, and a little later on in the season, I had again made arrangements for the trip. Indeed long before my leg was mended, my resolution to make another attempt had been come to. When Mr. Wymper, roaming about by himself one afternoon on the then unknown heights of the Matterhorn, slipped, and falling several hundred feet, met with an accident that all but cost him his life, he yet resolved to be the first to tread on the summit of the great mountain. Nothing could move him from his purpose ; nothing could move me from mine. The Channel of course had already been crossed in a balloon a fair number of times, whereas Mr. Wymper was aiming at a record in mountaineering. But as it happened, we too were to establish a record in ballooning.

On Monday, July 30, 1883, Simmons, whom I again chose for the trip, came to Maldon with his balloon, and at once set about repairing some damages which it had sustained at Brighton a few weeks previously. Composed principally of indiarubber and bird-lime—a queer combination this must seem to the non-aeronautic mind—it was one of the strongest balloons ever constructed. It was capable of holding 37,000 cubic feet of gas,—exactly the same quantity, by the way, as held by the balloon in which Burnaby crossed the Channel,—and when inflated it was seventy-five feet in height and forty-two in diameter. Directly I set eyes on it I felt assured of success, and only longed for an early start.

But that is exactly what we did not get. There was much delay in inflating the balloon, though the operation commenced so early as five o'clock in the morning. After breakfast I arrived on the scene of action, which was a paddock adjoining the Maldon Gas Works, and roamed about, growing after a while very impatient as the hours of daylight wore on apace. In the course of the morning we sent up six pilot balloons, of about sixteen feet in diameter, and the result was not at all encouraging. The wind was veering about, now north-west and now south-west, in a very fickle manner, and the fifth balloon went in a course which would take it straight up the North Sea! Simmons looked grave, as well he might. He was an intrepid aeronaut and had made upwards of four hundred and fifty ascents in his time, out of which more than half were solitary ones. He had had several very narrow escapes, and had descended into the sea no less than nine times—once into the German Ocean, once into the English Channel, and once into Lake Michigan. At the same time he had a laudable desire to live a little longer and make a few more successful ascents. The threatening-looking course taken by our fifth pilot balloon seemed to indicate that there would be every probability of his desire in this respect being unaccomplished, if he went up that morning into the heavens with me. He expressed his grave doubts as to the wisdom of our ascending that day, but was too courageous a man to actually decline to do so.

There remained, however, the sixth pilot balloon to try, and presently it was despatched on its journey. It took a more reassuring course than the fifth, and I adjudged that if our own behaved in the same manner, there was good ground for believing that we should reach Holland or Germany before dark. Simmons, however, did not look on things in such a hopeful spirit. He was in a dubious, head-shaking kind of humour, and was quite prepared for the worst. "Simmons, will you go now?" I asked him when the sixth pilot had floated away out of sight, and he replied in the affirmative. After that he never hesitated. At half-past eleven the inflation of the balloon was finished. The car was affixed, and then made captive to a tree in a hedge close to the gas works. Five hundred pounds of ballast in seven bags were stowed away in the car, and I made a small and useful addition in the shape of some sandwiches and cold tea. We had already tried on our life-belts for use in case we should fall into the North Sea, and nothing remained but to get in, and get off as quickly as possible. We ought properly to have started several hours earlier, as our safety must depend to a very large extent on the amount of daylight at our disposal.

At half-past twelve Simmons and I at last got into the car—the identical one out of which I lowered myself with my broken leg the year before—and the order was given to the score or so of men who were holding to let go. The order this time was promptly obeyed, and we went up in a lull between the gusts of wind. Greatly excited, and filled with admiration at the majestic manner in which we took flight, the great crowd of spectators, who had been waiting patiently for several hours, burst into loud cheers. The demonstration was kept up for some little while, and we acknowledged it by waving our hats. The undercurrents of wind were anything but strong, and as a result our progress to commence with was exceptionally slow. We were told that we were visible for over an hour after the start. Of a very different character was Simmons's ascent in the previous year; in that case the balloon had completely disappeared from sight in the matter of a few minutes, the rate of progress, as already pointed out, being from the outset quite lightning-like.

Flitting away over Osea Island and Asheldham Gorse, we soon found ourselves "at sea," though it was some time before we lost sight of the Essex coast. A beautiful "Kathorama" forthwith disclosed itself. The bottom of the sea could be clearly seen in every direction, each channel and shoal standing out in the clearest relief, though 9000 feet below us. The lightship east of the Blackwater looked the size of a flea, but, like every other object visible, it stood out most clear-cut. A man-of-war at Harwich was a bit bigger than a pea, and six steamers beneath us appeared to be on the point of a wholesale collision. Through the unspeakable stillness the bell on a buoy off the Blackwater was to be heard continuously ringing. A man perhaps never really knows what the most magnificent view is till carried

by a balloon into a perfectly clear atmosphere. However high we climb amongst the loftiest mountains,
there are always peaks in one direction or another to
obstruct the view. Nothing in a clear atmosphere
impedes the view which opens out to the aeronaut a
few minutes after his ascent.

But we had other things to attend to besides the
glorious scenery. We had to devote our minds to
the question of whether we were to reach *terra firma*
before night, or be carried away and drowned in the
North Sea. We flung out scraps of paper, and
noticed that they drifted a bit northerly. So long
as the course pursued remained a southerly or easterly
one we were fairly sure of reaching the Continent.
By two o'clock we had touched an altitude of 10,000
feet, and now for the first time found ourselves rushing into a dense mist to the south-east. An hour
later we were fairly enshrouded in it, and could see
nothing but each other and the balloon.

We enjoyed some effects as beautiful as the aurora
borealis. A perfect picture of the balloon presented
itself on the clouds. Every rope was faithfully reproduced, and our own forms were actually represented.
We opened our mouths to shout at our *vis-à-vis*
tearing along within a few yards of us, and they
opened their mouths as though to shout back at us.
The grappling cable which Simmons had let out was
distinctly reproduced in reflection or shadow running
to the phantom car that kept us company. At first
when Simmons drew my attention to this extraordinary effect I could see nothing, but coming over
to his side perceived it perfectly. Other curious
effects were noticeable. For instance, a blue serge

suit Simmons wore looked quite green for a while. The atmosphere above presently turned into a deep cerulean blue, and the gas up through the balloon could be clearly seen. The great dome itself, with its gores and diamonds, had a substantial appearance rather reassuring in a region of phantom effects. Meanwhile the silence continued to be, as was the case before we came into this dense mist, almost oppressive. We could well hear the beating of our own hearts.

These strange and beautiful reflections or images have been noticed occasionally by several other balloonists. It is not unlikely indeed that they are in various forms quite common. Monsieur Flammarion, when careering through the mystic realms of cloudland, was once startled by the sudden appearance of a rival balloon and rival aeronauts, at, as it seemed, less than a hundred feet away. The forms of the travellers in the rival balloon Flammarion and his companion speedily recognised as their own. The minutest details came out in this reflection, the thinnest ropes, and even the cords and instruments suspended thereto. Godard flourished the national flag, and the shadow of a flag was instantly moved by the spectral hand in the air. All around too they noticed curious concentric circles of various hues.

After two hours of silence and mist a faint sound smote on our ears. Could it be the surf on the coast of Holland or Germany? we asked ourselves. Slowly descending, we emerged just before five o'clock on the under side of the clouds, and at once caught sight of what we conceived and hoped to be the coast-line to the south-east. But a few minutes later this line turned out to be nothing more than one of the many shoals we had seen in the course of the day. Still the shoal was encouraging to this extent—it showed that we were no longer in mid-ocean. The next objects which engaged our attention were less deceptive. Several steamers and sailing vessels were within sight, the latter tacking and behaving generally as though they expected that their aid would be shortly required. If that were the case they were speedily undeceived. We left them far behind, and fell to discussing the very serious question —indeed it was almost one of life and death—as to whether our change in altitude had had the very undesirable effect of taking us out of our course east or south-east to one more or less due north. A streak appeared to the east, and though it remained indistinct for a considerable while, I had a fancy it was land. Presently, however, it began to grow dimmer and dimmer, and eventually turned out to be a cloud. There are mirages of the air as of the desert, as we discovered several times during our perilous journey through the clouds.

At ten minutes past six a rather startling thing occurred. The sun peeped out of the bank of clouds which encircled it, and under the influence of its rays, the balloon instantly took a wild leap heavenwards, carrying us in a single bound from 8,000 to 17,000 feet. In our mad career upwards we passed through what looked like a great field of glaciers and snow-covered mountains. The glories of Alp and Himalaya pale and sink to puny proportions beside the magnificence of that mountain-land of space. It was difficult to realize that these vast hills were built of mere cloud, so solid and immovable did they appear. The scene was so enchanting that we almost forgot the intense cold—the valve-line was frozen—and the danger we might incur by remaining at so great an altitude. The opening of the valve by Simmons, who was not inclined to risk his life for these "unsubstantial pageants" of the air, took us down towards base earth as quickly as we had shot up a few minutes before. The roar of the surf greeted our ears, and before our delighted vision spread a part of Walcheren Island (a spot patriotic Englishmen cannot as a rule regard with pleasure), and of the mainland of Holland, which shut us in on the north. We had thus securely crossed the North Sea, an aeronautic feat never before accomplished. Simmons was so satisfied that we were safe that he took out his sketch-book, and made a drawing of Walcheren and the town of Flushing which lay immediately beneath us.

Oftentimes the bringing of a balloon to anchor is a very troublesome and risky affair. As it was, we narrowly escaped striking the top of a cottage. The throwing out of some ballast just saved us from this disaster, which would not improbably have cost both of us our lives. After this incident all went well. We got our grapnel out, and having torn up an old fence or so, hitched on securely in a dyke. The car bumped about a little, and turned clean over once or twice, but this was a trifle ; for we managed to hang on to the guy-ropes till it righted itself.

A large crowd of people had meanwhile chased us from field to field. They came up and helped us to pack the balloon in the car, and afterwards escorted us back to Flushing with many signs of enthusiasm and approval. The only jarring note came from the owner of a fence we had considerably damaged. He mentioned large sums of money by way of compensation, but ultimately took a couple of sovereigns. Arrived in Flushing, we had just time to get dinner at the Wellington Hotel. Four hours after reaching *terra firma* we were on, instead of over, the water; and the following afternoon I was standing in my own hall at Champion Lodge. From an aeronautic point of view, complete success had crowned what looked at the outset a very risky enterprise. The Balloon Society's council met on Thursday, the day after the news of our success was wired to England, and under the presidency of Mr. C. Green Spencer resolved, "That the Society's gold medal be presented to Sir Claude de Crespigny, one of the life members of the Society, for the indomitable courage displayed in his voyage across the Channel yesterday; also that a public vote of thanks be accorded to him and Mr. Simmons at the meeting to be held to-morrow."

Burnaby's voyage across the Channel, differed a good deal from that of Simmons in 1882, as also from that of Simmons and myself across the North Sea in the following year. As I was meditating the trip myself, I was naturally very interested to hear all about it from his own lips. It seems that he first definitely made up his mind to cross the Channel when he heard of the failure of Brine and Simmons. Burnaby had little patience with people who decried every one as a lunatic, or a balloonatic, as he put it himself, who took any part in this pursuit. His view was that a man was no more a fool to risk his life in a balloon than to take part in steeplechasing or any other sport where a certain amount of hazard must be unavoidable.

Shortly after the failure of Brine and Simmons, he put himself into communication with the owner of a balloon, in which Mr. Powell, M.P., had once made an ascent. The balloon, he was told, would hold 36,000 feet of gas, and was in excellent condition. Its owner expressed a desire to go with Burnaby. But the latter declined this privilege, and decided to go alone ; for one thing Burnaby was seventeen stone, and one such a heavy-weight passenger as this is quite enough for the lifting-power of most balloons, unless the journey is to be of the shortest. Burnaby also declined to take a reporter for one of the London newspapers with him. The start was arranged for March 21, 1882, from Dover, and when the morning arrived the wind was found to be in the right quarter. The only hitch that occurred was in the work of filling the balloon. I have experienced difficulties in this matter in my own expeditions, as I shall show presently, and Burnaby found to his disgust that several hours had to be wasted. He had hoped to be off by eight o'clock, but had scarcely started two hours later.

As he went up the owner pointed to one of the cords, and suggested that if the balloon burst in the air, Burnaby might do worse than pull it ; he had an idea that the burst balloon might then come down in the form of a parachute. This was a nice kind of thing to set a man thinking about at the moment of his departure from the solid earth—and a pleasant send-off! Burnaby, however, was not a nervous man. As he sprang upwards, he appeared to be in considerable risk of striking a factory shaft which was in rather dangerous proximity to the spot selected for the ascent; but the collision was avoided by flinging out some ballast, and thus increasing the rising power of the balloon. He then rose rapidly to a height of between two and three thousand feet, and enjoyed a fine view of earth and sea. Though there had been frost overnight, the day was warm and pleasant. Being a stout man, Burnaby indeed felt the rays of the sun quite oppressive, and shielded the back of his neck with his handkerchief.

The balloon's motion was delightful, and the occupant congratulated himself that he was not experiencing the horrible qualms of sea-sickness on board one of the passenger vessels plying far below. The first striking incident in his voyage was a sudden and very rapid descent of the balloon. Throwing pieces of paper out, Burnaby observed that they fluttered in the air above. He therefore, to save himself from coming down into the water, began to throw ballast out. It was not until a considerable quantity of sand had been scattered that his barometer showed that the balloon was at length taking an upward turn. It did so not a minute too soon, for when his downward career was at length stopped, the balloon was within five hundred feet of the sea. This sudden descent was owing to the fact that the balloon had found its way into a region of cold air, which had compressed the gas.

Next Burnaby found his balloon had come to a dead stand-still! He threw bits of paper out of the car, and they one and all fell straight down into the Channel. He was thus, it was perfectly clear, becalmed in the air. Some fishing-boats were to be seen at no great distance off, and their crews made signs which Burnaby interpreted as friendly indications of a desire to take him on board, if he would come down into the water. But he had started with the set purpose of crossing the Channel, and of not alighting till he had done so. He therefore hardened his heart against the friendly advances of the fishermen, and stuck resolutely to his stationary balloon. For an hour he remained in this very aggravating position, but at length descended again within less than a quarter of a mile from the water, and then again reascended a little. Things, however, were no better at this lower altitude ; the balloon continued becalmed. What was to be done ? In order the better to consider this question, and to pass away time that was beginning to hang heavily on his hands, " the mad Englishman " took a cigar out of his case, and calmly lit up, regardless of the fact that there was a continuous escape of inflammable gas just above his head. He might just as safely have smoked in a powder magazine. Burnaby admitted the riskiness of the proceeding in describing it afterwards, and chuckled when he pictured what the discomfort of the owner of the balloon would have been, could he have seen what was taking place !

No change whatever in Burnaby's position taking place, and the balloon not catching fire, as might have been expected, the aeronaut resolved to ascend to a much greater altitude. He flung out a bag of ballast, which fell with a loud thud into the water.

10

Up shot the balloon to a height of 3,000 feet, and then again remained stationary. Out went another bag, and up went the balloon again, this time to an altitude of about a mile and a half ; but still the hateful calm. More ballast followed, and the balloon continued to ascend into the higher regions of the air. Very little ballast was left when Burnaby found himself at a height of about two miles. But at length in the midst of cloudland the balloon began to move, and, to Burnaby's great satisfaction, in the direction of France ; whilst presently, getting clear of the clouds, he was able to see most distinctly the town and harbour of Dieppe.

Full of spirits and fun over his successful voyage, the aeronaut, having descended to within a few hundred feet of the earth, over which he was now speeding, dropped some loose sand on a labourer working in a field below. The man started, looked all round to see where this had come from, and at length, perceiving the balloon, fell flat on his back. Others now saw the balloon, and cried out to its occupant to come down at once. This is often easier to say than to do in ballooning ; but after bumping the ground once with considerable violence and then reascending, Burnaby pulled the valve-line, and then, as he rushed down with great rapidity, threw out the remainder of his ballast in order to lessen the pace and force of the collision with the ground. He came to anchor in a ploughed field.

The natives were very kind and obliging, as Simmons found them when he ascended from French soil later on in the year, and vastly excited over the advent of the balloon in their midst. One old woman was especially demonstrative, and Burnaby placed on record her words. "Thank heavens, I too have seen it," cried she. "It passed over my house like the dome of a cathedral; and all my hens are still in convulsions of fright at its appearance."

The two ascents from Maldon, namely, in June 1882, and August 1883, may, I suppose, be regarded as the most sensational in my aeronautic career. It is a rather remarkable fact that almost within rifle-shot of my Essex house there have been two sensational ascents and two sensational descents. The former have been described; and as regards the latter, there was first that of Captain Alfred Paget, R.N., when the grapnel struck an unfortunate lad who was in its path and caused fracture of the skull; and secondly, the disastrous descent in a field very close to Champion Lodge when Simmons lost his life. Captain Paget's untoward descent near Maldon I was not informed of in time to go out and meet him and his companion and offer them the hospitality which one balloonist would naturally desire to extend to another. Simmons's death was a source of great regret to me. I had formed the very highest opinion of his pluck, resourcefulness, and experience.

Most tragic was Simmons's end. It occurred on August 27, 1888, at Ulting, near Champion Lodge. He and two other aeronauts made an ascent from the Irish Exhibition at Olympia, hoping to cross over to the Continent. Everything appears to have gone well till they tried to descend at Ulting. The grapnel caught in an elm tree, and Simmons seems to have made a premature attempt to reach the ground. The balloon came down with a bump, shot up again, and struck the tree. It burst with what was described as a terrific report, the car was dashed into fragments, and Simmons came by his end. So the dauntless aeronaut died in harness.

I recollect Simmons telling me that the only time he was ever in a balloon when the grapnel smashed, was in 1884, when he was with me. We ascended from Bury St. Edmunds, and came down near St. Neots. The ground was so hard that it smashed the grapnel! We dragged a long way before we got anchored, tearing an upright post out of the ground, as if it were a tooth-pick, and we only just missed being violently whirled into some telegraph wires, which would no doubt have finished us off all right. As it happened the balloon was burst from neck to valve, and the car stove in, but we ourselves escaped without injury, though we had to hang on to the guy-ropes for dear life to save ourselves from being hurled out as the car turned clean over once or twice.

We hovered over Bury during this trip for a considerable time, as motionless as Burnaby's balloon was over the Channel. At length I got tired of this kind of thing, and told Simmons to pull the valve-line. From an altitude of five thousand feet or so we dropped to perhaps three thousand, and soon afterwards found ourselves travelling at the very respectable rate of twenty-five miles an hour.

Not being myself a witness of the fatal accident which cost Simmons his life, I cannot safely offer any remark as to whether or no the disaster was the result of absolute carelessness. But though it is in the descent, as a rule, that most of the accidents occur, it is not by any means necessarily fatal to catch in a tree. Indeed it sometimes happens that a tree is the best place to come to anchor in. More than a hundred years ago, Mr. Blanchard, the Maxim of his day, in the company of Dr. Jeffries, an American, crossed the Channel from England to France for the first time in the history of ballooning. Before he and his companion had safely got over the water, their balloon began to descend with rapidity, and they only managed to keep up by flinging out their ballast and everything else in the car ; they even disposed of their hats and coats, though it was winter time. Fortunately the balloon appears to have changed its mind just before touching the water, and they were eventually taken up again, and carried away into the forest of Guieppe. Here one of the aeronauts caught hold of the branch of a tree, and the balloon's dangerous flight was successfully arrested without any accident. Blanchard's feat fired the ambition of a rival balloonist, Pilatre de Rozier, who at once resolved to cross the Channel from France to England. He fixed to the hydrogen balloon, by which the weight was to be borne, another and much smaller fire balloon. This, he believed, would enable him to alter his specific gravity as might be required. The fire balloon speedily set the fabric in flames, and Pilatre and his companion were destroyed. Fifty years ago an English aeronaut escaped from an explosion through fire in a truly miraculous manner. He alighted in his balloon upon a chimney on fire. The balloon caught fire and exploded, but the aeronaut dropped in the very nick of time down the side of the house, and thus escaped.

The most dreadful aeronautic position, perhaps, which it is possible to conceive was that in which Burnaby and a couple of Frenchmen once found themselves shortly after making an ascent from Cremorne. One of these Frenchmen had invented the balloon used, and was exceedingly proud thereof. It would probably have never ascended at all had not Burnaby, who volunteered to go with the theorists, slyly dropped some ballast out of the car. When about a mile and a half or a mile and three-quarters high, the appalling discovery was made that the neck of the aerostat, which should of course, in accordance with the usual custom, have been left open in order to allow of the gas escaping, was still tied up with a silk handkerchief. The balloon was now quite full, and the atmospheric pressure was rapidly decreasing as the aeronauts ascended ; whilst the gas, having no exit, continued to expand. The aerostat was constructed in such a way that it was not possible to get at the neck, and so unloosen the fatal handkerchief ; whilst, to make disaster doubly assured, the valve-line was quite out of reach. Under these circumstances, the only thing the aeronauts could do was to sit still and wait for their balloon to burst and dash them to the earth. To Burnaby death seemed absolutely certain. In a few minutes the balloon did burst, and instantly began to rush earthwards at a velocity that increased every moment. But by a piece of wonderfully good fortune, the balloon somehow in its headlong career downwards formed a kind of huge parachute, and the occupants landed unhurt in a field just outside the Metropolis.

By the way, Burnaby had a ballooning fad of his own, on which he dilated to me on one occasion. It was his ambition to reach a height far above that achieved by any other aeronaut, and he had an idea that this might be done by being clad in a kind of diver's dress to avoid the intense cold, and by taking with one a supply of oxygen, the lack of which defeats the balloonist ascending beyond a certain height. To have carried out this idea successfully—he never actually tried it—he would have had to ascend to a great altitude, for in 1862 Mr. Glaisher and Mr. Coxwell actually attained a height of seven miles. I have recorded the experiences of Simmons and myself at a height of 17,000 feet, which were not over-agreeable. But these two intrepid aeronauts, having three-quarters of an hour after their ascent from Wolverhampton reached to an altitude of five miles, calmly flung out sand till they attained a height of 29,000 feet. Before this was done Mr. Glaisher's sight had begun to fail, so that he could no longer read the fine divisions on his instruments. As they continued to ascend, the balloon rapidly spun round and round, and as a consequence the valve-line became so entangled that Mr. Coxwell had to climb up into the ring above the car to set it right. Mr. Glaisher became unconscious, and his companion was in almost as critical a condition. He had great difficulty in extricating himself from the ring, which was so piercingly cold that his hands were frozen. After a struggle he dropped somehow back again into the car, and there feeling himself becoming like Mr. Glaisher, insensible, made one despairing effort. He caught the valve-line—now unentangled—in his teeth, and, despite his dazed condition, held the valve open till the balloon at last began to unmistakably descend. When Mr. Glaisher was restored to consciousness, he found his friend's hands were quite black and powerless. The history of ballooning furnishes no more thrilling episode than this, and Mr. Coxwell's admirable presence of mind and perseverance in the direst of extremities must give him a high and enduring place in the ranks of aeronauts of all time. It shows what sort of a man Burnaby was, to think seriously of putting into the shade the exploit of these two balloonists.

Once Simmons's balloon ascended with such rapidity to the height of 30,000 feet, that he fainted away. Fortunately he had a turn of the valve-line round his hand when he sank insensible amongst the sand-bags, and this soon brought him down to a lesser altitude. He was thus saved in much the same manner as were Glaisher and Coxwell.

At various times different people have expressed a desire to go with me on a ballooning excursion. Don Carlos—to whom, by the bye, I was introduced by an excellent aeronaut, the late General Brine—has talked about it, and so have several steeple-chasers. One of the people who was quite ready to go a-ballooning with me was Lord Marcus Beresford. I asked him to go with me when I made an ascent with Dale from Lillie Bridge, but he was engaged elsewhere. Curiously enough we passed, by pure chance, over Tattenham Corner, and there was Epsom course spread out far below us ! I decided to come down, which we did on Walton Heath, three miles from the course. A number of spectators were soon alongside of us, and one fellow made a desperate endeavour to climb into the balloon by the neck. There was imminent danger of his tearing it, so I ordered him to desist. He took umbrage at this, and wanted to fight. I was not indisposed to do battle on behalf of the balloon, but his friends dragged him off. A little while later whom should we meet returning from a cricket match but Marcus and Jack Jones!

Little Dale I esteemed as a capital and most plucky aeronaut, though he had not the immense experience of Simmons. A very short time before his last and fatal ascent at the Palace, I visited Dale, and promised to go up again with him very soon. After Dale's death I was glad to be able to offer his widow a house-rent free for two years in South London, which offer, by the way, she declined.

Concerning Dale's death I had some remarks to make from the Chair of the Balloon Society, shortly after the accident, which were somewhat misinterpreted in several of the daily papers. I was represented as attributing the disaster to the fact that Dale ascended in a balloon made of inferior materials. But he was far too good an aeronaut to have done such a thing. It was and is my view, however, that he, being a poor man, kept his balloon rather too long for his own safety. The disaster occurred from the material partially rotting through being packed away damp; and it was found that nearly every bone in his body had been broken by the fall, as was the case with de Groof, the " flying man " impostor. For many years brave little Dale afforded, at the Crystal Palace, great amusement to many thousands of people.

My friend, the late General Brine, who made the
trans-Channel trip with Dale in August 1884, gave
a very useful and entertaining lecture before the
Society some years ago, in the course of which he
vividly described what may be termed the senti-
mental side of ballooning. " I have come here to-
night," he said, " to treat of ballooning in its scientific
aspects only, but I cannot bring myself to say adieu
without asseverating that in my humble opinion the
calling of the aeronaut has as many charms, if not
more, for the poet and the philosopher as for the
scientist. What sensation, for example, can equal
that experienced by the aerial voyager, when, in his
journey through the atmosphere, he actually touches
the very clouds which are the ' chariots of the Al-
mighty ' ? And what circumstances can be so much
calculated to impress him with reverential awe and
astonishment passing the power of speech, as when,
seated in his frail car suspended from a spherical
mass of inflated canvas, and riding triumphantly
over the summits of the loftiest mountains and along
the vast deep, he plunges into those mighty atmospheric reservoirs whence come the rain, the hail,
and the snow, and introduces himself to those heavenly
arsenals with all their attendant mysterious pheno-
mena, whence issue the lightning and the thunder-
bolt that strike such terror upon the earth ? "

Another aeronaut of that time was M. L'Hoste.
To look at, he scarcely conveyed to us the impression
of being a very adventurous or resolute man, but
his record was a good one. He twice crossed the
Channel, but a third attempt to cross from Dover
to Dunkirk cost him his life. On Nov. 16, 1887,

he and M. Mangot made an ascent. They were last seen about forty miles south of the Isle of Wight, and it was supposed that a storm of wind and rain which was raging at the time must have driven their balloon into the sea. No trace of it, any more than of Mr. Powell's, was ever discovered.

Up to the present time there have been, I think, about a score of trans-Channel balloon voyages, exclusive of MM. Blériot's and de Lesseps' successful flights on monoplanes, and Mr. Rolls' double journey on a biplane, and in the case of about half this number the start has been made from England. In addition there have been three trips from Dublin to England, and one across the Bristol Channel. In all, these trips have cost five lives. In seven cases the aerial travellers were cast into the sea, but picked up by vessels. Amongst the most notable voyages over the water within my own ballooning experiences were—

(1) Colonel Burnaby's, March 23, 1882.

(2) Simmons's, June 10, 1882 (when I broke my leg).

(3) M. L'Hoste's, Sept. 9, 1883.

(4) Simmons's, Sept. 13, 1883 (about six weeks after our voyage across the North Sea).

(5) M. L'Hoste's, August 7, 1884.

(6) General Brine's and Dale's, August 15, 1884.

Since the last-named date M. L'Hoste, as we have seen, has been drowned ; Simmons killed (August 27, 1888) close to my own house, and the scenes of several of his sensational exploits ; and Dale killed at the Crystal Palace on June 29, 1892. General Brine has also long since "joined the majority."

Thus of six balloonists who were all bent on crossing
and recrossing the water a few years ago, only one
remains to-day to tell the tale, namely, myself. With
Burnaby's end all the world is familiar. His fame
is as great and untarnished as on the day when
England first heard of, and mourned over, the loss of
one of her bravest soldiers. If any one were base
enough to ask of what avail to his land were
Burnaby's gallant deeds on the field of battle, there
could be no better reply than this—

"The greatest gift a hero leaves his country
Is to have been a hero."

The Channel trips have unquestionably been made
at a considerable sacrifice of life, but it is doubtful
whether ballooning is quite so perilous a pursuit as
generally regarded. In the course of ten thousand
ascents, in which fifteen hundred aeronauts were
engaged, it was calculated not long since that only
fifteen lives were lost, less than one in every seven
hundred ascents. I have not had an opportunity of
checking these figures myself, and probably they do
not include all the ascents made during recent years ;
but they appear to be on fairly reliable authority,
and, even if not perfectly accurate, help to throw
some light on the matter.

Ever since I saw the ballooning, ineffectual
though it usually was, during the siege of Paris, I
have always believed that the aeronaut ought to be
of great service in campaigns. It was my ambition,
even whilst I was lying helpless after the accident
at Maldon, to assist the British army in Egypt by
means of ballooning. I felt sure if I could make a

successful ascent or two I should be able to materially assist the General in command. Accordingly, hoping to be soon on my feet again, I wrote and proffered my services, but received a reply to the effect that it had been decided not to use a balloon at all in the course of this campaign. None the less I made up my mind that if I got well I would go out on my own responsibility and take my balloon with me. It was a great disappointment as the days and weeks wore on to find that there was no hope of my leg getting right again in time to accomplish this intention. The injury was a worse one than I had supposed. I may add that in my opinion, as in that of a good many others, a balloon would have been much more serviceable than the armour train which was actually used, and which proved no very great success.

After this date, it will be remembered, a balloon came into requisition at Suakin in March 1885. This was the first time a balloon was ever used by a British fleet at war, and about that period the question of whether dynamite could be thrown at an enemy by aeronauts was quite seriously discussed. Later on, in the year 1887, the British War Department conducted experiments at Chatham with a view of testing the use of captive balloons for taking observations in war time. It is rather more than a hundred years since a balloon was first used on the field of battle.

Considerable use might be made of balloons in war time for the purposes of photography. I made an ascent with Dale and two photographers from Lillie Bridge, our object being to take some good views of London, but unfortunately the atmosphere became clouded and we were not successful. We descended at Walton Heath without mishap, or indeed any notable adventure, and afterwards there was a lecture at the Society on an electrical stationary balloon which had recently been invented. Colonel Hope, V.C., seconded the President's proposal that a volunteer balloon scientific chair should be formed. Reference was also made to a question which should be of very general interest, namely, on the taking of observations from a balloon for meteorological purposes, which would enable weather forecasts to be made with much greater certainty and definiteness than at present.

Before quitting the subject it may be well to remind the public why it was that the ballooning experiments at Suakin, and also in Bechuanaland, proved of little use. These experiments were comparatively unsuccessful, I believe, because the wind happened to be almost invariably unfavourable for the purpose of the aeronauts. It may be readily understood that a captive balloon is only of use in the absence of anything like a strong wind. The department was under the charge of Majors Templar and Elsdale, who caused all the hydrogen gas to be conveyed to the scene of action from Chatham. The balloons were manufactured out of gold-beaters' skins.

I conclude with what may prove a useful tip to aeronauts, who have not made up their minds as to the best kind of liquor to take with them for refreshment, and with a ballooning incident not without humour, though I quite failed to see it in such a light at the time it occurred. I feel sure the blue ribbon army—though I am not yet exactly one of their number—would approve of the beverage I firmly believe in and always take with me a-ballooning—cold tea. I first learnt its virtue in my soldiering and sporting days in India. It is an admirable refresher for men engaged in any precarious or exciting occupation when alcohol is, or ought to be, out of the question. Bottled beer in the rarefied air into which the aeronaut plunges will, so Simmons assured me, nearly always burst.

As regards the humorous ballooning incident, it was this. On a certain occasion I had arranged to have the balloon I had hired inflated and ready for the ascent considerably before mid-day. When the appointed time arrived, however, the preparations were not nearly complete. An hour passed by, and the work of inflation was still unaccomplished. Daylight is almost above all other things precious to the balloonist, and here we were wasting the best part of the morning. Meanwhile as I waited and fretted big crowds of people poured into the field from which the ascent was to take place. I am not sure whether the railway did not run special and excursion trains to accommodate those who desired to see us start. It afterwards transpired that the enterprising person who was entrusted with the work of inflation had charge of the gas works through which the spectators passed, and had conceived the idea of charging them sixpence each. Naturally the longer the inflation of the balloon took, the larger his receipts. It must have gone against the grain to let us start before nightfall !

CHAPTER VI

NOW for a real downright pig of a horse commend me to Condor the Second. He was a horse of course of a vastly different calibre from Baron Hill, quite apart from the question of behaviour. Condor in fact could do almost anything he chose, but then he never did choose. I rode him for Jones on January 16, 1885, at Wye, when he was top weight by ten pounds. He could probably have won if he had cared to, but, as it was, got well beaten, only coming in third. Lady Mildred was first, and Madame Neruda, ridden by Mr. Goodwin, second, in this hurdle race, the Olanteigh Towers Handicap. Again on April 7 of the same year I rode Condor the Second for Jones, that time at Lewes. I was actually winning, when he suddenly took it into his obstinate head to stop short, and there was an end of it. I was top weight, or something like it, on the occasion, but this had nothing to do with my not winning, for he was not in the least beaten when he gave up. On the flat, as well as steeplechasing, Condor nearly always behaved in the same way. Webb, Arthur Hall, and other leading jockeys had been tried as his riders, and tried, as a rule, in vain. I asked Fred Archer, who had ridden Condor the Second more than once, whether the brute behaved in the same way with him, and his reply was, "Yes, always."

March 14, 1885.—Champion Lodge Hunt and Military Steeplechases. Once again we had excellent weather and a big attendance. In the first event, the Point to Point Steeplechase, Kaliph, owned and ridden by my brother, was alone backed. He won anyhow. In the Hunt Cup, Sporran was fancied. I made play on him for about three-quarters of a mile, after which we had a ding-dong race till a quarter of a mile from the winning-post, when Mr. Cooke's Hochheimer, ridden by Mr. Rodwell, forged ahead and won easily. Sporran finished third. In the Farmers' Plate I had a mount on Mr. Rust's Architect, and was again fancied. I jumped them all down, and finished at my leisure. My brother Tyrell won the Hurdle Race Plate on Elmina, who was made favourite, whilst Forester with myself up did not pass the post. After a rattling fine race for the United Service Cup, I was beaten on Coldstream by Mr. W. Cobbett's Maryx. The latter was ridden by Mr. J. Cobbett, and fell at the water-jump, but all the same managed to win the race. In the Consolation Steeplechase only two started, my brother and myself. I won on Sporran, by a little less than a length after a good race, though at first he refused the water. The owner of my brother's mount expressed great dissatisfaction at the result, and seemed to suppose the race had been thrown away. Thereupon I offered to ride the race again,

11

with my brother or any jockey in England whom he might select, on Nimrod, but the offer was not accepted, and the affair passed off.

Colonel, afterwards General, Byrne was invariably one of the Stewards at this meeting, as at others in the county. We all knew him as "one of the best." He was called in the Service "Gentleman Byrne," owing to the refinement of his manners. Many anecdotes are told which show that "Gentleman Byrne" did fairly earn his sobriquet. During the Fenian Riots he was in command of his Battery at the Curragh. Strict orders were given that no officer should go to Dublin without special permission of the General officer. This was very irksome to some spirited young fellows, one of whom resolved, come what might, to break through the regulation. He accordingly took his ticket for Dublin, and got into a railway-carriage, in the far corner of which sat a gentleman hidden behind a newspaper. After the train had started the paper came down, and revealed to the culprit's horrified gaze none other than one of the field-officers of the division. "Gentleman Byrne" recognized his travelling companion. But instead of reprimanding and afterwards putting him under arrest, he treated him with the greatest courtesy, and even offered to place at his disposal his own phaeton, which would be waiting the arrival of the train at Dublin.

One of the drawbacks of having a clinking good horse must always be that bores cease not to pester the owner as to whether or no he fancies it for various races. What struck me as a decidedly neat snub was administered by Byrne at Ascot one afternoon to a persistent bore. The would-be plunger rushed at the General as he was mounting the iron staircase to see his horse Amphion run, and asked could he give the weight ? " That is what I am now climbing these steps," replied the General most politely, with a wave of his binoculars, " to see."

The Point to Point Steeplechase has always been a favourite one with many local people at the Champion Lodge meeting, and the same thing obtains in other local gatherings. At one time we were rather hampered by the regulations of the National Hunt Committee, which tended to somewhat severely penalize riders who took part in these races. The whole question of the Point to Point came up in 1885, when the following motion was set down for a meeting at Weatherby's in the name of the Stewards : " Horses having once run in Point to Point steeplechases will not be qualified to run in races under these rules until a certificate of the Point to Point steeplechase in which they ran, signed by a Master of Staghounds or Foxhounds, be lodged with Messrs. Weatherby, who will register and advertise it in their Calendar on payment of one Sov., and a horse having won under these conditions will not be considered a winner under these rules. The certificate to be as follows : (1) I hereby certify that —— *bonâ fide* Point to Point Steeplechase took place at —— on —— day. (2) That not more than three steeplechases took place there on that day. (3) That the course was practically unflagged. (4) That the races were for *bonâ fide* maiden hunters only. (5) That no money was taken at the gates, or at any stand or enclosure in connection with the races.

(6) That the winning-post was placed within the limits of the country hunted over by my hounds."

It was no doubt time to take action in regard to Point to Point steeplechases, but I ventured to plead at the time for a little relaxation of this rather stringent certificate. We in Essex were accustomed to carry out this, the most popular race of the day, by ending on the run-in of the steeplechase-course, where everybody could see the finish with far more comfort than they would if the winning-post were elsewhere. Many hunting men will not sport silk between flags, but they are quite ready to put on their hunting coats for a Point to Point. It was in the interest of such sportsmen that I ventured to speak up for this particular kind of race. Personally I have never had a preference for any one class of race or steeplechase as against another. But some have strong views on the subject. A lady once remarked to me that she would far sooner win the Point to Point than the Ladies' Cup, it being " such a much more sporting event."

It is impossible to so organize your race meetings as to exclude all blacklegs and light-fingered gentry ; and almost the only jarring note in the chorus of approval which greeted these annual concourses arose from those who seemed to think that I was personally responsible for the occasional misconduct of undesirable visitors. There was some correspondence respecting the theft of a watch and chain from a clergyman who attended the meeting one year, and really I do believe that a few enthusiastic anti-sport folk considered I was responsible in the matter ! It was urged seriously that I ought not to advertise the meeting, because this brought down bookmakers and sharpers from town. As a matter of fact, one is bound to advertise meetings held under the ægis of the National Hunt Committee. I pointed out that you might as well hold the Stewards of the Jockey Club responsible for all the offences of a similar kind committed at Newmarket or elsewhere. But it is no use arguing with your anti-gambling, anti-sport faddist—any more than it is any good for him to argue with you!

The next day but one found me riding again at Chelmsford. On this occasion I had a mount on Sir Henry Selwin-Ibbetson's Deception, and won the Chelmsford Steeplechase. This horse was very bad at starting. He whipped round just before we got away, and lost a hundred yards or so. Fortunately I got off all right in the end, and made up for lost time, thanks chiefly to the consideration of the starter, who ran the other side of my horse and waved the flag at him. This had the desired effect, and I proceeded to make the pace a regular "cracker." Now Architect, the horse I had steered to victory a few days before, was in this race, and I was the unconscious agent of his destruction. The pace killed the old horse, and he fell dead on the course about a mile from home.

Next month I was busy at various meetings, such as Lewes, Harlow, Ipswich, and Plumstead. At the last-named I rode Sporran on April 11, but failed to score in the Open Military Plate, which was won by Mr. Lawson's Hay Fever. At Harlow I rode Romeo for Sir Henry Selwin-Ibbetson in the Essex Open Steeplechase, and again in the Consolation;

I was second in the former, which was won by Stud Groom, with Mr. Colvin up, and fell in the latter, which Mr. H. E. Jones secured on Knight. The Essex Open, by the way, I should have won save for a bit of bad luck. I got up beside the leading horse, and found I had got him beaten. But a few moments later Romeo blundered and lost the race. Deception, my winning mount at Chelmsford the previous month, won the Light Weight Hunt Cup in a canter, with I. Bailey riding. These steeplechases were of a private character, and held in connection with the Essex Hunt. The second day was a great one for the favourites, nearly all of whom came in first.

At Ipswich, on April 16 and 17, I did myself well, riding in three races the first day and five the second day out of a possible six ; the only race I could not get a mount in being the Harrier Hunt Cup, given by the Duke of Hamilton, for half-bred horses, *bonâ fide* hunted with the Hamilton Harriers during the season 1884–5. The first day I did nothing worth speaking of, but was more in luck's way on the second. I scored nothing on Romeo in the first event, a Maiden Hunters' Steeplechase. Starting favourite on a horse called Shylock, in a small field in the Essex and Suffolk Red Coat Race, I won by something like nine or ten lengths from Foxhound, ridden by Mr. Alexander. In the following race I rode a four-year-old, carrying 11 st. 2 lbs., Mr. Poole's Ariosto, against Soubrette and Stella, which also belonged to Mr. Poole. I was badly beaten, coming in second, however, as Stella stopped dead in the middle of a field before we had gone a great way. I was also second in the next race on my own horse

Sporran, being beaten by a length or so. It transpired in the weighing-in after this race that I had carried seven pounds too much, which made a difference, no doubt. The last race of the day, the Eastern Counties Hunt Cup, I won on Sir Henry Selwin-Ibbetson's Maid-of-all-Work, a rather nice mare.

I did not feel particularly in need of a rest after this pretty stiff dose of chasing at Ipswich, so went down to ride in the Isle of Wight. On April 21 were the Castle Club Races, and next day the Isle of Wight Hunt Chases. I returned home, however, without having scored anything, and after a day or two at Epsom, turned up at Sevenoaks on May 13. I rode a horse in Jones's stable simply for a certificate, and was told he could jump anything standing, but always made a rule of refusing the open ditch. The information was correct. I got him up to the ditch all right, and there the brute stuck. A perfect swarm of stable-boys came running up, and tried their level best with clothes-props to help me get him over the ditch, which he eventually did jump standing. The annoying part of the affair was that several of the well-intended, but ill-delivered, blows of the stable-boys fell on my shoulders rather than on the horse's quarters. So ended my spring chasing season of 1885.

In the autumn and winter of 1885 I did more hunting and shooting than chasing, but was as usual a good deal at Epsom. October 9, 1885, is a black-letter day in my diary. Cartridge, purchased in 1876, had to be shot. She was the cleverest of jumpers, with, as I have mentioned, a great reputation in Essex.

A horse which recalls much less pleasant memories than Cartridge is Forester, whom I was riding about this time. He was a purchase from Jones's stables, and never won me a race. I gave £200 for the horse, and at a time when half that sum would have purchased a clinking good animal called Standard, who soon afterwards won the Grand Military, or Amethyst, who won a big steeplechase at Worcester, and another at Leamington a little later on. Forester cost a good deal of money in all before we were happily rid of him, and he was the most expensive horse and biggest crock I ever possessed. He was given away to a friend as a park hack, and fell down dead not a great while afterwards.

A rough-up at Sandown early in March 1886 was disastrous to Red Hussar, a very fine horse indeed. Jones was anxious to give Coquette, belonging to his Royal Highness the Prince of Wales, all the schooling possible in order that she might have a good chance of winning the Grand Military Gold Cup, in which she was shortly to run. Bewicke was on Red Hussar, Fisher on Coquette, and I on Flushing. The ground was terribly hard, and we really ought not to have been out at all. Red Hussar, before we had gone very far, split a pastern, and had to be at once destroyed. The horse was so great a favourite that before he had lain dead for ten minutes almost every scrap of hair had been cut from the mane and tail by the mob to be kept by way of mementoes. How hard the ground was may be judged by the fact that there were something like *ten* broken collar-bones in Jones's and Iquique's stables, about half of which were snapped that afternoon. An offer to buy Red

Hussar had come from a high quarter very shortly
before this misfortune, and it was known that a heavy
sum had been named as the price.

This training disaster reminds me of a most unfortunate trial, the particulars of which were related
to me by an old chasing comrade. Returning one
evening from Wye, having most unexpectedly landed
an eight-to-one chance and upset a good thing of
Yates's with Sensier up, I strolled into the Naval and
Military Club, when a cheery hail from the depths
of an armchair, " Have you dined, old fellow ? "
revealed to me the beaming countenance of Billy
Morris—now, alas ! no more, killed, like Whyte
Melville, in a grip no bigger than a water-furrow.
Having told him I had dined, he replied—

" Well, bring yourself to an anchor, and let's have
some coffee, a smoke, and a yarn."

This suited me well, as I had as much respect for
little Billy's head as his hands, which were generally,
if not unanimously, admitted to be the best in the
British army. Amongst my steeplechasing acquaint-
ances there was not one his equal in observing and
graphically describing the incidents of a cross-country
event. Being connected with the same stable, a topic
of mutual interest was not difficult to find. As one
of our nags was first favourite for the big event at
Croydon to be decided the following week, I hazarded
a suggestion that it was a good thing for us. A
groan was the only answer.

" Halloa, old chap, what's up ; a twinge of rheu-
matics ? "

" Oh, of course you know nothing about it," was
the reply ; and forthwith Billy proceeded to unfold

his tale of woe, which I will try and relate as much as possible in his own words. " We're now at York, as you are aware. Yesterday morning a wire was handed me from Marcus, ' Come at once, do not fail.' The chief, with a merry twinkle, pretty shrewdly guessed what the game was, and at once granted leave. Though he doesn't sport silk now, you know what a bad one to beat he is with hounds. You remember what a cracker he led us with that good up-wind afternoon dog-fox from Lightly, right under your own windows, along the straight run-in of your private course, through South Wood, across the very best of your country, past Squarson Leigh's, with those fine horsemen, George Blake on Cartridge and Billy White on Tommy Dodd, riding knee to knee in a way which reminded one of the old days over the Middlewick course. By the bye, our brave old Chilblain was out that day, and your delight when the Tedworth Finder pulled the fox down in—where was it, Holland or Jamaica ?—for no fox-hunter had ever before seen the death honours of a fox in such a morass as was your East Anglian lagoon. But I'm rather running riot. Catching a fast train south, I'd time for a snack at the ' Spurs,' and to get comfortably down to Epsom Station, where our worthy trainer and jockey, Jack Jones, met me and soon rattled me up to Priam Lodge. There I found Marcus, and Jack's brother-in-law, Arthur Hall. Ensconced in Jack's snuggery, which is so tastefully decorated with many mementoes of his patrons' goodwill, a characteristic evening was spent discussing our battles past, present, and future—not the least important of which was that which had been the cause of my wire, viz. that C——, the favourite for the Great Croydon Handicap, was to be 'asked the question' the following morning, and we saw no particular reason why the noble army of touts should know more of the stable secrets than we could help. Jack, of course, was to ride the favourite, Marc old Woodcock, a most reliable trial horse, whilst Hall and I were to have the mounts on Q—— and T—— respectively to ensure a pace. Mrs. Jack had carefully locked the lads in their dormitories, from which durance vile they would not be released till C—— had satisfactorily or otherwise been through the mill. Weights having been carefully adjusted, about two hours before daylight we adjourned to the stables, saddled our horses, mounted and jogged along by the bye-lanes to Sandown, where everything had previously been quietly prepared. As day began to break we could distinguish the trees above and beyond the grand stand. Having filed on to the course, but little time was lost in getting into line and starting. Q—— jumping a bit the quickest into her bridle, led up to the first flight of hurdles, where she showed temper, and whipping round absurdly carried the others with her. So we laughingly returned to the starting post. No mishap followed a second attempt. The minor details of the trial will hardly interest you. Suffice it to say that it was a fast-run one. Hall and I had performed our allotted tasks, and were easing our horses somewhere opposite the lower part of the public stand enclosure, and, although at the wrong angle, watched the finish, so far as we could, with considerable interest. With one of his powerful rushes Jack seemed to come away from the half distance, and gradually overhauling game old Woodcock a few strides from the winning-post, landed C—— a clever winner. He subsequently ascertained it was three-quarters of a length. A gratified look had hardly passed between us, and a misty idea that the bookies' shekels were in my pocket, and that there would be no difficulty in springing that extra pony which would transfer that raking chestnut of Bob's from his stable to mine, and the following week the Rugby Venus Tankard from Hunt and Roskell's shop-window to my sideboard, when a remark from Hall arrested my attention. ' I don't like the way the master's dismounted ; hope there's nothing wrong.' Increasing our pace up the hill we found something very much wrong. C—— was on three legs ; he had broken down the stride past the post. The glorious uncertainty had indeed reminded us of its existence, to our great discom-fiture. Leaving Hall to make the cripple as com-fortable as circumstances would admit, a somewhat melancholy trio wended their way back to Epsom. On arriving outside the stables, Jack's face was a study at seeing the touts squatting about like so many peccaries, waiting the favourite's appearance for morning exercise. ' I hardly suppose the mischief has leaked out yet. Here, waiter, give me the "Special." ' By Jove, hasn't it, though ! look here, sixty-six to one offered. The acumen of touts is simply appalling."

This breakdown was naturally a bit of a facer, but fortunately just then the stable was in rare form, and by the time the so-called illegitimate season had closed, the winning brackets represented a for-

midable total, and the balance at Weatherby's a
correspondingly healthy appearance. Not a small
proportion of the brackets was earned in military
steeplechases, the winners of which were almost
invariably ridden by poor little Morris.

March 23, 1886, the date of the Chelmsford Steeplechases, was a blank day to me so far as the scoring
of any win was concerned. I rode, however, in five
races, and was placed in three of them. In the
Chelmsford Steeplechases Plate I started favourite
on Ubique, who broke down badly, the event being
won by Maid-of-all-Work ; favourite again in the
Roothing Steeplechase Plate on Mr. Poole's Heath,
was well beaten by Lady Bell ; second favourite in
the Essex Open Hunters' Steeplechase on Merrilegs,
was placed third ; an outsider in a Hunters' Selling
Steeplechase on Sporran, was second to Mr. Percion's
Matilda ; whilst in a fifth race was of course out
of it on that brute Forester—not a very satisfactory
day, considering I had ridden in five out of six races.

This year the Champion Lodge meeting fell on
April 1. I rode in six events that day, and in four
of them was second, being quite out of it in the other
two. The Ladies' Cup fell to Mr. Barkley's Problem,
the wretched Forester being second in this race, and
nowhere in the last event of the day, the Consolation.
Captain Henderson's Paleface, ridden by Mr. Pure-
foy, won the Hunt Cup, the only other starter being
Sporran, with myself up. Telemachus (Mr. Tippler
up) was first in the Champion Lodge Cup, and Flushing
second, both starting at odds of 4 to 1 against. Telemachus also won the Selling Hunters' Hurdle Race
Plate, beating Ariosto, my mount.

I did not ride again in April, but in both May and June following put in an appearance at a good few meetings, local and other. At Ipswich, on May 5, I won two races on a mare called Misunderstood— this despite an ugly fall in my second race that day, which so shook me up that it was scarcely easy to hold the reins. Fortunately Misunderstood had a beautiful mouth, and was very easy to ride. Both races, namely, the Shrublands Park Maiden Hunters' Steeplechase, and the Essex and Suffolk Red Coat Race of three miles " over a fair hunting country," were won by three lengths. In the first race I started second favourite in spite of my sprained wrist, and beat Sir Henry Selwin-Ibbetson's Lorna, the first favourite ; whilst in the second started top weight, and rather a hot favourite, if my memory has not failed me. Mr. J. B. Charters came in second on Garryowen. In the Military Steeplechase my mount was Pictus ; but though favourite he did not succeed in repeating his previous successes with me as his rider. Captain Lee Barber also had a nasty fall that day, breaking his collar-bone. The chasing came off on the old Ipswich course.

Talking of falls, I once came to much grief through trying to rise and remount when there was a horse close behind me. I got struck on the head and rendered unconscious as a punishment. It would have been far wiser to have lain still and allowed the horses behind to pass over me. A horse is as squeamish as a tame elephant about treading on a man. Once the Marquess of Queensberry riding in a race at Punchestown, came down when leading in a field of thirty-six. He lay flat, whilst the other horses passed over, or close to, him. There is no denying that it requires some patience to do this, but it is the only safe course to adopt.

This reminiscence of Queensberry as a rider recalls a rather quaint incident in his career as an owner of race-horses. He bought a horse called Morris Dancer for £700, and ran him several times. The horse was over-handicapped, however, and could do nothing. Quite disgusted, Queensberry at length resolved to try and get rid of the animal, and offered him to anybody who would buy him on the course after the last race. Everybody laughed at the offer, till at last a butcher ventured to say he would run to a five-pound note. Queensberry promptly closed with this princely offer. Shortly afterwards he was surprised by seeing the horse entered in two races, and handicapped no less than two stone lighter than he had ever been on previous occasions. Thereupon he wrote to the butcher, told him the horse couldn't lose, and asked to be allowed the mounts. The butcher was naturally quite willing, as the Marquess was a fine rider. So Queensberry rode in, and won both races, backing his mount in both events. He then offered to buy Morris Dancer back for £200. The butcher, nothing loath, consented. At once the horse got over-weighted again, and never afterwards won a race.

About now Blondin was astonishing, or rather re-astonishing, London with his tight-rope walking at the Albert Palace, and being in town on May 12, I repaired to Battersea one day to see the performance. I pressed him to take me across the rope; but he made excuse that the electric light was rather trying, and said he therefore could not accede to my request. He would only take his son across with him. It seems to have been a fact that his sight was not then what it had been a few years before, but knowing his extraordinary surefootedness I had not the least hesitation in making the request, and would have gone on his back without any misgiving. I should have made a point of not falling without at any rate carrying Blondin along with me, and Blondin, in my opinion, simply could not fall. He promised to take me across the rope on some future occasion should a favourable opening offer, but it never did.

Southwell, May 3, 1886.—Here I won the Hunters' Flat Race on my mare Imogene, starting at 5 to 1 against. She was by Queen's Herald out of Imogene, and trained by Jones. Captain Maudslay's Mercia, the favourite, was second, and Mr. Pidcock's Soudan third. This was one amongst probably many races won by a long and painstaking examination of the ground early in the morning. I found a shepherd's track, but so close to the rails that in sticking to it in the race I quite expected once or twice that my shins would get broken against the heads of some of the spectators who craned forward to see the sport, as people do when at all interested in an event. It was necessary to hug the rails for a good while, so as not to get off the track into the deep ground, through which the other horses were ploughing their weary way. The craning necks were no doubt one and all drawn discreetly back as I came up to close quarters, but in my hot haste I did not perceive this, and felt that an accident was almost inevitable.

As regards devices for winning a race, George

Fordham had one which in the case of a very close
finish was certainly not likely to confuse the judge
in a way unfavourable to himself. He would throw
himself forward almost between the ears of his horse,
and so seem to be first past the post in cases where
the race might otherwise have been adjudged a dead
heat, or even, it may be, given in his rival's favour.
Every inch in the case of a very close finish makes a
difference, and it is quite conceivable that the judge
seeing a jockey's colours first past the post would
award the wearer the race, even if his horse's nose was
beaten by an inch or two.

At Aylesbury, the same month, it fell to my lot
to ride another very ill-tempered horse—Quarter-
master Brown's Galloway. It was on the flat, but
Galloway suddenly took a fancy for a bit of steeplechasing. We went off the course, and over the
brook. It is scarcely necessary to add that he was
not placed in that race. At Wye, on June 17, I was
second to Chorister, ridden by Butcher, in the Selling
Hunters' Hurdle Race, with Imogene; and the following week was racing on the flat at Stockbridge.
Here I rode Imogene one day in the Hunters' Plate,
won by Amy with Billy Bevill up, but was not
placed; and Cutlet in the Andover Stakes, another.
Cutlet, the property of Arthur Yates, and trained at
Bishops Sutton, was, like Condor II., a perfect rogue.
He would scarcely ever try, but when he did was very
hard to beat. Sensier did once win a race on Cutlet,
not a little to his own surprise, starting at long odds.
In this race at Stockbridge, Cutlet was quite out of
it. George Lambton won on Lord Lurgan's Polemic.

When Billy Bevill, the rider of Amy that day at

12

Stockbridge, ceased riding, some years ago now, he was the oldest gentleman jockey, or at least the oldest known at all to the public, living.

Billy Bevill, like Fred Beauclerk, never believed much in his own oratorical powers. At a dinner at one of the Bibury meetings, Sir John Astley and others drank his health with acclaim. He got up to make a speech in response, and this is what he said : " I am very much obliged to you for having drunk my health, but I would a deal rather ride a race than make a speech." With that he sat down abruptly.

What an enjoyable affair used the " Hampshire Week " to be in those days ! The charms of the twin meeting over the Danebury Downs have been so often dwelt upon, that there is no need to repeat them here. Amongst the regular frequenters there were :—Lord Portsmouth, Caledon Alexander, Sir John Astley, Lord Falmouth, Henry Savile, the Duke of Hamilton, the Duke of Beaufort, Sir Frederick Johnstone, and Lord Alington, Count Kinsky, Prince Soltykoff, Duchess of Montrose, General Owen Williams, and Sir William Throgmorton. The passing years have made a sorry gap in the ranks of these patrons of Bibury.

Flat racing, as mentioned earlier in this book, has never been either my *métier* or my ambition. It lacks the stirring incidents, the hazards, and consequently the excitement of the steeplechase. Very few men have been strikingly successful, so far as my experience goes, both on the flat and across country, though now and again we come across a jockey, like Arthur Coventry, who is perfectly at home racing as well as chasing. Jim Adams might presumably have been regarded as decidedly successful in his day in both provinces. One mount in a big steeplechase—the Grand National—was enough and to spare for Webb, and Rickaby has also made a little chasing go a long way. Some who have grown too weighty to be any longer useful on the flat, take to steeplechasing with a certain amount of success, but they are few and far between. Steeplechasing of course has not the pecuniary inducements which are offered by flat racing ; it has no Jubilees and Eclipses. Nevertheless, Fred Archer always had a fancy to try his hand at a big cross-country event one day. He said he would ride in the Grand National before he died, but the intention was never carried out.

There was chasing at Wye in the early part of January 1887, but several meetings later on during this and the following month had to be abandoned owing to the hard frost. I went down to Savernake to ride in the Steeplechases, which it was intended to hold there, but the ground was too iron-bound to permit of their coming off, and we had to wait for sport till March 8. On that day the Rugby Chases were held. An interesting reunion to me at this meeting was that between myself and " Bay " Middleton. We had ridden just twenty years before, first and second respectively in the South of Ireland Military, and had not once met as antagonists on a racecourse in the interim. At Rugby " Bay " won a race on Punjab, and I one on Flushing. Twenty years is a good slice out of even a long sporting life ; but we both recalled our Irish contest very clearly, and not without some lively emotions. "Bay," by the way, though unlucky enough to lose the South of Ireland Military, which I was fortunate enough to win on Maid of the Mist, had won two races that day in the spring of 1867, one on Black Prince, the other on a mare called Sophy.

My win at Rugby was the Ladies' Plate. Flushing's success in this race seemed to show that a horse usually repays an owner for individual attention and supervision. Whilst at the trainer's this horse, who was rented from Billy White, was always singularly unfortunate ; whereas the first time he ran after removal to Champion Lodge, where we were able to train him ourselves, he won a race. Captain Elmhirst's Vanity Fair came in second, ridden by Captain Lindsey, who was beaten by a length and a half or so. A bad third.

Next day we turned to Loughborough to take part in the Quorn and Donington Hunt meeting. In a field of two for the Half-bred Steeplechase Plate, the betting was seven to four on my opponent, Mr. Lewin's Brunette. I was on Chatterbox, who was hired from a friend. Brunette won, but an objection was lodged and sustained on the ground of not being a maiden. The stakes therefore fell to Chatterbox.

Talking of disqualifications, it was once gravely stated that Wenty Hope Johnstone in a race in Ireland had appealed against five opponents, and got them all disqualified. Wenty was asked if that were so. He said, No, it wasn't, but told of a decidedly curious thing that had occurred in relation to this particular race. He had lodged an objection against the

"WENTY" HOPE JOHNSTONE.
(From "Vanity Fair."

favourite, which was allowed. Now the owner of the favourite was also the owner of the horse Wenty had ridden. Surely this case is an absolutely unique one !

One of the Louises used to write " Nothing " in his diary—even at a period when the fortunes of his kingdom were at stake—if there was no hunting. So a steeplechaser at times—during, at any rate, the steeplechasing season—may well set down the same word when he gets no sport worth speaking of. Thus " Nothing " at Chelmsford Chases on March 24, 1882, and ditto at 13th Hussars' Chases at Manningtree on April 12. On April 27, Greek Fire and I repaired to Thick Thorn. Greek Fire would certainly have been first instead of second in a fair race on the following day, had not my opponent ridden clean across, for which outrage he ought to have been disqualified at least as deservedly as Brunette. But the judge's decision was not upset. There is not of course the satisfaction, or anything like it, of winning a race through the disqualification of one's opponent as there is in beating all competitors in a fair-and-square race. It may be added that the jockey who spoilt Greek Fire's chance on this occasion in such an inexcusable manner was the merest amateur ; had he been a professional or a seasoned rider, his conduct would have disqualified him to an absolute certainty.

At Ipswich, on May 5, my colours were not prominent ; but on the 17th, Edensor won. The horse originally belonged to the Duke of Hamilton, who was present, and said he had never seen the horse looking better. He endeavoured to bolt off the course in this race—the Tradesmen's Cup at Bungay —with the evident idea of turning into the stables where he had slept overnight. But his rider did not see his way to accommodate Edensor, and instead the horse won the race. That was the last race for me in 1887, a trip to North America in search of other varieties of sport being arranged shortly afterwards.

Edensor would have had a great chance of winning the Grand National, in my opinion, if he had only been entered for that race. He was a beautiful jumper, and would not have carried more than ten stone on his back at Liverpool. Since passing out of Marsh's hands, Edensor had done a good deal of hunting, in our cramped Essex country, and the music of the hounds had probably made him take kindly to jumping. We had carefully "summered" him on the saltings, and got his legs as fine as a foal's. Had he landed upside of the leaders over the last fence at Liverpool, his fine turn of speed would have about carried him home. When in America I wrote to have him entered for the race ; but ought to have wired, for he had been sold before the message was received. Marsh, curiously enough, despaired of Edensor as a steeplechaser, and decided that he was only fitted for hurdle racing.

When in the winter of 1886 Mr. Stanley's African expedition was being arranged, I had every intention, could it be managed, of forming one of the party. We met and talked the matter over. Mr. Stanley's staff, however, was complete at the time, and moreover, whilst good enough to say that I was well fitted to be one of his party in nearly all respects,

he pointed out, what was perfectly true, that want
of Central African experience was a drawback. The
interview therefore did not promise good results, nor
was a second one with him and Sir Francis de Winton,
a few days later, more productive. What I ought
to have done was to have gone to the point of de-
barkation, and there in all probability Mr. Stanley
would have accepted me as a member of his party.
Friends who were aware of the offer I made to Mr.
Stanley of my services, have on more than one
occasion observed that it was very fortunate it came
to nothing, as otherwise there would have been an
ugly split between us, such as naturally occurred
in regard to Major Barttelot. But my interview
with Mr. Stanley was of a most friendly character;
nor is there the slightest reason in my mind to suppose that we should of necessity have fallen out had
my offer been accepted. Discipline should always
be one of the chief laws of life to every man who has
been in the Service; so much may be safely said
without making the least comment on the unhappy
quarrel which threw a dark cloud over this African
expedition of Mr. Stanley's.

Even more keenly have I had cause to regret
my lot in not being able to take part as a volunteer
in several of our little African wars. Unfortunately the terms of my father's will compelled me to
insure my life heavily about the time of my marriage,
and the insurance companies, as is well known,
are enabled to put on a very high war premium.
This shut me out of the various campaigns in South
and North Africa during the last twenty-five years
or so. In particular I was very keen to go to the

Cape as a volunteer at the time of Isandula ; but it was clearly intimated to me that I should be penalized by a very heavy and additional premium. I had therefore to stay at home, and fret over my baulked projects.

CHAPTER VII

IN these days of universal travel it is a difficult matter to strike what may be termed new ground. Indeed, it is almost impossible, and the nearest approach one can make to novelty is to pick out the spots least frequented by those two ubiquitous specimens of humanity, the sportsman and the British tourist. Bearing this in mind, and having received an invitation from an ex-sailor, I determined on a short tour through Florida, with Cuba to follow. So having written to S—— to meet me at Douglass's Tropical Hotel at Kissimmee, set about collecting my impedimenta, and engaged a berth by the Cunard boat from Liverpool to New York. Of course there are many ways of getting to the Stars and Stripes, and the traveller can have his choice of which line he will elect to travel by. Mine fell on the Cunarder, and there was no cause to repent it ; everything on board was most comfortable, and with fine weather we made a rapid passage, arriving at Sandy Hook almost before we had well cleared the Mersey—at least so it seemed.

From New York there is again a choice of routes.

You can take the luxurious vestibule train or the steamer to Jacksonville, where it will not be amiss to spend a couple of days at St. Augustine, in the palatial hotel, Ponce de Leon, built after the style of old Moorish architecture. From Jacksonville you will take the train to Kissimmee; or, better still perhaps, the steamer down St. John's River to Sandford, and then on by rail.

Arrived at Kissimmee, Mr. Douglass will, assuming that he is still in the land of the living, make you thoroughly comfortable in the Tropical Hotel at an exceedingly moderate outlay, and will put you in the way of obtaining either a steamer or boat to the best sporting ground, which is in the neighbourhood of Fort Bassenger and Lake Arbuckle.

On arrival at Kissimmee, I found all arrangements had been made by S——, who had also got punt and everything in readiness so that there was nothing for me to do but overhaul the shooting-irons and kit, and prepare for a start. While on the subject of shooting-kits, it may be mentioned there is no necessity to bring out cartridges, as a gun-maker in Kissimmee, called Farringdon, can supply every requisite; and, what is more, is particularly careful in loading. When ordering cartridges I found American wood powder by far the best, and can recommend it strongly. Flannel is the best material for clothing, and a stock of quinine should not be forgotten. These, however, are details.

On Tuesday, December 13, we left St. Elmo at 7.15 a.m., arrived at the south end of Lake Tokho-pekaliga at 1 p.m., and passing quickly through the canal into Lake Cypress, and on through a second canal, came into Lake Hatchineha, just as daylight was vanishing. Here we were lucky enough to hit off a sandbank studded with oak copse, and dry wood being plentiful, soon had our camp fire under way, and supper. The whiff of tobacco, and glass of Bourbon whisky which followed the evening meal, were both mighty acceptable, for we had had nine hours' hard rowing under a blazing sun, and were both fairly tired out. At least I can answer for it that it was with a feeling of deep satisfaction I curled myself up in my blankets for the night, and was quickly lulled to sleep by a chorus of frogs, with the occasional " ouf, ouf ! " of a somewhat consumptive alligator.

The following morning we were up betimes, and after an early breakfast packed our boat and made a move. Although there was no definite agreement made, I somehow drifted into the rowing, shooting, and timber-felling department while S—— " bossed " the steering, fishing, and cooking side. On arriving off Fort Gardner we came across a party of five Seminoles headed by Tom Tiger, a fine stalwart Indian, who we gathered was likely to be elected chief when old Tallahassee departed for the happy hunting grounds. Pocahontas, who married an Englishman named Rolfe, was reputed to have belonged to this nomad tribe. She was for some years in England, and rumour said that she was still living in a large cypress swamp to the south of Lake Okeechobee, called the Everglades. If this were correct, she must have reached a ripe old age, as she is said to have died in England in 1617 !

The Seminoles, though now friendly, fought gallantly under Tallahassee against the whites, and it took the American troops some years before they were enabled to thoroughly subdue them. Whilst we were palavering with Tiger and his followers a moccasin snake slipped off the bank and commenced to swim the river. With my first barrel and a charge of No. 4 shot I only managed to wound him, and back he came right at us. Luckily he was turned white side up at a second attempt, and he floated down the stream. The moccasins and rattlesnakes are the most numerous and deadly of the Florida reptiles, besides being exceedingly pugnacious, so it was just as well we did not get to close quarters. Having arranged with the Indians to bring us some skins, we continued our journey down the river into Lake Kissimmee, and camped under a hummock on a fine ridge of sand—a hummock being the local name for clumps of variegated timber.

The next day, the 15th, we paddled down to Floridelphia in time for the midday meal, and having arranged with our guide to meet us the following day on one of the neighbouring lakes, returned, meaning to ascend the Tiger River. But missing the entrance we were brought up in the " bonnet " (waterlilies), so had to give it up and make our way back to Floridelphia by the light of a new moon. Early in the morning, before daylight, we were forced to shift our quarters, for a heavy sea got up, and our punt became none too pleasant. After breakfast, however, we took Louis, a " cracker " (*i.e.* one of the local squatters, so dubbed on account of their powers of manipulating the stock-whip), as guide, and started for Tiger Creek, which we reached at noon, and at once commenced its ascent, little dreaming of the difficulties we should have to surmount, or the severe tax on our powers of endurance that would be required before arriving at its source. A strong current had to be stemmed, the turns were both numerous and sharp, and at times we were forced to use both axe and saw where the channel was choked with willow, bonnet, water-lettuce, flags, buttonwood, and maiden cane, whilst to make matters extra pleasant, at the most critical part, with a crack and a splash, overboard I went, if not "amidst the sharks and whales," amidst the thousands of alligators and snakes which inhabited the adjoining swamp. However, it is a long lane that has no turning, and we at last entered Tiger Lake, and skirting its eastern shore, beached the punt whilst Louis went off to a log-hut for a few necessaries. During the time he was away I took the opportunity of replenishing our larder, and managed to bag half-a-dozen snipe—a welcome addition, but one which very nearly cost me my life, for in struggling through some flags to gather one of my birds, my foot came right on the top of a huge moccasin, who was coiled up close to where it fell. Happily, he was as much frightened as myself, and dived out of sight instantly, at which I was very grateful, for my legs were bare, and had he bitten me it would without doubt have been fatal. On Louis's return we pulled round the lake till near Rosalie Creek, where we camped after dark, and spent a most unpleasant night, being much worried by ants, to say nothing of an aggressive centipede, on which S—— nearly put his hand. Saturday, the 17th, we were up before sunrise, and had a fruitless tramp of four hours through the swamp after deer and turkey. Probably old Tallahassee's hunters had been before us, as we saw plenty of signs, but beyond that nothing. The timber and undergrowth in the swamp were very fine, consisting of three different kinds of oak, black and bay gum, maple, ash, wild mulberry, pine, palmetta, and saw grass. After this we shifted camp, and all three took a stroll for duck and snipe—though what Louis expected to kill with a Winchester rifle, which was the weapon he selected, was only known to himself. That night we were visited by one or more members of the rat tribe, who managed to make a tolerable supper of three courses, viz., one boot, one sock, and one gaiter.

Next morning we returned in the teeth of a stiff breeze to Tiger Creek, and the steadiness of the punt in a nasty choppy sea quite astonished us. The unfortunate Louis proved himself a thorough landsman, and kept on bemoaning his hard fate, wishing between the paroxysms of sea-sickness that he was once again driving cows. Once he nearly came into collision with a moccasin snake in some bonnet, which fairly frightened him out of his life, and had the desired effect of keeping him a little quieter. On this journey I did not fall overboard, but varied the performance by stepping with my naked foot on to the spoon bait, and then, while trying to extricate the barb, drove the tail hooks into my other ankle. It may be imagined after this I was grateful to an Indian who accepted the machine as a present, and who certainly rated it far above its value. That afternoon we bid farewell to our guide, as we discovered that his knowledge of cooking far exceeded that of venery, and that his ability in emptying the pot was well in advance of his powers of replenishing the same.

In the evening we lit our fire close to where we had previously camped in the angle of two huge branches of a fallen oak, and were shortly afterwards joined by **Tom Tiger** and his nephew. We then proceeded to look for our supper, and were fortunate in shooting a couple of duck, which Tom and his relative helped to devour. Before supper commenced, however, the former gentleman amused himself by enshrouding his athletic form in my Inverness cape, and then suddenly remarked—

" You got yellow fever ? " some rumour of that disease, which had been raging in Tampa, having evidently reached his ears.

" No," I replied.

" Aha," rejoined Tom with pride, " I got measles," and removing the cape and opening the front of his hunting shirt, he showed me a plentiful crop of spots. " You think me bad ? What medicine I take ? " he then asked. But I was too flabbergasted to reply, for the Inverness was my only *robe de nuit*, and I foresaw that I must either make up my mind to go without it, and thereby contract a certain cold, or else run the chance of catching the measles by wearing it. Eventually the latter course was adopted, happily without any evil results.

In the middle of the night I was awakened by a heavy thud close to my right ear, and starting up found that our fire had undermined the branches of the oak, and that one of them had fallen with tremendous force within a foot from my head on to my rug, a jagged branch driving it quite half a yard into the ground. Had it been a few inches to the left it would have converted me into a jelly. This was about the narrowest shave I ever had of visiting the Great Unknown, except perhaps once, when a friend knocked over a brave Portuguese just as he had got his knife between my shoulder-blades. S——, who had coiled himself up in the punt for the night, also had somewhat broken rest, for in the small hours he suddenly found himself drifting out to sea, and had a hard paddle to get back. After breakfast we sculled to East Gardner, where for the next few days my time was occupied in supplying our larder with game from the prairie and pine-woods swamps, S—— having injured his foot, and consequently being unable to move far from camp. Leaving Fort Gardner we were taken in tow by the Arbuckle steamer, which landed S—— at St. Elmo's wharf shortly after midnight, and myself at Kissimmee City about half-an-hour later. Kissimmee, notwithstanding the high-sounding title of city, is nothing more than a straggling village, whose morals are looked after by a mayor and two policemen, or rather a marshal and his assistant. Marshal Bailly was a fine old Georgian who, besides being riddled with Northern bullets while serving under Lee, was ruined by the abolition of slavery without compensation. However, we found him a host in himself, and the short work he made of a rowdy cowboy or a refractory nigger was beautiful to behold. It seemed to me a pity we could not hand over Trafalgar

Square to his keeping for a short time with the same freedom of action that is extended to the constabulary of the Republic. Here I remained for a short time before going on to Cuba, feeling better in health than ever before in my life ; and no wonder, for camping out in the fine climate of a Florida winter is most enjoyable, and with a liberal commissariat, consisting of fish, venison, and other varieties of game supplied daily by rod and gun, supplemented by a few tinned provisions, coffee, flour, rice, potatoes, hog and hominy, which we took with us, together with the constant exercise from sunrise to sunset, sometimes commencing before the former and ending after the latter, made one feel like a new man. To any one who is fond of sport, and is feeling a little out of sorts, a trip to Florida may be confidently recommended.

When in Havana on my way home from Florida, I not unnaturally desired to play some part, if possible, in the bull-fights which take place there. It would have been a pleasant ending to the excellent small sport we had been enjoying in America. There was a demand for picadors, as a good many men employed in that capacity had recently suffered severely and fallen out of the ranks, but a very inadequate supply. Regarding this as a good opportunity to "cut in," I offered my services as picador. But the bull-fighters, if jealous of each other, were even more so of a stranger and outsider. They traded on their reputation of being the only people who could face the bull, and they would no doubt have lost prestige if an outsider had been allowed to act as picador, and had proved at all successful in

13

that capacity. Accordingly they would not hear of my taking any part in the fight, and I was obliged to go away unsatisfied. No Englishman had ever acted as picador over there, and I had hoped to establish a record and precedent.

This short sojourn in the West Indies reminded me of sailoring days spent there more than twenty years before, and especially of the shameful way in which Governor Eyre was treated by, one regrets to have to say, the English Government. The controversy concerning Eyre was reopened some years ago in one of the newspapers, and a member of the Carlton Club wrote vainly trying to prove that the leader and instigator of the mutiny—which, had it not been effectually crushed out by the Governor's promptness, might have resulted in a general butchering of all the whites in the island of Jamaica—was quite unjustly hanged. My memory is pretty vivid in this matter, as we were almost in the midst of the mutiny, and received the most accurate account of all that took place. About the guilt of the ringleader there can be no possible shadow of doubt in the mind of people really conversant with the affair; though it may be admitted that there was a slight, or what may be called a technical, irregularity in the way he was captured and executed. The Mutiny Act was not operative over the whole of the island, and the leader of the rebellion was seized just beyond the line where the Act ended. It was somewhat like shooting a burglar a yard outside your house, instead of actually within it. Eyre probably saved the whites from a wholesale slaughter, and in reward he was dismissed, and, what was even worse, never given a post elsewhere. The whole thing was a shocking miscarriage of justice. Eyre was on one or two occasions on board our ship to consult the Admiral, and I recollect well enough taking him ashore in the boat in my charge.

Though prevented from taking an active part in the bull-fights in Havana, I saw several exhibitions there, and later in Portugal. To many English people, even sporting people, the idea of going to a bull-fight as a spectator is a repellant one. But we ought to clear our minds of cant in discussing the frequently agitated question of cruelty in sport. After seeing a good many bull-fights, and talking with people who are well versed in the matter, my conclusion is that it entails *far* less cruelty than several sports which are in high favour in this country. Take battue shooting, for instance. I am not going to preach against it, by any means—though I do consider it a somewhat luxurious form of sport, and infinitely prefer to make a small mixed bag over a good dog—but it is idle to gainsay the fact that these monster days amongst feathered game mean a great deal of acute suffering. However deadly the shots, a percentage of the birds get wounded, and creep away out of reach of beaters and game-gatherers to endure much prolonged suffering.

Now in bull-fighting the pain endured by the animals is probably small compared to that endured by the wounded pheasants and hares. There is no question whatever about the bull itself thoroughly enjoying the sport. The pheasant does not want to be shot at, nor the fox to be hunted, but the bull does want to fight. It is the beast's nature. He is pricked a good deal, no doubt, and rendered furious in consequence ; but what is his pain in comparison to that of a pheasant with a broken wing or leg ? Next to nothing. Then as to the horses : they are, it is true, injured, and finally killed. I am the last in the world to view with approval brutality towards horses, and should not fail to intervene where possible and practicable. But the lot of the horses used for bull-fighting purposes is infinitely preferable to the lot of the wretched animals that are doomed to drag the ordinary Spanish diligence. Two blacks do not make a white, but if you approve on behalf of the horses of doing away with bull-fighting in Spain, you ought to approve even more of reforming the existing state of things in regard to the Spanish diligence.

The cruelty of the drivers is well-nigh incredible. It might almost disgust some of the worst drivers of hansoms in London. The Jehu of the diligence indeed knows no mercy, and many who have travelled in Spain by road must have noted the fact that when opportunity offers he will usually prod the wretched animals on a sore place. The stick with which he belabours his horses is of a very hard wood, and used with no little force. In a single stage a horse can, and often does, suffer more pain than is likely to result from the wounds received from a bull's horn in the arena.

No doubt this view of bull-fighting is a little out of the common. Bagot and Churston, my shooting and yachting companions in the Mediterranean, came to a very different opinion after they had seen a fight at Malaga, which, by the way, certainly does appear to have been a very sanguinary affair ; but, depend upon it, there are plenty of people who, if they went out shooting and saw hares and pheasants suffer, would be quite as much upset by the sight as by an ordinary bull-fight. Bull-fighting as practised in Portugal is certainly in some respects a more artistic performance than that of Spain. The horses used are much finer, and altogether too good to be exposed to the certainty of injury which the Spanish animals incur. The riding too in these Portuguese performances is very pretty. Bagot has given a good description of a Lisbon fight in his little book on Shooting and Yachting in the Mediterranean.

"After the usual preliminaries, and march past," he writes, "the ring was cleared, and in came *El Toro* with padded horns and a piece of board strapped across his forehead. Then appeared two Portuguese noblemen riding their own horses (rare good-looking nags, too), and the fun commenced, the object of each rider being to plant a small banderillo, in the shape of a rosette, in the bull's neck, and get away before the bull knocked himself and horse head over heels. There was some very pretty play and good riding, and the entertainments was varied with other feats, such as riding the bull bare-backed, getting into a barrel, and letting the animal roll it about the ring, vainly trying to get at the man inside, who, having made the bull perfectly furious, would wait his opportunity, and jumping out run like a hare for the barrier with *Toro* in hot pursuit. One individual was just a moment too late, and the bull caught him before he could get over, and hove him fairly into the middle of the spectators following himself clean over the barrier amid shouts of laughter. However, nothing worse than a few bruises was the result, and when we got back on board we all agreed we had spent a very pleasant evening, and that Lisbon bull-fighting is worth ten of the Spanish performances."

In that excellent book, *Wild Spain*, Messrs. Chapman and Back give a glowing picture of the commencement of a Spanish bull-fight, which will help to show even the most prejudiced that there is something in "tauromachia" other than brutality. "What a spectacle," write these authors, "is presented by the Plaza at this moment! One without parallel in the modern world. The vast amphitheatre, crowded to the last seat in every box and tier, is held for some moments in breathless suspense: above, a glorious canopy of an Andalucian summer sky: below, on the yellow arena, rushes forth the bull fresh from his distant prairie, amazed yet undaunted by the unwonted sight and the bewildering blaze of colour which surrounds him. For one brief moment the vast mass of excited humanity sits spellbound: the clangour of myriads is stilled. Then the pent-up cry bursts forth in frantic volumes, for the gleaming horns have done their work, and *Buen toro! buen toro!* rings from twice ten thousand throats."

The performances which I witnessed at Havana, and tried to take part in myself, were only fairly good. There was a good deal of carnage without any superlative display of skill. The best men, for instance, Espartero, who came by such a tragic end in the arena at Madrid not a great while ago, or

Xerezano (that is, a man from Xeres), would not find it worth their while to settle in Havana, when they can make an income far exceeding that of the best-salaried Spanish minister by staying at home. A bull-fighter's income in Spain does not compare ill with that of a first-class jockey on the flat in England. There is no doubt that a great number of the *habitués* at the Spanish bull-fights are of a decidedly brutal turn of mind. As a very prominent and successful bull-fighter remarked, they are never content unless the most difficult and most dangerous feats a man can accomplish in the arena are constantly being repeated. If an *espada*, having achieved a feat requiring a superlative display of skill and courage, does not do the same thing again when he next enters the arena, the audience feel aggrieved; whilst, if he continues to attempt the same feat, he is almost bound in the end to come by his death in the arena. Having won a great reputation, the bull-fighter cannot afford to rest on his laurels. He must preserve it by constantly redelighting his admirers with his most daring and clever devices, otherwise he will soon fall in the popular estimation.

To regard the Spanish bull-fight as a merely brutal slaughter, without any redeeming feature, is to show oneself ignorant of the sport, and equally so of the history and traditions of this ancient country. It is idle to deny that the office of matador or *espada*, as well as that, in a lesser degree, of picador, demand the exercise of skill of the highest order, besides bravery and perfect coolness. No Englishman, who is accustomed to think highly of such qualities, can see a first-class matador overcome a very active and savage bull in the arena without a strong feeling of admiration. A matador carries his life in his hand, with a vengeance, when, single-handed and on foot, he challenges to mortal combat an infuriated bull. Should his courage, or his eye, or his feet fail him at the supreme moment, it is all over. Mr. F. C. Selous once related a stirring adventure he had had with a wounded lion. The animal, mad with pain and anger, came rushing upon him with the evident intention of exacting a deadly vengeance. Had he turned and fled, or lost his nerve and resource in any degree, probably nothing could have saved him. But he stood perfectly still, and merely yelled for the dogs to be let loose. His boldness caused the red-hot courage of the lion to cool, and the brute turned tail. There were cheers when Mr. Selous reached this point in his story. Englishmen cannot restrain a feeling of generous admiration for conduct of this kind, and they never will. Conceive, then, what feelings must animate thousands of susceptible Spaniards, when they see one of the popular favourites perform some feat in the arena that requires an amount of bravery at least equal to that needed by a lion-hunter, and infinitely greater skill. The most exciting of all sports are those in which the human element plays the chief part, and in which the greatest pluck and resource are called for. Nothing in ancient or modern times, except perhaps the exhibitions of the Roman gladiators, has ever come near a first-class Spanish bull-fight in this respect.

Then again, people who are ready to stigmatize the Spaniards as utterly brutal because they love the bull-fight, have not perhaps considered how inextricably bound up with the ancient traditions and history of the country is the art of " tauromachia." We often talk about horse-racing as a national institution in England, and it no doubt is so. Compared, however, with the bull-fight, it is, after all, the merest mushroom growth. Its traditions are great, and it has numbered amongst its ardent supporters not only princes of the royal blood, but statesmen of the highest prominence and popularity. But for centuries the chief performers in the Spanish bull-fights were many of the foremost noblemen and grandees in the country. It used indeed to be part of the " liberal education " of a Spaniard of distinction to have graduated in " tauromachia." Charles I., grandson of Isabel, killed a bull in fair fight in the arena in his day.

When the Bourbons succeeded to the throne of Spain, bull-fighting gradually went out of fashion amongst the Spanish nobility, that is so far as the taking any personal part therein as matador or picador was concerned. This was not because the Bourbons were shocked at the custom, but rather by reason of their effeminate character. They " Frenchified " the Spanish nobility in this and other provinces. But even the secession of the nobles and grandees from the arena could not lessen the popularity of the bull-fight. There arose a class of professional matadors or *espadas* who took their place, and have ably filled it since. To judge by the incomes these men earn, and the enormous audiences that crowd to the various arenas to witness first-class performances, bull-fighting has quite as strong a hold on the affections of the people to-day as it has had at any previous period in the history of Spain.

One more word concerning the charge of brutality which is brought against the Spanish bull-fight, and I have done. To those who do not even admit that in the *toréo* there is frequently to be seen what has been well described as "an unrivalled exhibition of human skill, nerve, and power," it is no use appealing. But the question may be asked of those who do admit that great skill and pluck are shown by the best *espadas*, whether pain inflicted on the brute creation under these circumstances is not, at any rate, more excusable than pain inflicted where there is no such exhibition. There is surely nothing in the nature of an "unrivalled exhibition of human skill" in potting pheasants, even if they are "rocketing" birds. Moreover a wounded pheasant, in all probability, suffers more pain, or, at any rate, usually suffers it much longer, than a horse in the Spanish bull-ring. We may feel for the horse more because we esteem it as a much better and more intelligent creature than the bird; then, too, the size of the creature injured has a great deal to do with the size of our grief. We forget how "the poor beetle, which we tread upon, in corporal substance feels a pang as great as when a giant dies."

Before arriving home I stayed both in Spain and Portugal. Whilst at Madrid, an attempt was made to get up a little boxing match, in which I was to play the part of a principal. The fact was the chief picador, or the man who in Portugal answers to the picador, was rather a bully, and had on several occasions knocked about the local police and other people into the bargain. So there was a desire to enlist some one who would " take it out " of him. I was urged to take on this bullying bull-fighter, and professed my willingness to give, or receive, a hiding. But it came to nothing, as the man would not be induced to risk his big local reputation as a pugilist.

The 60th was at Gibraltar at this time, and I accordingly stayed there a while on my return home, and did some fox-hunting with the Calpe Hounds. It is rather a poor substitute for hunting with English packs. We were not allowed to gallop over the cultivated ground, and the " going," where one could ride, was of a dreadful character, the ground being mostly rocks. English horses could not stand it, but the country-breds which were used were certainly a very clever and useful breed.

I left Spain on January 31, 1888, arrived at Plymouth on February 4, and after a day or two in town to see what there was to be seen after my long stay abroad, returned home, and recommenced fox-hunting. Frost militated against steeplechasing, so there was no sport for me to speak of till the Chelmsford meeting on March 15, 1888, when I got home first in the Galleywood Steeplechase on Brown Tommy—my first win for a long while past. Descending the hill, we had to pull up and *trot*, so deep and sticky had the Derby digger made the stiff clay. In the ascent of the hill, the three leading horses were rolling from distress—a terribly severe finish that ! Brown Tommy was a ten-to-one chance. The Toad, ridden by Mr. Tippler, led up the ploughed fields closely accompanied by the favourite, Sir Harry Selwin-Ibbetson's Burnouse, but soon after turning into the straight run in, Brown Tommy came to the front, and won by a little over a length.

In my next steeplechase I again started the outsider of the party, this time on Imogene. It was March 27, and a cruel day too for steeplechasing. A perfectly blinding snowstorm swept over the course, and was twice straight in our faces, so that we could not see our next fence till close up to it. This was the Solent Maiden Hunters' Steeplechase at the Grange Club meeting. Imogene was trained at Arthur Yates's stables, at Bishops Sutton. There were two good jockeys in that race, Escott and Dollery, but they certainly rode under great disadvantages. Half-a-mile from home Imogene came out full of running, and heading the favourite, Cope (with Dollery up) won easily. Didn't the bookies cheer as she came in! Imogene had probably not been backed at all, as it was generally understood that Cope, which had been backed for a lot of money at Sandown, and was trained in the same stable, was much the better.

On the same day I once more started at ten to one, riding Spangle in the Alverstoke Selling Hunters' Flat Race. I had Spangle on racing terms. He could only get placed second, so my spell of good luck with rank outsiders was broken. The race was won by Sir I. Duke's Passing Shower, which started at something like three to one on—at all events a hot favourite. There was chasing again next day at Winchester, in which I scored nothing, Imogene being very sore after her previous exertions; and this ended my little Hampshire riding expedition, with the exception of a couple of days' sport next month in the Isle of Wight. There were the Castle Club races on one day, and the Isle of Wight chases on another. Spangle and another were schooled and sent down for those events, but without any good result.

Spangle, however, won the Tradesmen's Plate a week later at the Bungay Steeplechases. It was rather a good race that. Kelvin, the favourite, ridden by Mr. C. Thompson, made a desperate bid for victory, and once in the straight—Spangle having worked to the front after blundering at one fence—we had an exciting race neck-and-neck almost up to the post : won by half a length. Spangle was disqualified a long while afterwards, as it turned out that he was in the flat-race forfeit list.

To fall twice in a field of five and yet win the race, is a thing one does not expect to do often in a lifetime. On May 3, 1888, I did so, when riding Brown Tommy in the Essex and Suffolk Hunt Cup at Colchester. Owing to recent floods the course was in a very rotten condition, and as a consequence every horse but one came down! Five started, namely, Captain Hawkshaw's Lady Cherry, ridden by owner ; Mr. Wright's Patrician, ridden by owner ; Mr. Dunnet's The Toad, ridden by Mr. Percy Tippler ; Mr. Charteris' Countess, ridden by owner ; and Brown Tommy. They laid six to four on the last-named. Countess alone kept up, but she ran off the course. Brown Tommy won by a distance.

I rode in all the races but one that day. In the East Essex Hunt Cup, won by Mr. Colvin with Cossack, the second favourite, Zither, refused ; nor

could I do anything in the Middlewick Cup won by
Hochheimer, which Mr. Percy Tippler steered to
victory. In the Military Steeplechase, Cerise, with
myself up, walked over. Four horses entered for
the race, including my own; Coloony did not
start. All the favourites, save Cossack, the second
favourite, won that day.

The summer, autumn, and winter of 1888 were
spent between Essex, Hampshire, Portugal, Spain,
France, and London. But there was no riding to
speak of in any of these places. Reference has been
made in this book to the difficulty of keeping oneself
thoroughly fit when leading a London life. About
this period I discovered a pleasant way of getting
exercise, namely, sculling on the Serpentine. It may
be strongly recommended to jockeys, and, for the
matter of that, to anybody who cares for aquatic
exercise. You may frequently have the Serpentine
to yourself early in the morning, for very few people
seem to care for rowing and sculling there except
the shop-assistants and their lasses on Saturday and
Sunday afternoons. One other cross-country rider
has occasionally sculled on the Serpentine to keep
himself fit, namely, Roddy Owen; whilst only a
few hours before his death I met Sir Robert Peel on
the banks in his whites, though I cannot say whether
he was going on the water. There is also swimming
to be got in the Serpentine, or Long Water, as all the
world knows, at certain hours, even in the depth
of winter. I asked a friend to enter me for the
contest held there last Christmas day, and as I should
probably have been made limit man owing to age,
ought to have had a good chance of winning. But

he could not find out about it in time, and the opportunity passed.

Even those who love neither bicycle nor tricycle may admit that wheeling is another excellent way of keeping fit when in London for any length of time. Not a few officers in the Guards used to be seen disporting themselves on "safeties," and amongst other ardent cyclists was Lord Queensberry. " Q," as his intimate friends called him, once spun up from the Star and Garter, Richmond, to his place in town in forty minutes. A punch-ball used to be one of his favourite methods of taking exercise, and that, again, if one has a suitable room for it, is a rare good way of keeping oneself fit in town.

Friends often chaff me about my habit of taking exercise in all manner of queer ways, and for going out for a walk or run without a hat. Now Sir Thomas Barrett-Lennard, of Belhus hunters' fame, did really take his exercise in an uncommon manner. When he felt that he was growing too fat, he would take off his coat and waistcoat, put them in his carriage, and run home briskly by the side of the horses. Sir Thomas was so fond of doing this kind of thing at all hours, that more than once he was chased by his own keepers, and on one occasion all but run in by a vigilant policeman, who actually captured the coatless baronet, and was not for some time to be persuaded that his doings were of a lawful character.

Sometimes I was yacht-racing in the orthodox fashion in the Solent (when I usually managed to go to sleep during what to some appeared the exciting part of the day) ; at others playing racquets, a grand game at which I have usually managed to hold my own, though certainly not a " flier " ; and at others, again, turning up at bull-fights in the Peninsula, or races in France. But in the spring of 1889 I addressed myself again to steeplechasing, taking part chiefly in East of England meetings. At Colchester, Woodbridge, and Ipswich, I rode without winning anything, and on May 2 we had our own steeplechases.

In the summer of 1889 I tried to make up for my rather unsuccessful chasing season in the earlier part of the year, by sport in the water. I won a veterans' swimming race in Essex, and on the following day went to sea in an open boat.

It has been suggested that I may to a certain degree have inherited my love for, and ease in, the water from my grandfather. Captain Augustus de Crespigny was known by the sobriquet of "the Newfoundland Dog," owing to the number of lives he had saved. In those days they did not give away medals for the saving of life in quite the lavish style they do now. It was then not only a great but a rare distinction to gain the medal of the Royal Humane Society. For instance, in one year only two men won it, namely, my grandfather and Richard de Saumarez. Curiously enough, a de Crespigny and a de Saumarez were awarded the medal at a much later period. De Saumarez, it should be added, got also the Albert Medal. He effected a rescue in the Canton river in the face of great danger, there being sharks all around him as he swam.

On one occasion Augustus de Crespigny's enterprise in saving life at sea won him the generous admiration of the Commander of the French Fleet, engaged with our own at the time of an action off Cadiz, in the year 1810. Augustus went to the rescue of five men, who were in imminent danger of being drowned owing to the sinking of the *Achilles'* barge. To accomplish his purpose the rescuer had to pull under the very muzzles of the enemy's guns. The French Commander happened to be an eye-witness of the incident, and was so pleased with the conduct of my ancestor that he at once bade his men desist from firing.

To the luxury and ease of the orthodox style of yachting I never could take very kindly, though from time to time a little of it has come my way. As practised at the present day it is altogether too destitute of adventuresomeness. Everything is done for one by the crew, and as a consequence it tends to inaction and inglorious ease. But going to sea in an open boat, or even cruising about in a small yacht, and doing the major portion of the navigation with one's own hands and head, is a vastly different matter. For the former I have always had a distinct taste, which was not even cured by an adventure in 1889. I had been out in a small boat from Portsmouth on that day with my wife and a friend. As the afternoon advanced and it came on to blow, I put in and landed them at Langston Harbour, and then put out to sea again, intending to get into Portsmouth that evening. But it came on very choppy, and as a result I spent the whole of the night tacking about Spithead, with a dinghy in tow, which greatly increased my difficulties. Of all forsaken places, Spithead at night to a man in an open boat,

14

very hungry, and with nothing but a bit of brown bread to munch, is about the worst. I finally anchored off the New Pier at daybreak.

In June 1889 I procured a ship's gig, made her more or less seaworthy, and set out from Heybridge with a man-servant—who was much more at home with a horse than in a boat—as crew. I managed the navigation myself, and before Westgate was reached, we had gone through a series of interesting adventures. We ran ashore four times, carrying away bowsprit, after-shrouds, main and top-sail sheets, and splitting the mainsail. The 28-footer, however, which was named the *Star*, held out gallantly, and after putting out my man, to his obvious relief, at Westgate, and having the *Star* repaired by a coastguardsman, I again went on my watery way rejoicing, and bound for Portsmouth. I was out by night as well as day, and before reaching her destination the poor *Star* was little better than a wreck. At Shoreham my wife came aboard, and went on with me to Portsmouth, though the accommodation on the boat was not very tempting for ladies.

Another time my son and I successfully crossed the Channel from Folkestone to Boulogne in half a gale in a small boat, though it seemed once or twice as though we must get capsized. My father, by the way, made rather a famous passage across the Atlantic in a yacht of ninety tons, called the *Kate*. He was in the company of Sir S. Clarke, and the trip was talked and written of a good deal, because the *Kate* was the smallest yacht which had up to that time crossed the Atlantic. The *Kate* still exists, and is worked at the present time as a fruit-vessel—rather a come-down.

At one time during the *Star* trip I came to the conclusion, knowing the coast pretty well, that we must be hard by the Reculvers, where there are some rocks, so trusted my man with the helm, telling him to steer whilst I examined the chart. It was night-time, and the work of examining the chart was not easy. After a few minutes' searching I became aware that we were boxing the compass, so wild was the steering. I then saw that it was perfectly hopeless leaving my companion to the helm even for the shortest time, and resumed it myself, remarking cheerfully, " Well, we'll chance it : I can swim all right myself." We escaped the rocks, perhaps more by good luck than good judgment. My companion, when safely ashore, let it be understood that he was very glad he had been once to sea in an open boat, as it was a thing to have done, but vowed that he had no intention of ever trying it again. Considering that he could not swim a stroke, and that on the first day we began by splitting our mainsail, it was not altogether to be wondered at that he resolved in future to stick to *terra firma*. Had he accompanied me the whole way to Southsea, the last state of that man would probably have been worse than the first.

After leaving Ramsgate at three in the morning, I was for twenty hours at the helm. At length, at Eastbourne, sleep claimed me for its own, and I dozed off, but woke presently to find myself half overboard.

A rather eventful trip was that in a little half-decked craft called the *B'nita*, which a friend was so good as to lend. My companion in this case was, however, a man who well understood navigation, so that the entire burden did not fall on my own shoulders. We set sail from Southampton in the middle of May 1890, our destination being Plymouth. Starting at about ten a.m. we were caught in a storm of wind and furious rain in the afternoon, and had to put into Christchurch as best we could at five o'clock. It blew W.S.W. so hard next day that it was not possible to leave till the morning after. It was blowing very hard again when we reached St. Albans Head, where we had to drift through stern foremost. Ultimately we got into a harbour, which neither of us could at first recognize. It turned out to be Torbay.

The wind, which was blowing quite a hurricane in the night, played havoc with the little craft. By 1.30 a.m. it had carried away bowsprit and top-mast. I was lying down asleep for awhile when this wreckage was going on, but was roughly awakened by a broken spar, which threatened to knock a hole in the boat. We then had to clear away the ruined gear and get inside the breakwater. But this was about the toughest, and not the least risky, job of the kind which I have ever experienced in a small boat. After a struggle, however, we managed to get inside, and were then all right. It had taken about three-quarters of an hour to get a matter of two hundred yards, or thereabouts, so strong was the wind. Shortly after daylight we were at length able to land. The poor *B'nita* looked a perfect wreck— so much so that it is questionable whether her owner would have recognized her in her sad plight. We waited next day for a new bowsprit, and for the wind to moderate. Starting from Torbay at 10.20 a.m. on May 22, the seventh day after leaving South-ampton, we arrived at Keyham, and made fast to a buoy by nine o'clock that night, and anchored at the Catwater on the 23rd. Early in June I returned to Devonshire, and brought the *B'nita* to Cowes. The passage back was accomplished without any adventure or incident of particular interest.

CHAPTER VIII

TO EGYPT AND BACK AGAIN

In July 1889 I started for Egypt as a volunteer to join General Sir F. Grenfell, a fellow-officer in the 60th Rifles in India. An engagement had already taken place between the British troops under Colonel Wodehouse and a Dervish force at Argain. The latter were defeated and driven to the hills, but not without some severe fighting, as the total loss of British troops showed—no less than six hundred and seventy being on the list of killed and wounded. The Dervishes continued hostilities from their mountain fortresses, and it was accordingly decided to send out reinforcements under Sir F. Grenfell. The opportunity for volunteering seemed a really promising one, so on July 11 I hurried up to town, took my ticket for Egypt, got together with all despatch a small kit, and started for the East on the following morning. There was not an hour to be lost, if one was to make sure of getting to the front whilst hostilities were still going on. Brindisi was reached on July 14, and left at midnight on the same day. Just outside Brindisi the train caught fire, and we all but missed the steamer. The mail indeed passed us as we were engaged in putting out the flames. Curiously enough, a few days afterwards we were in

214

another fire outside Assouan : some cocoanut matting for camels got ablaze and burnt with great rapidity. On the 18th we arrived at Ismailia on board the P. and O. steamship *Peninsular*, and a special train conveyed us thence to Cairo. Here I stopped the night at General Sir J. Dormer's, dining with General de Montmorency, who was preparing to join Grenfell at Assouan in the course of the next few days. The General entertained us at the Khedival Sporting Club, the *menu* of which was irreproachable. The dinner was an *al fresco* one, and a more enjoyable evening can scarcely be imagined. We sat drinking our coffee and smoking our cigarettes in the midst of most charming scenery. I left Cairo on July 19, in the company of Hickman of the 19th Regiment, who was attached to the Egyptian army, and reaching Assiot, embarked on board the *Tanjore*. We passed Mensheyah, Keneh, and other ports where there were troops ready for action, and arrived at Assouan on the 23rd. After dinner that evening with the Egyptian mess, I saw Grenfell, who accorded me a hearty welcome.

It was when we were bathing next day in the Nile that my desire to get to the front and see active service in some capacity or other was broached. To my chagrin the Sirdar pointed out that it was impossible for him to allow any one not attached to the Army of Occupation to do this. " The only way," said he, " you can accomplish your ambition is to get some English newspaper to appoint you its special correspondent." The Toski affair was so sudden and so soon over, that none of the great dailies —though there was time and to spare—sent out a representative. Now "the Shifter" had actually asked me to send to his paper any items of interest from the scene of action, so playing my last card I said to Grenfell, "I am war correspondent of the *Pink'un.*" He could not help laughing at this, but thought, with due respect to the paper in question, that such a qualification could scarcely be allowed to pass muster. What was to be done? Happy thought! Wire to Lady de Crespigny and get her to find me an appointment. Pending a reply, the only thing to do was to fret in inaction at Assouan, and, what was worse, to see Grenfell off on July 29 from Shellal, beyond which point it was not permissible to advance. "I think Njumi," said Grenfell as he departed, "is in a hurry to get to Paradise, and that we can accommodate him." It was pretty clear indeed to most of us that Njumi was playing a very risky game, and one likely to get him into an awkward fix. He would have been wiser to have taken up a position at Abou Simbel, where he might have given the Sirdar a good deal more trouble.

All this while the heat was frightful. I can stand a fair amount of roasting myself, but had to admit that Assouan was the vilest spot I had ever been in. There were no Eastern appliances for keeping oneself cool. The one cooling thing was to lie down in the muddy old Nile, which was not even fringed at Assouan with bulrushes. Whilst waiting at Assouan we heard that our troops had captured Njumi's head doctor. This man's methods were simplicity itself, his rule being kill or cure. The doctor's stock-in-trade consisted of a barrel of oil and a long knife. If the former failed to cure the sick he cut their throats with the latter, and so prevented the hospitals becoming too crowded.

I filled in the time after seeing Grenfell off, and whilst waiting a reply from Lady de Crespigny, by a trip or two up the river in the steamers *Okmeh* and *Amkeh*, and by accompanying some of the troops who had not yet pushed on. All the Mounted Infantry were still at Assouan at the commencement of August, together with some of the cavalry and two companies of the Welsh regiment. A ride down the Nile to meet the infantry was rather a pleasant manner of passing away the time. Skirting the river, we had to pick our way rather carefully under the date-trees, amongst the innumerable native huts and wells, but were able to return at a swinging canter along the cultivated land on the edge of the desert, with the irrigation ditches for obstacles. Right cleverly the little Arab horses negotiated these ditches. You might almost have imagined yourself at times schooling on Epsom Downs!

On other days the cataract was ascended in the two vessels referred to. The *Omkeh* got through without a mishap, but the *Amkeh* was not so fortunate. She struck the rocks several times, and must have filled a good percentage of her twenty-four compartments. As one steams, the distance from Assouan to Philæ is seven miles, the rise being seventeen feet. A stern-wheeler is capable of making fair headway except up the narrow gut of the rapid, which is 250 yards long. To pass this we required some hundreds of Egyptian soldiers on our bow-rope, and as many Berberines under the sheik of the cataract on our four guy-ropes. On the second day the bow-hawser and a wire guy-rope suddenly snapped simultaneously, and at a critical moment. We looked perilously like getting broadside on and capsizing, after the fashion of the ill-fated gunboat *Kirbacan*. That vessel, it may recollected, was raised at a cost of some thousands, and then sold to Messrs. Cook for £100. We eventually got out of our difficulties, and passed the rapids, to the astonishment apparently of the natives, who cheered loudly.

These rapids have long borne amongst Englishmen an evil reputation for danger. It was during our trip on the *Amkeh*, and whilst waiting for a native boat to get out of the way, that I landed and ran up the side of the rapid with the determination to test the matter on my own account. The question of whether or no it was possible to dive into the rapids, swim down the narrow gut, and land without assistance, had already been discussed between myself and several of the officers. It was asserted that only one Englishman, or more properly Scotchman, namely, Montgomery, R.N., the boxer, had ever made the attempt, and that he had not actually swum the narrowest part of the gut, but had put his swimming powers to the test further down the rapids ; nor did the natives in my presence, notwithstanding their fine swimming powers, ever dive in and swim down at this particular point. But I resolved to make the attempt, so dived in and swam down the narrow gut to within a few yards of the exit. Then having gone far enough to convince myself and others that the thing was quite practicable, it only remained to get into one of the eddies at the side, and so into the quiet water, where a landing was effected with ease. The rush of the water in the narrow gut is tremendous, but it is not broken, as, for instance, below the Niagara Falls; and the one thing necessary was to keep oneself afloat, and to nicely calculate the force of the stream so as to be able to get into the quiet water. I was in excellent condition at the time, and therefore felt absolutely no fatigue, and after landing walked back to the boat.

The chief danger incurred by a strong swimmer in these Nile rapids is that of being, through an evil chance, drawn into a whirlpool before he can get a full breath. Personally, I have swum in almost all parts of the world, and in every variety of water, and don't think the Nile is so particularly dangerous, although the natives have an idea that if a man once dives down he can never come up again alive. As for the crocodile danger it is *nil*, at any rate at this point of the river. Besides, crocodiles are like bears —they much prefer clearing out of a man's way to attacking him. They invariably do so on land, and, I believe, statements notwithstanding to the contrary, that their behaviour is much the same in the water. Sharks, too, often act in a similar manner. When stationed at Barbadoes we used to bathe on one side of the bay in perfect safety, though it would have been great folly to bathe on the other, because there the sharks fed on the offal from the slaughterhouse, and were ravenous for blood.

The Nile incident was talked about a great deal at the time, and, so far as I know to the contrary, it has never been repeated. But I achieved a more difficult, though perhaps a less sensational, bit of swimming once at Portland.

There is a beach there called the Chesil, on which the surf beats with great force. So furious, when there is a sea on, is the suction of the retreating waves, which tear down with them the beach, that it has usually been considered quite impossible for even the strongest swimmer to effect a landing. When it was known that I had resolved to essay the task, a boat was in readiness to effect a rescue if necessary. A tripper had got into trouble at the Chesil only the day before, and it was therefore deemed wise to take precautions. I went out through the waves, and then in coming back hovered as it were pretty close to the shingle, waiting for a small wave to get in with. A few short, quick strokes brought me in with the fifth or sixth wave—a small one—and I succeeded in running up on to the beach, although the shingle rolled away a good deal from under my feet. The use of the head and the feet was more necessary than that of the arms. During heavy storms the strength of the waves at this place is prodigious ; and tradition has it that a ship was once swept clean over the Chesil Beach and into the Bay.

A good many people, having heard—often through unreliable sources—of these and other adventures, have chosen to set me down as either a man quite reckless of life and limb, or an advertiser on a big scale. To have won, even without meriting it, either of these reputations is scarcely a matter to be " wept with tears of blood." There is at least nothing dishonourable in holding one's life cheap, however small the stake played for ; whilst in an age of self-

advertisement some tolerance ought to be extended
to one who makes himself known by courting danger
whether in earth, sea, or sky. As a matter of fact,
I cannot lay claim to either distinction, having never
actually courted danger for its own sweet sake ; and
never risked my life and limb for the paltry purpose of self-advertisement. However, there is a
wide difference between risking your life through
pure ignorance of its value, and shunning danger
when by so doing you must soil the escutcheon of
bravery, which should be the most precious possession of every good Englishman. Indifference to
danger in a good cause, and especially where a man's
honour is at stake, is absolutely essential. Could
our ancestors, the makers of England, had they not
been actuated by some such principle as this, have
put together this great Empire ? Surely never !

This may seem no more than a truism, save perhaps
to that miserable party of men known as the " little
Englanders." For myself, I must go further, and
declare that it is necessary, unless we are to perish
like the Romans in the lap of peace and luxury, that
some of us should strive to keep alive the reputation
which Englishmen have always had of greatly daring
and suffering all things. Surely where there is a
daring deed to be done in any part of the world,
an Englishman should leap to the front to accomplish it.

It needs but little reading between the lines to
discover a sentiment similar to this running through
much of the best patriotic literature of our country,
and through almost every page of our history. Deeds
of daring strewn so plentifully through the story of

England impart to it an imperishable glamour. The heroic exploits of Richard the Lion-hearted must appeal to young hearts for ever, as must the courage of Falkland and many another great Englishman on the field of battle. Even from those who swear by Cromwell, and condemn the Stuarts and all their ways, the despairing courage of the Cavaliers and of the Jacobites may almost draw a tear. The charge of the Light Brigade down the North Valley, was it wild and useless ? Yes, it may have been, but no brighter gem sparkles in the crown of the nation.

Swimming and riding were all very well in their way, but it was not exactly for these pursuits that I had come out to Egypt. It was therefore a cause for rejoicing when the message came from my wife that I was appointed to act as Special Correspondent of the *East Anglian Daily Times*. We had already heard various rumours concerning Njumi and his movements. One was to the effect that his health was good, and that he was still advancing ; whilst another asserted that he was badly diseased, and had to be carted about in a barrel of butter—an awkward position for the leader of a Dervish raid. It would now be possible to get to the front, and find out the true state of things.

So at length, after more than a week's anxious waiting, I was able to tell De Montmorency of my appointment, and on Saturday, August 3, to wire to Grenfell to the same effect ; and then to start up the Nile in a felucca from Shellal, which was reached from Assouan by train. We reached Abuhor, a distance of forty-eight miles, on the first day ; Kostambe, a distance of sixty-three, on the second ; and

Tabbel, eighty-eight miles, on the third, which was Bank Holiday. Before this a hitch had occurred. The crew got fairly beaten owing to the amount of work they had to do when the wind dropped. What was to be done ? The captain and owner of the felucca recommended that the sheik of a village we had reached should be asked to supply men to tow us up to the next village. The sheik was approached, and declined, saying he had no spare men. Fortunately I was armed with a Colt's revolver, and I asked, " Shall I shoot the fellow if he persists in his present attitude ? " The reply was prompt and decisive, " Certainly, shoot him." The rascally sheik was informed of my intention to shoot him for insubordination if he did not instantly alter his tactics. In a moment his demeanour underwent an entire change. Nothing could exceed his desire to oblige in every respect, and accommodate himself to my requirements. After the revolver argument had entered into the controversy there were any number of men at every village ready to tow us along where a fair wind was lacking. As a result we actually kept for awhile well ahead of the Army of Occupation, which was advancing in steamers under De Montmorency.

On my way up the Nile I seriously considered whether it might not prove of real assistance to Grenfell to cut the telegraph wires. It was the recollection of the way in which Sir Evelyn Wood had been hampered and harassed in Africa by the Government a few years before, that made me think about this ; but going into the matter, it occurred to me that in the case of Sir Evelyn Wood, Mr. Gladstone held the reins; whilst Lord Salisbury was now in power, and not very likely to repeat the blunder of his predecessors. Had Mr. Gladstone been in power I should most certainly have set to work to cut the wires, and burn down the telegraph-posts. My crew no doubt would have rendered all the necessary assistance.

When off Maharakka, on the evening of August 5, I observed, first to my astonishment and then to my intense vexation, a flotilla consisting of steamers, barges, and a dahabeah, flying the white flag with the red cross coming down stream. It must mean this, that it was all over " bar shouting " with the Dervish raid and Njumi. The ill fortune, which had on several occasions pursued me when intent on seeing some active service, once more dogged my footsteps, despite the fine opportunity that had at length apparently presented itself. We were hugging the east shore at the time this flotilla came in unwelcome sight. The boats were well in the current on the other side of the river, and as the Nile is not exactly a trout stream, there were no means of communicating with them. Clinging to the vain hope that my apprehensions might be wrong, I carried on towards Korosko, resolving to try and gain some reliable information on the way. A few miles from Samooah we stopped at a small village where there was an Egyptian officer and man. As most of the Egyptian officers speak either English or French, I looked to this one for information. To my surprise, however, it was not the officer, but the man, who was able to reply in somewhat broken French to my inquiries. We learnt from him that Njumi's force had been completely routed at Toski. Later on further tidings came to hand, which told how Njumi himself had been killed, together with fifteen Emirs and fifteen hundred men, at the loss of a very few of our troops. There were probably amongst those who fell or fled at Toski not a few fighting Dervishes, such as broke into our squares a few years previously. The genuine Dervish was an extraordinary specimen of humanity. He and even his camp-followers were utterly callous of pain, and laughed at amputations. A stranger told us of two incidents which came under his personal observation in relation to these folk, men and women. He was ready to swear that he had one day found in a palm-tree a man whose leg he had amputated twenty-four hours before, and that he had seen a woman grinding corn the day subsequent to his having taken off one of her legs at the thigh and one of her arms above the elbow ! He succeeded in telling these tales without a smile.

The fun being all over, we turned back after three days' real hard work in striving to keep ahead of De Montmorency's troops. A large percentage of head and light winds are but poor allies in the business of overcoming a rising Nile with constant rapids. At eight o'clock in the evening, with a good moon, I resolved to head for Assouan, though expecting remonstrances from my boatmen. It turned out, however, that they were one and all only too anxious to get back again to their wives and homes. On we went at once. The men rowed vigorously—with such oars too !—through the night, singing after their quaint fashion. I had lately been enjoying the melody of such artistes as Battistini, Nevada, and

15

Regina Paccini, so that the Arabic boat-song palled a trifle after a while, but in its way it was not devoid of a certain beauty. It took twenty-four hours to do the eighty-two miles to Shellal, notwithstanding the current and rapids in our favour. We were caught in a vicious little squall in the " Gates of Kalábsheh," and very nearly capsized. This was the only incident of much note during the homeward journey. I had one most narrow shave, which made my blood run cold when I thought of it for a long time afterwards. On the look-out in the night for game of any sort along the banks of the river, I barely escaped putting a bullet into the head of a camel which suddenly appeared behind a jackal that offered a tempting shot on the skyline. It might have been hard to live down the ridicule sure to be attached to any one for shooting one of these long-suffering and very non-combatant beasts of burden.

In the Nile, some miles above Shellal, poor Major Turnbull lost his life. He fell overboard at night, and must have been taken under by a whirlpool just after he had called to his companions in the dahabeah that he was all right. Early on the morning of August 7 we shot the cataracts in the felucca in company with Chaplain-General Collins; recovered the body of Turnbull terribly disfigured, and buried it with all military honours at Assouan. The body was in the shallows, where I had foretold it would be found. It was discovered by his company dog, who, with an intelligence rather above that of an average human being, induced some of the men to accompany him back to the spot where the officer was lying.

The Egyptian question has been discussed a great

deal of late. This is scarcely the place to deal with such a matter, but I cannot help remarking that my experience of the country and its inhabitants has led me to form a strong opinion against evacuation. The Egyptians are utterly incapable of self-government, and if left to themselves they would speedily slip back again into all the old evils of bribery and corruption, which appear to be inherent in nations under Mussulman rule.

On August 12 I embarked at Alexandria on board the *Cathay*, and was at Brindisi on the 15th. Here I wired to Don Carlos to expect me in Venice in a couple of days, and upon arrival there found a beautiful gondola waiting to take me to his residence, the Palazzo Loredan. The Palazzo, where Don Carlos resided, is finely situated, with extensive views of the Grand Canal ; and it contains, amongst other interesting things, one of the most perfect private armouries in Europe. I was able to add to it on the occasion of my visit in the shape of a Colt's revolver—the very one which had brought the unruly sheik to his senses—and a Dervish sword.

There was only the afternoon and evening to spend at Venice ; but I was not at all averse to my host's agreeable proposition that we should bathe. At Lido we swam about for a good while near the shore, when suddenly Don Carlos exclaimed, "Now we will go for a swim," and struck out as if with the intention of crossing the Adriatic to Fiume. This was rather more than I bargained for, as I was getting very cold, and not unnaturally so after the grilling in Egypt. After a time, however, my host thoughtfully asked me whether I felt at all cold, and upon my replying in the affirmative, somewhat to my relief instantly turned towards the shore. Venice was left shortly before midnight, and London reached on the evening of August 19.

After my return from Egypt I contented myself with hunting and shooting, taking part in no steeple-chasing whatever in the autumn and winter of 1889. In the first few months of 1890 I addressed myself to hunting, chiefly in the New Forest, and in the spring and early summer to cruising about the coast in a small boat.

It does not often fall to one's lot to get through a " mill " in the midst of a run. But this rather novel experience did once fall to my lot when out cubbing with the East Essex. The hounds were running, when I rode up to a gate, on the other side of which were a ploughman and two men in a cart, one of whom was a renowned local " bruiser." I remarked to the ploughman that he might have opened the gate seeing the hounds running, and the others took this in ill part. A volley of oaths told me that one of them was more than my match in blasphemy, so I made no further comment, and intended to pass on without more ado. However, to my surprise the man got out of the cart in no time, and expressed a desire to kick me. I dismounted of course, and prepared to do battle. He was a huge fellow, fully six feet in height, proportionately broad, and on the upper ground. Retreat, however, was out of the question, and it only remained to make the best of what looked like rather a bad bargain, more especially as my right arm had not recovered from a compound fracture. We went for one another hammer and tongs, and at the onset my antagonist got rather the best of it. After the first burst we stopped instinctively for a moment or two, glaring at each other in the way men do under such circumstances. In that brief interim I saw that his great flanks were heaving. " O ho, my friend," thought I, " at any rate I'm more than your match so far as condition is concerned." Almost directly afterwards I landed him one on " the point," and the contest was over. He never showed fight after that, nor did his companion, who was invited to come down and try his fortune. " What's good enough for my friend," he remarked, " will do for me." Several members of the hunt had come up whilst we were at it and formed a ring. The fight over, we mounted and were able to rejoin the hounds, which were still running. I cannot recollect whether or no we killed our fox.

Later on in July, I took the *B'nita* from Ryde to Folkestone, and then crossed the Channel to Boulogne. The trip took four days. It was not so eventful as one or two other excursions of the kind which I have made in small boats in the open sea ; but it may be not without interest, in case others should desire to make the same trip in fine weather, to give the time of starting, and the number of miles covered each day. On the first day we sailed at 1.35 p.m. and arrived at Selsea Bill at 7.50 p.m., a distance of fourteen miles ; on the second day Selsea was left at 4.40 a.m. and Brighton reached at 8.20 p.m.— distance twenty-three miles ; on the third day we left Brighton at 3.35 a.m. and reached Folkestone 4.30 p.m., a distance of fifty-seven miles. Folkestone was left at 4.10 p.m. on the fourth and last day, and

Boulogne reached at 10 o'clock that night—distance twenty-five miles. Thus, the total number of miles being one hundred and nineteen, the average a day was just under thirty.

I was a good deal in Boulogne in July and August of this year, and did some pigeon-shooting, though the sport was not worthy of much notice. One day, being in form, I managed to knock my competitors, who were Frenchmen, one and all well out of it. Thereat arose a good deal of soreness and grumbling, which was only stopped by some one explaining, " Oh, but de Crespigny is one of ourselves. His name should tell you that."

The year 1891 was an uneventful year so far as steeplechasing was concerned, but next year it was possible to settle down once more with a will to cross-country sport. On March 24 I found myself again on the steeplechase course that ought to be at least as familiar to me as any in the country— Chelmsford. It is not easy to say how many times I have ridden there, but I know that twenty years ago my total was sixteen, covering about forty miles. The calculation was then made for the purpose of showing that steeplechasing was not nearly so dangerous a pursuit—so far as fatal accidents went—as many seemed to imagine. In those sixteen steeplechases I fell only twice, and was in neither instance considerably hurt. At the same time it has happened that my worst tumbles have been on courses other than Chelmsford, such as Lingfield and Hurst Park.

Corrèze has turned out the best horse I have ever had the fortune to own and train in England. We bred him ourselves out of Wild Georgie by Young

Citadel, and he was the mare's second foal. Wild Georgie was originally bought to ride as a Yeomanry charger ; and her pedigree has already been touched upon. Young Citadel (1872) was a direct descendant of Brutandorf, and a writer commenting on this has remarked, " There are very few, if any, horses now at the stud representing this line ; and so good-looking is Corrèze that he will be valuable for transmitting it, and so reviving an almost extinct but very valuable branch of the Blacklock family." Young Citadel was by Lambton, son of The Cure, son of The Physician, son of Brutandorf. We first made up our minds that Corrèze was really useful when he won a four-mile trial at Captain Aiken's, where he easily knocked out Profit, a horse that went the first two miles with him—and also The Sikh. The latter would have been my mount at Liverpool, had he not unhappily broken a blood-vessel in that trial.

Corrèze came out as a good horse rather slowly ; at least he did nothing very much in his first few races, though not always very lucky. On April 18 I got a nasty fall with him on the course outside the Cavalry Barracks at Colchester. He crossed his legs after landing over the brook, came down, and gave me concussion of the brain. As I was carried past my second son, a yokel remarked, " Wonder whether he's gone to 'eaven." In about twenty minutes I came round, not much the worse for the toss. Two days afterwards, April 20, was my forty-fifth birth-day. It is pleasant to win a race on one's birthday if it can be managed. It was managed on that day, for going down to Woodbridge, I won the Orwell Hurdle Race by three lengths on Marcus Beresford's, afterwards Lord Decies' Amber, riding of course as one naturally does on another man's horse—unless told to make your own pace—to orders. Gondola was second ; Topper third. In the following year, too, I won a race on my forty-sixth birthday.

From Woodbridge it is not a far cry to Ipswich, where there was some steeplechasing two days later. I did not excel there, but was more in luck at Chelmsford, on the 28th winning the Selling Steeple-chase on Mr. Ditton's Old Ben, beating the favourite —Major Peter's Barbiana, who was ridden by Mr. Cheney—by a length or so.

In the winter of 1892 Corrèze was not a very good second in the Essex Open Steeplechase at Chelmsford on Nov. 30, Mr. Clayton's Grab All, the favourite, who was then in good form, being too much for him. Corrèze indeed was not at all fancied, and started a rank outsider. At Bury, a week later, in the Suffolk County Steeplechase, Corrèze was going strong, and seemed a winner all over, when, three fences from home, Fugleman, whom I struck into, crossed, and this brought us down. Next time I rode the horse was at Hurst Park on Dec. 10, starting as outsider in a field of five, and getting second to Sensier, who won on Mr. Ryall's Kynaston. This was over a three-mile course, as was also the Essex Open Steeple-chase. Corrèze has always been rather a stayer than a speedy horse, and does not run up to his form over short courses such as two miles.

In the early part of 1893 it fell to my lot to get knocked about a good deal on one or two courses, but I was able fortunately to soon shake off the effects of my falls, and to enjoy a good deal of sport.

January 21, 1893, was a day much more fitted for skating than riding across country. Indeed skating was actually going on within a stone's throw of the course at Lingfield, where we were steeple-chasing. I received what at the time looked like a very ugly fall.

When my horse fell there was another close at his heels, but knowing the man for whom I was riding believed my mount ought easily to win, I took no heed of this in my anxiety to be up and doing again. So I rose at once, and as I did so the off fore plate of the horse behind struck me a heavy blow just over the eye. I was of course insensible for a while, but came to before the stretcher was brought, and was led away between two friends, one of whom, by the way, was relieved of his note-book by a member of the light-fingered fraternity as he leant over me. A policeman on this occasion offered to try his surgical skill on me, but I flatly refused to submit myself to his tender mercies. Ultimately they plastered me up, and, when I arrived home, my own doctor bandaged and sewed me up properly with cat-gut.

Three or four days later I was out and engaged in rolling my cricket-ground, which, by the way, is an excellent way of keeping oneself in condition. I followed this up with a Turkish bath, and the day after was, though still in bandages, quite fit to ride Corrèze and Birdseye at Hurst Park. But I did nothing, as the former fell in one race at the ditch, and made such a hole in the fence that my old friend, Sir Matthew Wood, the then Secretary, threatened to send me in a bill for damages; whilst the latter only managed to come in fourth in an open selling race.

Though now and again I have had a little brush not of a particularly unfriendly character with sporting writers, I have to gratefully acknowledge that the sporting press has, on the whole, always dealt by me in a very kind manner. There were some allusions to this accident at Lingfield, one of which may be reproduced :—"Neither broken bones, concussion of the brain, nor a severed artery can take the gameness out of Sir Claude de Crespigny. What with his ballooning, his boxing, his racing, and his other lively pursuits, Sir Claude has been knocked about as much as most people. Last Saturday, whilst riding in a steeplechase at Lingfield, his horse fell, and he was kicked on the head by another animal, sustaining concussion of the brain and a severed artery. He was carried home, and his wounds were found to be of so severe a character that they had to be sewn up. In less than twenty-four hours, however, Sir Claude was writing to the editor, saying that he was doing well and hoped to be in the saddle again before long." The letter referred to was the following :—

" Turkish Bath, Northumberland Avenue,
Jan. 25, 1893.

" DEAR SIR,

" My daughter, who has just started for Exeter, has handed me your kind letter. Yesterday my M.D. considered danger from erysipelas had passed, and let me out for an hour (which I took on a stone roller on the Champion Hill Cricket Ground). To-

day I've had a good spell in the Turkish bath; to-
morrow shall go down to the country for a gallop,
and on Friday hope to sport silk at Hurst Park
Steeplechases.

"C. Ch. de Crespigny."

Aiken and I went down to Warwick on Feb. 6,
when I rode in the Warwick Handicap Steeplechase,
starting an outsider on The Sikh. The horse however
was placed second, though well beaten by Wenty
Hope Johnstone, whose mount was Mr. Irving's
Champion, the second favourite. This was described
as quite an old jockeys' race, for between us and our
horses it was calculated that our total ages amounted
to over a hundred years !

After this race we tried to get up a match between
Wenty and myself over a four-mile course at Sandown, and on the same horses. Wenty was to give
a stone for the beating. I should have fancied The
Sikh on these terms, but the match never came off.

In the seventies the 7th Hussars—the old Regiment
of both Wenty Hope Johnstone and Billy Morris—
the 9th Lancers, and the Guards supplied most of
the soldier jockeys that could hold their own both
inside and outside the military circle. When River-
escat won the Grand Military, the 7th had no less
than five jockeys riding in the race—namely, John
Drye Barker, Baby M'Calmont, Marcus Beresford,
Billy Morris, and Wenty Hope Johnstone. This reminds one of Eton pretty well monopolizing one of
the 'Varsity boats, as she often has done. Probably
no regiment has ever been quite so strong in jockeys
as the 7th was at that period.

Billy Morris—known in the 7th as Billy Morgan—was, in my opinion, the finest soldier jockey of his time, and he could ride under ten stone. He rode more than once in the Grand National, and when up on Downpatrick was first on the racecourse. Twice he won the Grand Military, each time on Chilblain, and once the Irish Military on Witch Hazel. Billy was immensely popular amongst all racing men, amateur and professional alike. There is a dark cloud about his end, which can now never be thoroughly cleared away. It has always been a belief with some of us that he was hustled in the hunting-field where he came by his death, and left to an untimely end. A friend and soldier colleague of his says—" Billy was found lying with his collar and shirt undone, and his pin stuck in his coat. His neck was broken. Hard by, his horse was tied to a paling. How it happened, or who saw it, is a tale that has never been told. A bold horseman and a good soldier was poor Billy Morgan."

Old Chilblain wound up his career in peace and honour at Champion Lodge. He had his horse-box, shed, and four acres of paddock, and a companion for some time too in the shape of a lamb. This animal followed Chilblain as faithfully as that of the poet did Mary, and a great affection sprang up between the two. Whichever left the box first the other immediately followed, and at the same pace. The horse and lamb grazed alongside of one another, and when the horse lay down, the lamb followed suit. They became, in fact, inseparable—a remarkable instance of Platonic affection between two animals.

CORRÈZE.

In several instances during the spring of this year Corrèze had bad luck, losing races by little unforeseen accidents. Thus on March 3 he was leading in at Sandown Park in the National Hunt, when he blundered at the brook, and went on his head and knees. He recovered, but I had to jump the next two fences without one of my irons. After the blunder I felt the off-leather getting longer and longer, and speedily perceiving what had occurred, made a desperate endeavour as we were passing the stand to adjust the buckle. This was ultimately done, but not till we had passed the stand. Corrèze made a dash for the big gate instead of bearing to the right, and this lost so much ground that it was impossible to make it up. The winner was Van der Berg, with Cuthbert Slade up. Corrèze had started an outsider; subsequently he turned the table on Van der Berg.

On March 8 we repaired to Gatwick, and I rode Corrèze in the Harkaway Steeplechase, but had to put up with a beating from Lily of the Valley, with Dollery up.

In a hurdle race at Windsor on March 13 I came down pretty hard with Robert Dudley. It was a case of slight concussion; but I jumped up, interested to see what was winning, and was so stupefied by the fall that I found myself looking right in the opposite direction to the winning-post.

The streak of bad luck which pursued me for part of this spring season of 1893 was not broken through on March 23. At Chelmsford, I went over the Galleywood Course carefully beforehand, and ought to have won the Chelmsford Steeplechase. It sometimes happens that when a horse has been doing stiff fences, he fails altogether over a much easier country. I feared this might happen at Chelmsford, and it did. Corrèze was going well, till he took it into his head to hit the rail of the fourth fence, not more than a foot above the ground, and came down. It did the horse good, and made him careful afterwards.

The next steeplechase of any note was at Kempton early in April, when Corrèze was second to Abyssinian in the Twickenham Steeplechase. That race was lost by one of those little chances which rarely get recorded in the press reports, because they are not noticed. Abyssinian was going very unkindly, and he would have certainly gone clean into the middle of the brook, if it had not been a mere splash, and have probably finished up the race there had I not come up alongside, which helped to keep him straight. He then got out of his difficulties. Dollery, who was up on Abyssinian, saw how well I had served him by accident, and said afterwards, "You gave me that race, Sir Claude."

The same week Corrèze was tried again at Lingfield, but was not placed in the Lingfield Grand National, won by Excelsior. He had not fully recovered from a slight touch of the influenza, which attacks horses sometimes as it does their riders. This race told me something, as it enabled me to about gauge The Primate's form, which came in useful later in the year.

Bewicke, Dollery, and I rode down to the post just before this race, and commenting on Dollery's success in the Grand National on Cloister, Bewicke said, "By the way, I was the first to tell you that you'd won that race." "Were you indeed, sir?" quoth

Dollery ; " well now, I recollect I did hear somebody halloaing out, and could not think where the sounds came from." Bewicke had been shouting out from underneath his horse, The Primate, quite forgetful of his fall in the excitement of the race.

At Woodbridge, on April 19, 1893, the ground was so hard that for once in a way it was actually necessary to decline mounts. This was done not so much out of regard for my own safety, but for that of two horses, Sprig of Myrtle and Robert Dudley, which had been brought down for me to ride. They were accordingly sent back to Ipswich for the Chases to be held there a few days later.

On April 20 Corrèze won easily enough in the Open Military Steeplechase in the Household Brigade meeting at Hawthorn Hill. He started favourite—six to four on—and was well in, carrying 11 st. 4 lbs. against Lord Tullibardine's Mazzard, 13 st. 3 lbs. (ridden by owner), and Mr. Tilney's Willoughby, 12 st. 7 lbs., ridden by Captain Milner. At the same time, two miles was not the proper distance for Corrèze. He has always essentially been a stayer. On March 10 of the same year, I rode him over a two-mile course at Sandown in the Open Handicap Steeplechase, won by Tenby. In this race we knocked out a prominent G. N. candidate, Sarsfield, who was served up a hot favourite, but had apparently lost all form.

An incident that reminds one rather of the kind of judging one looked for in India, when I was steeplechasing and racing there, occurred at Ipswich on April 21, 1893. I was riding Robert Dudley for Mr. Loftus le Champion. He had backed the horse for a small sum for a place, and had been so fortunate as to get a very good price, something like five to one. White Heather—owner up—was first ; Candytuft, second ; and Robert Dudley came in third, having fallen at the water-jump. He was a hundred and fifty yards or thereabouts behind the second horse. But the judge left his box, and consequently Robert Dudley was not given a place, though he was third. I remonstrated, but it was of no avail, and Mr. le Champion not only did not receive, but actually had to pay ! It was an act of culpable carelessness. I went into the judge's box myself after the race, and found that one could see easily as far as Nacton corner. Now Robert Dudley had passed that point long before the winning horse passed the post, so there was really no excuse whatever for not awarding him the place he had fairly won. It need hardly be said that it was merely an act of carelessness on the part of the judge, but it was an undeniably gross one. A pretty uproar there would have been if the public money had been on the horse to any extent. That day I was not altogether displeased to see a horse disqualified. The owner had asked me to ride for him some time previously, but said he could not find me. As I had ridden in the previous race, the excuse was somewhat lame. The jockey, not having walked round the course, missed a fence, and so the good thing fell through.

CHAPTER IX

MORE SPORT IN SPAIN

The racing memory, unlike the political, is not by any means notorious for its shortness, so that there is no need to do anything but skim very lightly over the history of steeplechasing during the remainder of this and the next two seasons. April 1893 was one of the driest on record, and the ground was like iron. I took part in no more cross-country sport till the autumn, when there fell to my lot a win or two in a few events, such as the Army and Navy Steeplechase at Hawthorn Hill—Corrèze's second win there—and Dormans Steeplechase at Lingfield. At Hawthorn Hill, Corrèze got the better of Father O'Flynn, ridden by Mr. C. Grenfell the owner, and of Emin, who started favourite, also ridden by his owner, Lord Molyneux.

The biggest events in steeplechasing, even including the Grand National, are, despite the undoubted popularity of the sport, mere drops in the ocean compared with the monster prizes to be won on the flat. My own mounts have rarely brought me in anything over two figures, so that December 9, 1893, the date of the Great Sandown Steeplechase which Corrèze won, was quite a red-letter day in my calendar. Even here the stakes are not excessive, but the event is a

big one in its way, and what was particularly satisfactory about the winning of it, from my point of
view, was the fact that the Prince of Wales, as the
late King was then, cordially congratulated me on
my success. His Royal Highness was present at the
dinner given by the Sports' Club to Lord Dunraven,
and spoke to me most kindly about the race. It
was permissible to remind the Prince that I had once
had the honour of training in his old stable, namely,
that of Jack Jones.

The Primate, carrying 12 st. 7 lbs., and ridden by
Bewicke, started rather a warm favourite. Corrèze,
with 10 st. 13 lbs., was backed at nine to two—Fairy
Queen was second favourite—but I believed him to
be better than Primate at the weights, as I had had
some opportunities of judging, and was not much
surprised, therefore, at the result. Then Primate did
not behave over well in the race, swerving at the first
fence, and never jumping too well. Corrèze, on the
other hand, jumped well, and stayed well. Before
the last fence was negotiated, Corrèze had the favourite nicely settled, and Fairy Queen being unable to
stay home in the run in, he won by a couple of lengths.
Corrèze, after this, began to be talked of a good deal
for the Grand National ; but a break-down in training
later on robbed him of the great chance he would
otherwise have had in that classic steeplechase.

Of all the smart steeplechasing performances I
have ever seen—and their name is legion—not one
surpasses Bewicke's in this race. Glancing round,
one espied Primate down at the fence by the pay-
gate. He looked to me, in the hasty glance which
I was able to take, stretched out almost spread-eagle

fashion on the ground.   Yet the rider never lost his
seat, and scarcely had the cry of a fall gone forth
amongst the spectators, than he had Primate up
again, and was pressing Corrèze hard, having only
lost a few lengths by the mishap.   It seemed, and it
actually was, a marvellous achievement of Bewicke's.
No one with knowledge of steeplechasing, who saw
the incident, can ever forget it.

The *Sportsman*, in commenting on Corrèze's win
in the race, referred to his rider in tones so eulogistic
that my native modesty quite prevents me repro-
ducing them here!   But there was one passage in
the article in question which was so much to the
point, and so true, that it may be well quoted for the
guidance of young and ambitious riders; "His victory is, in my humble opinion, a salutary example
for the younger division who are not unfrequently
lacking in go. . . .   Practical horsemen are well
aware that race-riding over a country or hurdles is
impossible except for a man who is thoroughly fit
and constantly taking riding exercise.   But the
modern Sybarite is far too apt to luxuriate, and try
to ride at Sandown upon occasions, when, as almost
invariably happens, he makes a lamentable show,
and then, forsooth, complains if he is criticized in
the papers.   These gentlemen should understand
that when they get up to ride at a gate-money meeting
they offer their performances as value for the public's
money, and are therefore most legitimate objects of
criticism.   If they would but make themselves fit
to ride—if they want to ride—as Sir Claude de
Crespigny does, we should have a better prospect,
and be spared that terrible barrenness of soldier riders,

which was marked when that good horse Partisan could not run at Sandown because there was no soldier capable of riding him." Without going the length of this somewhat severe criticism of our soldier riders, it may be readily conceded that the reference to men who try to ride without keeping themselves in the proper condition is quite justifiable.

Throughout the winter season of 1893 and '94, there was abundance of riding for me at several meetings in the South, such as Hurst Park, Kempton, Portsmouth, and Bury St. Edmunds. At the last-named I met my old friend the Duke of Hamilton, with whom I have in days long past had many a pleasant revel, for the last time on or off a racecourse. He gave me a lift in his special. It seems but yesterday that I saw his Grace, " the Mate," and C. Blanton (their trainer) chatting cheerily on Stockbridge racecourse. " All, all are gone—the old familiar faces ! " "Angus," as he was always called by his intimates, was one of the kindest-hearted of men, and his loss will be deeply felt round Easton. The cheers which invariably went up when the cerise and French grey caught the judge's eye in the van showed how he was appreciated by sport-loving Britons.

A bloodless victory was mine on Badminton at Hurst Park on January 3, 1894, when the horse ridden by Oates, my single opponent, bolted before the start. The brute actually ran four and a half miles before the jockey regained control over him, and was then totally unfit to do any more racing that day. So Badminton was permitted to walk over.

Perishingly cold, by the way, was that third of January. The ground was so hard, moreover, that very few jockeys would think of riding. Of course I had to wait at the starting-post with Arthur Coventry whilst Star in the East went through this performance. Before long my hands got so numbed that it was difficult to keep hold of the reins. Seeing this, the starter, with real good-nature and self-sacrifice, lent me his gloves. What sort of weather it was may be judged by the fact that on the following morning the thermometer showed something like nine degrees below zero in an exposed place.

We were offered seventeen hundred pounds for Corrèze in Feb. 1894, just before his running second to Nellie Gray in the Prince of Wales' Steeplechase at Sandown. I could not do better in this race than leave Van der Berg behind ; but next month Corrèze ran prominently in the Grand International at Sandown till he pulled up lame after going two miles—a great disappointment.

Early in 1895 the opportunity offered of once more turning for sport to Spain. I formed one of a jovial little party, and had a great time in the land which, though little known to sportsmen, has turned out nevertheless a very paradise to the few who have been fortunate enough to enjoy shooting and fishing over the best preserved ground and water. Some letters which were written to a friend from the Peninsula, and during our voyage home, will perhaps serve to give a fair idea of the variety and novelty of a short sporting trip in—to use the words applied by Byron to a contiguous country—" this delicious land."

"*El Cuco, Jerez de la Frontera,*
"*Jan.* 25, 1895.

" MY DEAR D——

" After a rough passage to Gibraltar, and another to Cadiz *viâ* Tangiers, we have duly arrived at Don Pedro's, who has not only received us with princely hospitality, but has also given us a suite of four rooms overlooking the Bull-ring and the Alcazar of the Duke of San Lorenzo, besides providing us with a great variety of amusements prior to our starting on Monday for the Palaccio de Oñana, the Comte de Medina Sidonia's hunting-seat in the Coto, which marches with the big preserves of the Comtesse de Paris. The Coto has an area of two hundred and fifty square miles, so that each gun requires two horses. Don Pedro's stable is full of nags, and we have been trying which we shall select for our trip. Dinner-parties, dances, a masked ball, lawn-tennis, pigeon-shooting, hunting, etc., made our stay very pleasant ; but best of all, Don Guillermo Garvey, the owner of the finest stud in this part of Spain, if not in the whole country, has placed his horses at my disposal. My riding opportunities are therefore unlimited, and my knees already as raw as mutton-chops. To-morrow I am going to school Lindo—a grandson of the Duke of Hamilton's flying Leonie—whom I shall hope to ride in the big steeplechase at Madrid, over a country adjoining the Jerez race-course. After the ride we intend trying for a lot of snipe, which we flushed out hunting this afternoon. I am also in hopes of getting mounts at Cadiz, Jerez, San Lucar, and Seville. *Wild Spain*, by Chapman and Buck, gives a capital account of the Coto shoot.

" Yours, C. C. DE C."

" *El Cuco, Feb.* 11, 1895.

" Yesterday we did our pigeon-shooting. In the big prize—two Spanish horses—I had bad luck, three of my birds falling dead just out of bounds. However, I won the next sweep in a field of thirteen, and then failed in two others. There were only four birds left, and the light had become so bad that we could barely see the traps. I was in favour of stopping, but O'S—— asked me to shoot for him against their two crack shots. I consented, and shot first. My bird—a white one—went up like a rocket, and I got him with my second barrel against the sky. The others were much less fortunate, getting dark, low-flying birds that went straight away like rabbits ; so not unnaturally they missed. Thus the shekels became ' Colorado's,' as we now call him.

" The name arose this way. The keepers cannot pronounce our names, so adopt their own nomenclature, and as the glare and constant exposure have made O'S.'s jolly old face as red as the rising sun, they have dubbed him ' Colorado.' I am ' El Baron.' We were rather amused the other day. O'S—— had just shot a stag, a fine beast, when one beater asked another to whose gun it had fallen. ' Rubio's,' was the reply. We arrived at the Palaccio after dark, and at dinner a voluntary sweepstake of from one to five dollars was agreed upon for each beast shot with ball—stag, boar, lynx, or fox. I barred paying or receiving over the last-named, but consented to shoot them, as they do undoubtedly destroy many fawns and young pigs. I don't know whether you are going to publish this, but if so, trust it won't be welcomed as a damaging admission on the part of an ardent fox-hunter by enemies of Reynard at home. You recollect that tale Townsend told us the other day in Essex, about the farmer who was ready to swear that owing to a dog-fox getting into the pen, half the young lambs were born with fox heads ! But to return to Spain. A fox did come racing past me, so, hardening my heart, I put a ball from my smooth-bore behind his shoulder, dropping him in his tracks. At that moment, by way of judgment, a noble stag trotted by on my other side. To drop my gun and pick up a Reilly Express took but little time, but instead of a steady broadside, it was a more hurried and diagonal one : result, a miss, profanity, and a spirit of dejection. Luckily I shortly afterwards got a ten-pointer. . . . Nine hinds had passed me, when at length I espied a stag. I was outside gun, and he was just outside the pine-wood over seventy yards off, with very uneven ground between us, so that his head, neck, and top of shoulder were alone visible. I heard my bullet strike home, and saw the hinds going off without him, so concluded it was all right. On going up after the beat, there he lay, the bullet having entered just behind the ear, and fractured the base of the skull."

"*El Cuco, Feb.* 14, 1895.

" We leave here on Monday for Gibraltar, driving by special diligence from St. Fernando to Algiers, and take Orient boat on Tuesday for England, arriving in London probably on Saturday. There was a ball here to-night, and one close by yesterday after some theatricals, through which I slept profoundly ; in fact they do say that I snored so loud that two friends led me from the room to an adjoining one, where I lost gloves to the belle of Jerez.

" There is an old custom much appreciated at Coto, and that is crowning a man who has killed his first stag, either at the Palaccio, or Marismilla. A crown composed of paper and forest flowers is made, and placed on his head by the local beauty. The successful sportsman sits in a chair of state, and the beauty having crowned him, the musicians with their mandolines, playing the Royal March, head a procession comprising Don P——'s army of retainers and all their women folks. Then the fun commences, and sevillanas and songs last till the small hours, the women being provided with wine and cake, and the men with wine and cigars. Both males and females, the latter playing castanets, dance with considerable grace, and much delight the onlookers.

" When ' Colorado's '—' Rubito ' (little fair one) a woman called him yesterday in Seville—turn came, he was splendid, his good-humoured face smiling all over—the sun and unlimited '47 Solera, which we drank like water, had made it mahogany-coloured—with a Henry Clay Sobremesa, as big as a spinnaker-boom, in his mouth, and his crown worn like a forage cap. His head being swollen by mosquito-bites, he looked a perfect picture of King Cole. At the finish the procession departs as it entered, playing the Royal March. On our last day ladies joined us from Jerez, one of whom shared my butt during the two drives she was with us in order to see the sport. Twelve hinds, two fawns, and a stag passed us. I got the stag, though he did not fall to the gun. He was a long shot, and had both bullets through him, but a bit far back and low. He crossed a lagoon, where a dog bayed him. We followed, horse and foot, but before we got up he broke his bay, when we were obliged to race our hacks to our felucca on the Guadalquiver, in order not to miss the train to Bonanza. However, Manuel the keeper tracked this wounded stag for three miles, and finally secured him. During our first drive, an officer of the French Cuirassiers, who accompanied the ladies, not only fired at hinds whenever he had a chance, but also down the line, which was quite contrary to regulation. His first shot whistled just over our heads, whilst the second struck a tree very near us. It was lucky that his other cartridges misfired.

"One day Pepe Larios, a keeper, and I had rather a good gallop after an ape which was to be turned down, but which got away with a chain and collar. Pepe had a hog-spear, and tried, but unsuccessfully, to pin the chain to the ground. We eventually pumped our quarry, who ran under a low pine-bush. I jumped off the faithful Saturno (who has carried me for so many miles, and whom I saw again to-day apparently none the worse for all his hard work), and gripped the chain, whilst Pepe slipped his long Jerez knife under the collar, and set him at liberty."

"S.S. 'Himalaya,' Feb. 20, 1895.

"We left Gib. yesterday, and are having a fine passage, so, bar accidents, may expect to reach Plymouth on Friday morning, and Tilbury about noon on Saturday. On Sunday we had a day at the bustard, and found great quantities, but unhappily they flew too high. Our party, including

one lady, started at 8 a.m. for a point about fifteen
miles from the Cuco, and Don P—— drove a team
with a party of ladies to lunch, which we thoroughly
enjoyed on a hillside in most perfect weather. Riding
to our last drive I came across a dead snake, not
killed, so far as I know, by one of our party. This
was only the second I'd come across, the other being
in the Coto ; José followed its track in the sand, and
halved it with his big knife.

"It was getting dark when W—— killed his first
bustard. Benitez, his shikari, is considered the best
bustard hunter in the Jerez district. He has an
exceptionally fine collection of eggs, and I should
think could supply collectors with rare specimens
at a moderate price.

"Our nags had done a hard day's work in the
deepest of ground, and we were many miles from
home. I and a companion, being merciful to our
beasts, lagged so far behind that one of the party
came back to ascertain whether an accident had
occurred, or we had been tackled by anarchists, who
are pretty numerous just now, owing in some degree,
no doubt, to the fact that the recent heavy rains
have thrown many men out of work. Not long since
four were garroted in the big square. It was with a
certain relief that at 8 p.m., after a very long day, I
led Saturno up to the stables, where he had a well-
earned rest ; to my surprise he had all his shoes on.
When at daybreak next day I went round to bid
the horse farewell, it seemed like parting with an
old friend. Our return was welcomed by frantic
bounds and barks by gallant little Vampiro. The
dog received no less than twenty-one wounds from

a boar, whilst defending his master, Don P——, who was on his back fighting with heels and fists, till at length when all but exhausted he got the brute by the hind legs, and threw him on his side. Luckily Juanillo came up in time to hang on to the boar, whilst Don P— slipped his knife into him, and so ended a desperate encounter. Poor little Vampiro's entrails were out, and his life was despaired of. However, the wounded canine hero was sewn up, and, marvellous to relate, recovered. He is now an honoured pensioner, but is never allowed to go to the Coto, for they are sure he would be as willing to give his life in defence of his beloved master, should occasion arise, in the future as he was in the past. That boar's head is the first trophy of the chase which catches your eye in the entrance-hall of the ' Cuco.'

" Juanillo is the finest specimen of a Spanish forest-keeper I ever came across. He is always ready with his dogs (only two or three mongrels) to tackle any boar on foot. To watch his opportunity, have the boar by the hind legs on his side, and a knife into his ribs, lungs, or heart, is the work of an instant. It is not difficult to guess the penalty of failure with an old tusker. The other day, when the boar was on foot, it was a refreshing sight to see Juanillo slip off his mule and keep abreast of the dogs, watching his opportunity to dash into the jungle the moment the quarry was bayed. When one looked at that simple brave forester, and recollected some of the feeble specimens of manhood that are to be seen crawling about Piccadilly and Regent Street, a feeling of contempt and indignation arose, impossible to suppress.

" The pace was pretty warm in the above-mentioned
run, and no less than three guns were in jeopardy of
being lost. First I jumped over a gallant Colonel's
gun—as he wore an eye-glass he was dubbed by the
keepers ' Looking-glass ' (in Spanish) ; then I saw
' Colorado's ' second horseman with his gun turn end
over end on his horse. After killing the boar, Don
Pablo D—— on looking into his bucket found it
empty ; but that keen sportsman, Delmé Radcliffe,
rode his heel line back for three-quarters of a mile
and recovered the gun.

" On Monday we left by an early train for San
Fernando—both direct boat and train service with
Gibraltar having broken down—and where a special
diligence was awaiting us. With five mixed teams
of horses and mules we covered the fifty-eight miles
to Algeciras in under ten hours, the usual time being
fifteen. The roads here and there were awful—composed of soft deep clay with pine boughs stretched
across ; but the main part of the distance would have
been fairly sound travelling had it not been for occasional large holes, which not only jolted the vehicle
till it nearly capsized, but strained the springs to
their utmost. The country between San Fernando
and Algeciras is decidedly varied. At the start many
parts reminded one of the Coto ; then the lake opposite Mariana and the mountains beyond recalled
memories of Switzerland.

" Both ' Colorado ' and I agreed that never again,
if it could be avoided, would we make a forced march
by diligence, as the cruelty of the driver and his
assistant, who keeps jumping off to flog, and prod
with a pointed stick, the unfortunate team, passes

credulity. It only confirmed my oft-expressed belief that to be killed, even if death was not immediate, in the bull-ring, is kindness itself compared to the sufferings of a hackney horse in Spain. Take, for instance, our last team from Tarifa to Algeciras, the most severe stage of our journey. These were the most ragged lot of the five, consisting of three mules and three horses ; all had been down, and were galled all over. At starting the team could scarcely move, despite the free application of stick and whipcord. Long before reaching our destination the galls on each wretched beast of burden had become open wounds, and woe betide the animal that stumbled ; when the near leader did so, and cut open his already blemished near fetlock, it passed our comprehension how he recovered, and was able to continue the horrible journey. Having knocked the piratical porters down from seventy-five pesetas to sixty-two and a half for transporting ourselves and baggage about three hundred yards to our launch, for which ten would have been ample remuneration, we steamed over to Gibraltar, where Delmé Radcliffe, the worthy scion of a fine old sporting stock, hospitably entertained us at a farewell dinner at the Bristol. This Delmé is a grandson of the author of that noble work on fox-hunting, and, you will recollect, near relatives of his lived in the Tedworth country. The hospitality and kindness we received at Jerez were quite beyond praise. ' See Naples and die ! ' What nonsense ! ' See Jerez and live ! ' is much more to the point."

After my return from Spain I availed myself of such opportunities as arose for steeplechasing in the spring. Several good friends offered me mounts. A rather severe attack of influenza, or something of the kind, got a grip of me in March, but shaking it off without great difficulty I went almost straight from my bed to the saddle without any evil effects, and rode in two steeplechases and a hurdle race at the Sports' Club meeting at Hurst Park. No good there ; but better fortune at Warwick in May, where I won a race on Fred Cotton's Sophism, a real good thing. Curiously enough, Wenty Hope Johnstone and I scored in the first and last races respectively of the Warwick meeting. May 10 was rather an interesting day from a family point of view, as my son and I were pitted against one another in a match at the Plumpton meeting. He had beaten me in a steeplechase not such a long while before, but I had my revenge in this match. Cotton's Burgundy, my mount, started a very hot favourite, and indeed my son had no chance whatever on Mr. Erskine's Sappho, who refused at the first fence, and never finished the course.

I should not forget to mention that in August 1897 I had five magnificent days in the Austrian Tyrol as the guest of Prince Blücher. We were accompanied by Count Schaffgotsche, and succeeded in getting forty-six chamois. In subsequent years I have had some grand shooting with the Prince at Krieblowitz, and taken part in the annual shoots at neighbouring castles.

CHAPTER X

NATURALLY enough, when the Boer War broke out I was anxious to be in it! My eldest son Claude was at the front with the composite regiment of the Household Cavalry, and two of my other sons, Raul and Vierville, were about to follow him, the former with the 3rd Battalion of the 2nd Grenadier Guards, to which he had just been gazetted, and the latter with the Imperial Yeomanry under Colonel Paget.

I suggested the idea of going out to Lady de Crespigny, and not only did she immediately fall in with it but proposed to accompany me herself, and do a little nursing.

A few days before we sailed I received the following telegram from Claude's regiment:

" Hearty Congratulations upon Mr. de Crespigny's courageous action.
                    "ARMSTRONG, *Corporal-Major.*"

At the time I was quite in the dark as to what the telegram referred to, but I soon found out when I got my morning paper. Perhaps it would not be out of place to give the account of the incident in the words of the correspondent of the *Mail*, who wired from Rensberg as follows :

" During the advance of Colonel Porter's brigade on Friday, January 19, a detachment of the Household Cavalry which formed the advance guard under Captain Ferguson, was ordered to reconnoitre the kopjes to the north-west of Kleinfontein. The party, which was commanded by Lieutenant de Crespigny, had almost reached the top of the kopjes, when it was met by a heavy fire from the Boers. Trooper Kemp's horse bolted. Trooper Jaager was wounded, and his horse ran off. Lieutenant de Crespigny, whose horse was twice hit, took that of Shoeing-Smith Coulson, and rode back to save Jaager. The latter was too exhausted to mount, and the lieutenant bade him hold on to the stirrup leather. Meanwhile they were subjected to a heavy fire, and the horse was twice wounded. Lieutenant de Crespigny then dismounted and took the other stirrup, both men thus continuing their retreat. Another trooper then came up and took Jaager behind him on his horse, the lieutenant waiting until Coulson came up with his wounded charger. Lieutenant de Crespigny's action is spoken of as one of the most distinguished bravery."

For this he was recommended for the V.C., a recommendation which was lost in transit between the Brigadier and Divisional Commander, and was subsequently refused by the Army Council, which did not come into existence until four years afterwards. Is there any precedent, I wonder, for the rejection of a recommendation from the Commander-in-Chief, supported by the Divisional Commander ?

17

I was naturally glad to find that the boy had had a chance of distinguishing himself, and had not failed to make use of it. No doubt he found that the experience gained in steeplechases and in the hunting-field came in useful, and probably there were plenty of others who found the same thing. Indeed, as was once remarked by Sir Hussey Vivian, who commanded the Hussar Brigade at Waterloo, the value of sport in this connection cannot be over-estimated ; and men who have been good sportsmen at home are the men who will do best and show the greatest amount of resource when on active service.

The horse he was riding at the time was " Carlist," an old steeplechaser, which had given us seven falls in six steeplechases ! My boy had a very bad fall when riding it at Newmarket, and was " knocked out " for a long time. I remember Prince Christian saying to me, " If I were you, Sir Claude, I would either shoot or sell that horse ! " Well, in this case he got a little of the shooting that the Prince suggested.

We sailed for South Africa on February 3. On our arrival at Cape Town the first thing I did was to witness a boxing match ! It was the middle-weight championship of South Africa, and they very politely made me a member of the club and asked me to act as referee. I declined the invitation to officiate in that capacity, as one of the pugilists was a 60th Rifleman, but I thoroughly enjoyed the sport, which was capital. I have seldom seen a closer contest.

To return to the war. I made all speed to get to the front. Of the actual fighting I didn't see as much as I should like to have done, I'm sorry to say. I got to Kimberley soon after the relief, and found the garrison in a surprisingly cheerful condition, considering all they had been through. Lady de Crespigny, by the way, was the first lady to enter Kimberley and Bloemfontein. At Kimberley I stayed at the Sanatorium, where Cecil Rhodes had also stopped, which had been fitted up as a redoubt. On March 7 my eldest son was severely wounded in the engagement at Poplar Grove. The occurrence was reported in the following dispatch from Lord Roberts :—

"POPLAR GROVE, March 7 (7.35 p.m.).

" We have had a very successful day and completely routed the enemy, who are in full retreat.

" The position they occupied was extremely strong, and cunningly arranged, with a second line of entrenchments, which would have caused us heavy loss had a direct attack been made.

" The turning movement was necessarily wide, owing to the nature of the ground, and the Cavalry and Horse Artillery horses are much done up.

" The fighting was practically confined to the Cavalry Division, which, as usual, did exceedingly well, and French reports that the Horse Artillery Batteries did a great deal of execution amongst the enemy.

" Our casualties number about fifty.

" I regret to say that Lieutenant Keswick, 12th Lancers, was killed, and Lieutenant Bailey, of the same regiment, severely wounded. Lieutenant de Crespigny, 2nd Life Guards, also severely wounded.

" The remaining casualties will be telegraphed to-morrow.

" Generals de Wet and Delarey were in command of the Boer forces."

Lord Roberts ordered a special ambulance to take my son and one other man who was also severely wounded (and subsequently died) to Bloemfontein, the remainder of the column being moved to Kimberley.

Lady de Crespigny and myself shortly afterwards arrived at Bloemfontein, and found our son in hospital, badly hit but quite cheerful.

I might mention that Lady de Crespigny and myself were granted a special pass into Bloemfontein to see our boy. His condition for some days was extremely critical. Lord Roberts was kindness itself, and paid the patient several visits. He supplied him with eggs when none were to be got for love or money; and Prince Francis of Teck also showed his kindness in the same way.

A good deal has been said about the explosive bullets used by the Boers, and there is no doubt that they were used, and pretty extensively too. But I fancy the explanation lies partly in the fact that many of the Boers who had been commandeered for service brought with them the same cartridges which they had been in the habit of using when hunting—these being of an expansive character. As to their having fired upon the white flag, I must confess to having seen shells falling among the ambulance wagons at the Modder River. It is the sort of thing one doesn't easily forget.

I brought home with me a good many trophies of the campaign of one kind and another. One of these was a cartridge wrapper which I picked up in the Boer trenches, which bore the following inscription :

" 1° cart S.A. Ball for the Martini-Henry Rifle,

or machine gun, Ely Bros., Ltd., London," showing that in some cases the enemy were actually potting our men with our own cartridges.

I saw an incident at Bloemfontein which showed the sort of stuff the Naval Brigade were made of. Early one morning in the great square, I met the big naval guns, each dragged by thirty-two oxen. They were led by mounted naval officers, with a variety of royal yard and spinnaker boom seats, and escorted by blue jackets with the usual breezy roll which passes muster for marching when they are ashore. I hardly had time to walk half a mile up a hill to visit a wounded Grenadier, when these veritable "handy" men had run the heavy ordnance up a high kopje, and were sitting at ease ready to defend the town like the grand watch-dogs they are ; and it must be remembered that the enemy were pretty close at the time.

But every branch of the forces was doing good work, in spite of the stay-at-home critics, for some of whom one can have nothing but contempt. I wonder what these same critics would have felt if they had actually been at Magersfontein, where there was such a terrible loss among the Highlanders—as the Boers caught them in quarter column before they had time to open out into loose formation. They would probably have died of sheer "funk" where they stood.

A little "live" experience would have done these critics good. They might have discovered that the open veldt opposite Boer earthworks is no great catch when it is as dark as a wolf's throat, with a fusillade of rain striking you from the clouds and another of Mauser bullets from the trenches.

All this talk by the stay-at-home critics about "feather-bed" soldiers was just so much silly nonsense. I had lunch with the Duke of Teck about eight miles from Bloemfontein, and he was living on the commonest rations. As a great surprise there was a hot cake to finish up with. It was a curious sort of cake, made by the Duke's soldier servant. The Duke had himself been taught how to make it by an old Boer woman who took a great fancy to him at T'bancho, and had passed the information on to his servant, apparently with rather indifferent results. All we had to drink was cocoa; there was no wine or spirits. Another time I came across the 10th Hussars, after they had been out all day, and with them was old "Bobby" Fisher, whom I have often ridden against. He said I must have something with them, but, when he came to look, all he had was half a loaf of almost uneatable bread. There was an officer attached to that party, the late Lord Kensington, who would think nothing of giving 500 guineas for a polo pony! His breakfast consisted in smoking a filthy pipe full of Boer tobacco! I met, too, an officer whose father owns one of the finest feudal castles in Scotland; and all that he had to eat was the inside of a black potato. But they were not complaining. Amongst the non-commissioned officers and men a similar spirit prevailed. I gave one man a piece of chocolate, and he was as grateful as if I had given him an order for the Savoy.

In spite of all that has been said about Buller's inaction before Ladysmith, I can testify from a letter received by my eldest son in hospital, from one of Buller's aide-de-camps, that he was fighting on

SIR EVELYN WOOD, V.C., G.C.B.

[p. 262

thirty-one days out of forty. Mention of Ladysmith reminds me that Sir Harry Smith (whose wife gave her name to Ladysmith) when Governor of Cape Colony gave me his sword-belt. I was quite a lad at the time, but after the war I hunted it up, and sent it to Sir George White, as a small token of my admiration for his gallant defence, when he kept the Union Jack flying so long and in the midst of so many perils and privations at Ladysmith.

As to the Volunteers, I remember a speech made by Sir Evelyn Wood at Maldon, to the 2nd Vol. Batt., Essex Regiment, in which he referred to a letter he had received from Major-General (as he was then) Smith-Dorrien, writing from Komati Poort, in which the latter said : " I have now been associated for a year with the Volunteers. Taking the mounted and dismounted men, I cannot want to have a better, more willing, more daring, more go-ahead lot of men, and I shall be glad if I can get the same sort of men that I have had with me heretofore."

Sir Evelyn, by the way, had one or two rather amusing things to say about his first acquaintance with Smith-Dorrien. He described how, eighteen years before, he was outside Alexandria, and their lines were being menaced by a division of Arabi Pasha's army. Smith-Dorrien was then a lieutenant, and he sent him into the Khedive's stables, about eight or nine miles behind them, to get horses. The lieutenant returned with twenty-two horses, three mules, and a donkey. He put some of the soldiers on these—most of them had never been astride an animal before—on saddles which he had got from somewhere, and away he marched with them at night, most of them not riding, but holding on to the animals, as there was plenty of accommodation between the saddle and the neck. They went out to the front, engaged the enemy, of whom they shot three, and from that day the latter ceased from troubling!

Two or three years afterwards, when he was trying to raise the Egyptian army, he came across Smith-Dorrien again. The latter had been practically turned out of his regiment through rheumatism of the knee, and when Sir Evelyn agreed to take him on, the doctor remarked that he had done wrong, and taken on a " dead head." " Well," said Sir Evelyn, " I'm willing to back my own judgment. I'd rather have him with one knee than most men with two."

Among the officers with whom I came in personal contact were General French and Lord Dundonald, both of whom did much brilliant work. Lord Dundonald went out to South Africa on his own hook, and the authorities would not do anything for him at first, but they soon had to recognise his sterling qualities. All sorts of reports were circulated about Lord Methuen; but I saw him, and he was as well as possible. With regard to Magersfontein, it is said that the order given to the Highlanders was intended for the Foot Guards. It was dark at the time, and they were afraid to " flash " the orders.

I also met General Gatacre, General Brabazon, Colonel Quale-Jones, and Colonel Babington, each of whom had been stationed at Colchester. I saw Sir William Gatacre at Cape Town, prior to his departure for England; but nothing passed between us in reference to the General's recall. He was too good a sportsman to complain, and I did not mention the matter, but I felt very sorry for him.

One day I had a long ride with General Stephenson, formerly in command of the Essex Regiment. It was rumoured that the Boers were trying to take a water tank ; and as we were riding along we met someone whom it was thought was Lord Stanley, the Press Censor, now Lord Derby. I rode up to him to see if he had any later information he could give us, when I discovered it was Dr. (now Sir Arthur) Conan Doyle, and a very fine fellow I found him.

An incident that I witnessed after my return to England impressed me very much at the time, as showing the sort of spirit that imbued the men who took part in this war. I was on my way to see my son Raul off at Southampton.

With us in the carriage were Lord Alan (now Earl) Percy, and the late Mr. Meeking, who lost a brother in the 10th Hussars. As we crawled past Pirbright in a South-Western "express" we found that the Grenadiers had voluntarily turned out on the canal, which is near enough to the line for Raul to recognize several of the men, and they cheered their officers as only British soldiers and sailors can cheer. When men have such a feeling of affection and respect for their officers one realizes how strongly *esprit de corps* still exists, especially in our crack regiments, and how it was that the Grenadiers remained with an unbroken front in South Africa, when other regiments on either side were " disorganised," on an officer saying, " Remember, men, you're Grenadiers ! "

There can be no doubt in my mind that faulty scouting accounted for many of our disasters in the early part of the war. Scouts are to an army what frigates were to the fleet in Nelson's day ; and every-one remembers that gallant sailor's remark when, in the bitterness and despair of his fruitless search for the French fleet, he declared that at his death, " Want of frigates " would be found stamped on his heart.

I did a good deal of scouting work myself, by the way. I went with Porter's Cavalry, and though I really was a " visitor " I scouted as a private when I was required. I saw the Boers on several occasions, but we did not get very close to them. My eldest son was in about two dozen actions—he was under fire every day almost—and he told me that he hardly ever saw a Boer. They are undoubtedly clever at that sort of fighting ; but they wouldn't meet our fellows in the open.

A letter received after my return to England from a Maldon man, who was serving under Colonel de Lisle, shows the sort of tactics that De Wet and his men pursued. " I notice by the papers," he says, " that some of the people have a very good opinion of De Wet. If they knew as much about him as we do, they might think differently. We have often met De Wet's convoys and captured them, but not the leader, for the simple reason that as soon as our men were sighted he has bunked off, leaving his men to get on as best they can. Of course, while we are engaging them he has time to pick up a few stragglers, who are in abundance. He once more repeats the so-called smart ' tactics,' this time on another column, loses his men, and once more bunks, which is very easy to do in Africa, even if he had twice the number of columns on his track, because his friends, are in every part that he directs his attention to. We are also handicapped, as the enemy have so much in their favour. They seldom wear uniform ; they know every kopje ; they also practise what the British soldier is not allowed to do."

While with Porter's Cavalry I assisted in rescuing a large number of our wounded after Broadwood's disaster at Koorn Spruit. We were only just in time to save them, and we had to bury numbers of dead. I was under fire on this occasion, and a Boer shell passed quite close enough to my head to be pleasant.

There were several amusing yarns current about the Boer women. One of them became so affectionate towards the officer who escorted her to Cape Town, that her husband was positively delighted when he and his wife were safely shipped for St. Helena !

The men who did the scouting work (to return to our " muttons," as they say), were good men and true enough, but the majority of them were town-bred, and new to the game, and no match for the Boers, who are past-masters in this department. There were plenty of men who had served in former years who, to their everlasting shame, did not offer their services in the war—men who by accident of birth, education, and inclination, should have proved the best scouts we had—men who have devoted much of their spare time to the ordinary sports of English country gentlemen, and who have probably, in addition, shot big game either when serving abroad or travelling.

There were some in my own county of Essex, who have made the profession of arms their study, but who had retired from the service and were under sixty years of age. Joubert and Cronje were sixty-five! And I remember the case of a fine old New Zealander, whom I knew, who, at the age of sixty-five, when refused in his native island on account of age, though in humble circumstances, paid his passage to the Cape, and enlisted in the Duke of Edinburgh's volunteers. The last I saw of him was being carried in a stretcher over the side of the *Canada, en route* for Netley Hospital.

Surely some of these gentlemen could have formed the nucleus of a corps of scouts from among their tenants and retainers—men who might have saved us from such a disaster as Sanna's Post—men who would have been prepared to sacrifice their lives to save their comrades. And the men of Essex, who fought under Stephenson and others, proved themselves second to none. Knowledge of drill would have proved absolutely unnecessary, but a want of that knowledge doubtless made men, who would have been admirable scouts, diffident about joining either the Yeomanry or the Volunteers.

These feather-bed soldiers doubtless consider themselves aristocrats, but as such they should be wiped out, as were the effeminate French aristocrats during the latter days of the Bourbons. If we are to have aristocracy, let it be the genuine article, sprung from the loins of such men as Winchester and Airlie.

Of aristocrats of the right sort I am glad to say there are still plenty and to spare, as this war fully testified. There comes to my mind, amongst others, the name of Lord Rosmead, the son of a distinguished father, who had made a great name for himself in South Africa. The moment England was in a tight place, the son volunteered to go to the front, and endeavoured to add some further lustre to his family escutcheon with his sword. I had the pleasure of meeting him several times out in South Africa. On one occasion, on the Orange River, I found him making use of very strong language at being forced to lead a life of what he considered to be inactivity ; but a few days later I met him again at Bloemfontein, where he had done the most sensible thing a man could do to see active service—he had got on the Staff of General Hutton, of the 60th Rifles. While General Buller and other 60th Riflemen were " giving the Boers what for " on the Durban side, General Hutton was " giving them hell " on the other. The march from Bloemfontein to Pretoria was no kid-glove picnic. Lord Rosmead lost no less than eight horses on the march and during the fighting, which was a pretty good indication of the hot work he had been through.

This is the sort of thing that helps to make and keep England what she is. Personally, I think that every able-bodied Briton should qualify to defend his country ; and I do not consider a male to be a man till he has done so. We might take a lesson in this matter from savage nations. It is a dream of mine that one day we may see the institution in England of " Schools of Instruction for Home Defence," in which each individual could select the branch most interesting to him, including marine mining. Of course to remain a first-class nation we must retain the command of the sea. But this being secured, I think, if some scheme of the kind I have suggested were carried out, that, should occasion arise, England might be depleted of its active army, and the country's defence might safely be left in the hands of the citizen soldiers.

I cannot quit this subject without referring to a speech made by the then Lord-Lieutenant of Essex, in the course of which he remarked that he was not sure that our Army officers had taken their duties quite as professionally as he would have liked to have seen them. I took the matter up in public very strongly at the time, and my very natural indignation at the aspersions cast on the British officer as a class must be my apology for referring to the matter again here.

I saw plenty of instances in South Africa of the serious way in which British officers performed their duties, and of the hardships which they had to undergo. On one occasion, at Karee Siding, Broadwood's Brigade were engaged from seven in the morning until seven in the evening of the following day, —thirty-six hours !—without so much as the bite of a biscuit.

There is a story that some foreign military attachés were being conducted round Woolwich Arsenal, and saw some men who were working with pick and spade, and dressed in common canvas suits. One of the attachés remarked to the officer conducting the party, " Convicts, I presume ? " The officer replied, " Oh dear, no ! they are British Artillery officers." That explanation caused the Attaché to observe that he could now quite understand why the British Artillery was the best in the world.

But after all, the British officer needs no words of mine to vindicate his honour—his own deeds

KOZAK.

are the most fitting criterion by which to judge him.

The war cost me a very dear friend in Major Henry Shelley Dalbiac, who was killed in the fighting outside Senekal, while with Sir Leslie Rundle's force. Dalbiac had been in the Royal Artillery, and served as a Captain in the Egyptian war. He was badly hit at Tel-el-Kebir, and when the doctor told him he had only a quarter of an hour to live, the gallant " Treasure " offered to bet him a fiver he was a liar ! He retired from the army in 1887, but when the Boer War broke out he went out as Captain in the Imperial Yeomanry.

Poor Dalbiac ! He was the best of friends, and a true sportsman. Old Kozak belonged to him, and he used to ride him with the West Surrey Staghounds. When Dalbiac went to the front he left Kozak behind, declaring that he was far too good a horse to get shot ; and after his death in South Africa I purchased the horse for old acquaintance' sake, and many is the race I have ridden and won on him since.

One of the first events after my return to England was the revival of the Champion Lodge Steeplechases, after a lapse of about ten years. The event was interesting to me in two ways, one being the fact that it was the thirty-fourth anniversary of my first winning mount, and the other that I got home a winner in the first event—the Champion Lodge Cup —on the back of poor old Dalbiac's Kozak.

I won two other races on Kozak early in the same year, 1901—the Maiden Hurdle Race at Colchester, and the Nimrod Cup at the Hawthorn Hill meeting.

At the East Essex Hunt Point to Point Races in March, by the way, my son Raul had what might have been a nasty spill. His horse rolled over just after clearing the second jump, and his rider lay mixed up, as it seemed, with the animal's hoofs; but beyond a slight injury to his shoulder he was quite unhurt.

In the autumn of the year I held what I called my annual South African Picnic, a shooting party which consisted entirely of men who had been out in South Africa, including on this occasion Lord Rosmead, General Sir Evelyn Wood, and General French.

One of the best runs I ever remember having occurred with the East Essex Hounds in December, though unfortunately it came to an untimely ending. We were only a few minutes in South Wood, when a grand up-wind dog fox flew, and ran through Captain's Wood, Maypole, and the north end of Eastlands, by Wickham Bishops, to Chancery, Strutheath, Westhall, over Braxted Park wall—a feat very few foxes who have been travelling with a killing scent, in heavy ground, for over half an hour, are capable of performing—then across the park over the farther wall, followed by a single hound, into Tiptree Springs, before entering which, by the keeper's request, when the hounds had fairly earned blood, they were stopped, much to the disappointment of every good sportsman, at the best Saturday run of the season being so spoilt. Think of this, in the middle of December! Supposing a few pheasants were moved by hounds from a covert which was going to be shot the following week, they could easily have been tapped back, and everyone knows that pheasants fly all the better after hounds have drawn a run through the coverts. However, there it was, and we had to swallow our disappointment as best we might.

It was about this time that I had an adventure which was a bit of a novelty, and didn't come under the head of any of the things I had tackled before in the course of my varied experiences. This was a stand-up fight with a monkey, and it happened in this way. My youngest son used to keep a couple of monkeys in a cage at Champion Lodge, which stood to one another in the relationship of mother and son. On the occasion in question the young monkey had escaped from its cage, and no one could re-capture him, try as they might. At last my services were called into requisition, and a fine dance he led me ! However I got him eventually, and took him back to the cage. Thereupon the mother monkey, imagining, no doubt, that we had been ill-treating her precious offspring in some way, flew out of the cage, leapt on to my shoulder, and promptly went for me tooth and nail. The way she pummelled me would have done credit to Pedlar Palmer, the bantam lightweight, in his best days. She planted her feet under my chin, got hold of my head, tore my scalp, fairly lifting it up, altogether giving me an awful mauling. I have stood up to a good many men in my time, professional and amateur, but I had never tackled a monkey before, and 1 don't know that I ever want to again. The result was a liberal application of arnica and bandages, and it was several days before I could even wear a cap.

Kozak laid another victory to his credit in April 1903, when he carried my son Raul home a winner in

the Grenadier Guards' Challenge Cup at the House-
hold Brigade Steeplechases. Another horse of Raul's,
Woodlander, ridden by the Hon. G. Douglas-
Pennant, came in third in the same race.

I remember that in the month previous to this,
I rode Old Calabar in the Grand Military at Sandown,
but he refused at the first ditch, and I pulled him up.
I then took him back a short cut across the park,
but in jumping the rails of the course he smashed up
the whole obstruction, and brought me down in a
heap.

Races succeeded one another with great regularity
during the seasons of 1903 and 1904, but I can recall
no very noteworthy incident that is worth recording,
and a mere repetition of my racing engagements
would become tedious. It is enough to say that I
was still feeling as " fit as a fiddle," and going as
strong as ever.

In 1904 my son Vierville and I enjoyed some
pigsticking and shooting in Morocco, after a fearful
fall he had had with the Pytchley the previous year.

There is rather a good story up against me in
connection with the Essex Summer Assizes. I was
foreman of the Grand Jury, and Mr. Justice Kennedy
was the Judge. We had been hard at it all the
morning, and as I was particularly anxious to catch
the three o'clock train from Chelmsford I left it to
two of the other gentlemen, Mr. Thomas Kemble and
Mr. D. J. Morgan, to take the last of the true bills
and the usual presentment into court. The docu-
ments were handed to the Clerk of Arraigns, who at
once noticed that they had not been signed by me as
foreman. The Judge said it would be necessary for

the foreman to sign them before the Grand Jury
could be discharged. "But, my Lord," exclaimed
Mr. Kemble, amidst the laughter of the Court, "our
foreman's bolted!" "What's to be done?" said
Mr. Morgan, *sotto voce*, to Mr. Kemble. "I'm sure
I don't know," said the latter. "Well, I do," said
Mr. Morgan, suddenly: "I'm going to catch Sir
Claude, or we shall be kept here all night."

Suiting the action to the word, off he went, rushed
downstairs, commandeered the first policeman he
came across, and told him to "run like the devil to
the station, find Sir Claude de Crespigny, and bring
him back to the court!" Off rushed the policeman;
but Morgan, thinking, I suppose, that he might not
prove a good "stayer," bolted after him, and found
him meandering up the street. Using his sonorous
voice to the full, and gesticulating wildly, he again
urged the policeman to catch me, with the result
that the latter broke into a trot, and was lost to view.
When, a few minutes later, Morgan reached the
station, the train was just about to start. "Jump
on, sir!" cried the porters. "Not much!" replied
Morgan; "I want Sir Claude de Crespigny." And in
the distance he espied me, safe in the arms of the
policeman, who was resisting, as politely as possible,
my somewhat vigorous attempts to board the train.
There was nothing for it, so I had to go back; and
loud was the laughter that greeted me when I re-
appeared in the Shire Hall.

CHAPTER XI

IN the early part of 1905 I went out to East Africa
for a little big-game shooting, and had the luck
to arrive just in time to join the Sotik punitive
expedition, so that I was able to combine a certain
amount of fighting with some excellent sport. For
an account of this trip I don't think I can do better
than to refer to my diary, and relate my experiences
just as I jotted them down at the time, while the
incidents were fresh in my memory. The first entry
is, I see, dated May 14, 1905.

"S.S. 'Sybil,' VICTORIA NYANZA.

" Last Monday a patrol of an officer (Capt. Barrett)
with fifty men of the Uganda Rifles, with a Maxim,
were sent to defend the settlers who have been
threatened by the Sotiks, forty miles north of Njoro
Station. A large force, under Major Pope Hennessy,
consisting of from three companies to a wing of
Soudanese, will follow early in June.

" The forest through which the troops will march is
very thick, the grass high, and too damp to burn, so it
will favour the enemy ; who, doubtless, will endeavour
to ambuscade us, and will in all probability,—as they
have never yet met disciplined troops—fight well

with their poisoned arrows and spears, for at least some time, against our Metfords, minus the magazine and Maxim.

" If the advance guard does not get porcupined it will be very lucky.

" So far as can be judged there will be a far bigger job on a little later nearer this lake, with the Nandi tribe, but as I propose leaving the country after the Nairobi races in July, I shall hardly be able to take part in it.

" We are making a steeplechase course, so as to be able to have some cross-country events in conjunction with the flat races.

" This morning I visited the Ripon Falls, one of the most beautiful spots on earth. The falls are —in addition to being the principal source of the White Nile—the dam of this lake.

" The fall is about 25 feet, I should think, and a vast volume of water rushes down it. Some plucky fish, like our tench, scaling about 4 lbs., were trying to jump it. None, however, as far as I could see, got more than half way up, and then they fell back.

" This lake (Victoria Nyanza) would make a perfect paradise for an artist who was fond of sport. As its altitude is over 3,500 feet above sea level, the heat is not excessive ; neither would his expenses be excessive. Return passage £100, shooting licences £50, hire of dhow (say) 50 rupees a month.

" He would have an everlasting variety of sport and scenery—bold rocky headlands, hills of volcanic construction, mountains which remind one of the Austrian Tyrol, occasional native huts surrounded with patches of cultivated ground, and finely-timbered forests, with jungle which is in many parts impenetrable to man. For example, at Ukerewe there was a huge animal. It might have been anything smaller than an elephant. There were eleven of them close by. It jumped up within five yards of me, but so thick was the undergrowth that I could not make out what it was—probably a boar. Luckily, it broke away from me, for had it charged it would have been a bad look-out for my Swahili gunbearer and myself, as my chance of knocking it over would have been rather remote.

> " *S.S.* ' *Sybil,*' Bukoba,
> *May* 17, 1905.

" Yesterday we arrived at Bukoba (German Territory), and were hospitably received by the officers at their rather primitive mess room.

" At Entebbe, having been most cordially welcomed and entertained by the Commissioner, Colonel Sadler, and Judge Ennis, I visited ' The Sleeping Sickness Hospital '—the only one in the world of any importance. There is a small one at Kisuma. This disease, which has only been known for three years, has been alluded to in the European press, but it has attracted very little notice, though out here it is pretty freely discussed, as no one, either white man or native, has ever recovered from it. Whole districts have fairly been wiped out with it. For instance, near Jinga (Ripon Falls), 30,000 died, and many of the islands in this lake are now uninhabited.

" The disease is conveyed by the tsetse fly, in appearance like a horse-fly,—the same insect that worries the bullocks to death in South Africa. It is computed that no more than two per cent. convey the fatal germ. It is at present doubtful if it actually springs from them, or whether they convey it from fish. The hospital staff consists of two officers of the Indian Medical Corps and two professors.

" I saw about a dozen patients, mostly prisoners in chains, as but few natives care to come into hospital. Knowing that they must die they prefer, to use their own expression, ' to die in the grass '—i.e. they return to their homes, where they are more or less looked after by their own people ; but as the nourishment they receive is less than they would receive in the hospital, it lessens the number of their days, which never exceed two years.

" In the earlier stages the patients seem very fat and jolly, but there were two very nearly gone—one almost, and the other quite insensible. The doctor said they could not possibly last more than three or four days. A German was down with the disease, but I did not see him. Only about four Europeans have died from it up to now. We had on board a first-class passenger, an Italian, bound for his native land, whom the German military doctor at Bukoba has pronounced infected. I shall endeavour to ascertain his future.* There is nothing to indicate to the ordinary eye that anything is wrong at present, but the glands of the neck are, I believe, the infallible tell-tale.

* Apparently he was wrongly diagnosed, for after remaining some months in his home at Florence he returned to East Africa.—C.CH. DE C.

" At the hospital they have about forty monkeys inoculated. About half die inside two months, the remainder being considerably emaciated before recovery. I wonder if your home doctors know anything about it ?

" Bukoba, which is gradually developing, is of a certain historical interest, as the officers' quarters were built by Emin Pasha, and there are the remains of a camping ground once occupied by him and Stanley.

" Glass being a scarce commodity, the windows of the messroom, and commander's quarters are filled in with old photograph plates.

" On the 18th we arrived at Muanga, the German station at the south end of the lake. It is in a magnificent rocky position, and almost completely landlocked, which is decidedly a consideration when it blows hard.

" Both crocodiles and hippopotami swarm. They are far more plentiful than foxes in Essex.

" Yesterday, when washing clothes, a native was killed close to where we are now anchored. The German Commandant was promptly on the spot with his rifle, so the remains of victim and crocodile, minus his head, received simultaneous burial.

" A singular incident happened on board the boat a few months ago. A $14\frac{1}{2}$-foot python crawled up our gangway when at Pt. Florence, close on midnight, and was shot by the chief officer. The body sank, but was fished up with a boat-hook, and the python's skin is now in the possession of the captain's wife."

I see I made a slight error in my last entry. The

Soudanese patrol was sent south of Njoro, not north. The fact is, I find it much more difficult to ascertain the points of the compass when bang under the equator—I have crossed it three times during the last few days—than in our northern latitude, though at night one can see both the Great Bear and the Southern Cross.

"May 20, 1905.

" Yesterday a Hampshire sportsman and I endeavoured to revenge the death of the native, and, I think, may fairly claim to have done so. First disturbing a small colony of monkeys from an india-rubber tree, which had been freely tapped by natives for the valuable sap, we took up our position in the shade above some rocks on which the crocodiles would be likely to sun themselves. Unfortunately for us, whatever we killed fell into the water, especially a large lizard, whose body I was particularly anxious to recover, as its hide makes excellent handbags, etc. ; but, alas, he doubtless made a *recherché* supper for a voracious crocodile.

" We shall probably finish our ' round-the-lake ' cruise on Wednesday, the 24th, and on the following day I shall hope to return to the happy hunting grounds of the plains round Nairobi.

" S.S. ' Sybil ' Bukoba, June 2, 1905.

" The Sotik punitive expedition, under Major Pope Henessey, K.O. Rifles, was previously inspected and addressed by Sir Donald Stewart, K.C.M.G., who was accompanied by his A.D.C., and rode with them for the first four miles, witnessing how the men took up their positions when the ' Alert ' was sounded. His

Excellency found the force drawn up in the most imposing formation—600 Masai warriors in a single line near Njoro Station, in the shape of a balloon with neck and valve open, the post of honour being held by forty lion-killers, with their lion-skin head dresses, shaped like Life Guards' helmets. To the south-west, in quarter column, were six officers and 235 K.O. Rifles. The advance was also witnessed by Lord and Lady Delamere (the latter riding with us for some miles), Lord Cole, Mr. Jackson, the Sub-Commissioner, and Mrs. Jackson. The first day's march was an easy one of eight miles, so as not to distress the porters, and our route through the forest was facilitated by trees which had been blazed last December. It was pretty rough walking through virgin forest, composed principally of cedar and juniper trees, with exceptionally thick undergrowth.

"Having arrived at our camping-ground, we at once proceeded to form a double zareba of about seventy-five yards square with barbed wire outside, and the troops and levies were warned of their night duties.

"I was rather amused when some young warriors were ordered to reduce the interval between them-selves and the group on their left. 'Not likely,' they replied, as the men on that flank were old warriors, who would steal their rations during the night.

"A Masai warrior is not supposed to drink during the day, when on the war-path, though I saw some of them with their heads in a stream and then wiping their lips; so they make up for their self-denial by filling the skins of the bullocks killed that day and mixing with the water the bark of cedar crushed with a knobkerry. Let's hope it tastes better than it looks.

" Our camping-grounds are somewhat similar—an open grass plot with a few scattered clumps, near a stream, inside a frame of splendid forest timber, our zareba being out of arrow-range from the belt.

" We naturally hoped to be attacked by daylight, so that after the rifles and maxims have done their work our levies may annihilate them with the spear.

" In the course of a day or two we hope to be joined by two attachments, which will make up our strength to 400 rifles and 900 spears. The estimated strength of the enemy is between 3,000 and 6,000, one-third with bows and arrows, and two-thirds with spears.

" It is improbable that we shall be attacked by daylight, failing which we are in hopes that it may be on the night of Monday, June 5 ; and I hope that our outer zareba may be, as it is to-day, composed of bamboo, near which we are encamped (and through which we marched, it being fully forty feet high), and barbed wire, as this will give both bayonets and spears, who are mixed alternately, an excellent chance ; but I do not suppose our levies will be allowed to pursue in the dark.

" The tents of the C.O. and myself are placed in the front face, between the two zarebas, immediately behind a maxim.

" We are packed fairly close inside our seventy-five-yards square, for in addition to the rifles and levies we have 200 porters and 200 cattle.

" The Masais laager inside their spears and shields, in groups of about a dozen, and keep their fires going, rain or no rain, all night long—which must be comforting as there is frost every night, we being at an altitude of 9,000 feet—but till the fires get red-hot the smoke is rather trying to European eyes.

" Our casualties up to now are one porter deserted, and two soldiers wounded by a cartridge exploded in a camp fire.

"*June* 4.

" We arrived to-day at what we call ' Fort Barrett,' the zareba having been built by a captain of that name in the K.O.R. It is situated above the farm of a settler named Nielson, who is acting as our scout in the Sotik country, and on a huge rolling plateau adjoining the Sotik forest.

" From what we can gain from our prisoners we may commence exchanging shots in about two days.

"*Kericho, Kisumu Province, June* 26, 1905.

" The duties of the above force are nearly at an end, and it will probably concentrate at Molo, on the Uganda Railway, about July 3 or 4, with the remainder of the cattle, sheep, and goats.

" I had to leave to fulfil an engagement to a big game shoot on the Athi River and plain, and shall arrive at Nairobi on the 28th.

" Major Pope Hennessy, K.A.R., may be congratulated on having done all that might have been expected of a capable leader and experienced bush-fighter, and he was ably seconded by those immediately under him—officers from nearly a dozen British regiments, now attached to the 3rd Battalion K.A.R.

FORT HALL.

" The results are, so far, roughly as follows, but the total will probably be augmented during the next few days : Cattle, 1,500; goats and sheep, 4,000; Sotiks killed, 50. The last item we had hoped to make 500, but its accomplishment was somewhat difficult, as our progress was not unlike that of the Turks and Greeks, viz. :—' One army marching while the other ran away.'

" The captives will at any rate pay the expenses of the expedition, and reimburse our friendly Masais for their loss in killed, captives, and cattle when raided by the Sotiks. It will also be a lesson to the latter, but whether a sufficiently severe one or not will rest with H.M. Commissioner.

" There can be but little doubt that the Lumbwa and Boret tribes, to whom the Sotiks are related, though ostensibly friendly to us, connived at the cattle of the latter being driven into their countries.

" It is more than likely that ere long a stronger force, say two battalions, divided into four columns, may have to give all three a nasty knock before settlers will invest in land in these parts; also that the Nandi tribe will throw in their lot with their coloured brethren.

" In parts our advance was extremely difficult, even for officers who had no weights to carry except their revolvers. They were wearing nailed shooting-boots, and had both hands free to hang on to bamboos when climbing up or sliding down narrow paths at an angle of 45 degrees. You can understand what the strain must have been on the porters with their naked feet and 60-lb. loads.

" At times we advanced perhaps half a mile in the

hour when cutting our way through the virgin forest ; at other times, in the open on an old game track, we put in three miles an hour. Then, again, we might march for hours over prairie composed of long grass, dotted at irregular intervals with small clumps of timber and bush.

" The distances of our marches varied as much as did the nature of the ground.

" As an example, I will take the last two days between the Sotik Post and this station. Having encamped close to a waterfall thirteen miles from the former—there are twenty-six rivers and streams between the two—we marched from 2.45 a.m. till past 11 a.m. (I don't think these primitive hours would suit some of our lardy-dardy swells who have been slap-dashing at Ascot during the past week.) After about six miles, my section, consisting of 31 rifles and 9 porters, headed for this station, while the main body swung to the right towards the Mau Escarpment. On arriving here a scout says that I did them a good turn, for a body of the enemy with cattle, who intended circling round Kericho into Boret country, immediately on seeing me, turned sharp to the right towards Mau, and, I hope, into the Major's arms.

" Before reaching my camping-ground on the Merri-Merri river, I met a Soudanese officer with some rifles, Masai levies, a prisoner, and some captured goats, three of which I annexed for my men's dinner, a luxury which they appreciated, as they had nothing but a little flour and rice in their haversacks.

" Starting at daylight, which is some considerable

time before sunrise, I got here in a little over four hours.

" As a proof that the show is not exactly grouse-pie and '92 Moet, I had to do it on a tiny piece of dry bread and a few spoonfuls of cold coffee out of a jagged sardine tin, so my waistbelt was fairly loose when I met the collector, Mr. Ainsworth, at the river which flows below the encampment. Although I had a pony, I think it always best to march with one's men.

" Nairobi, July 21, 1905.

" Having rested two days at Kericho, which is a small up-country station with a strong boma and two watch-towers, which would make it pretty secure from any ordinary attack, on July 27 I did the sixteen miles to Fort Ternan on the Uganda Railway in four and a half hours, which, considering that one escarpment was the stiffest going in the whole month's march, was not bad travelling on foot, and, I hope, justified the report of the corporal—whom I had sent on ahead two mornings previously to announce to the sub-collector the strength of the party he was to expect. On being asked the name of the officer in command, he replied, ' I don't know his name ; he may be an official from Nairobi or Mombasa ; he is a bit old, but he can go.'

" For the whole month, all day and every day, I wore a light pair of shooting-boots, by Dowie and Marshall, of the Strand, cut like ammunition boots, to facilitate pulling on and off in wet weather, and we crossed some forty streams ; they had Scafe's patent soles and about thirty medium-sized nails, and at the finish signs of wear and tear were almost imperceptible.

"I have in my possession three photographs—a good one of Masai levies, and a moderate one of some K.A.R.'s crossing a stream. The five former are lion-killers, and wear lion-skin head-dress, which I fancy must be pretty hot, as on one occasion I saw a warrior in charge of a prisoner making the latter wear it. One might have imagined it just as likely that Lord Roberts would tell off an orderly to carry his Field-Marshal's baton. I have also a photograph of Sir Donald Stewart's horse 'Whale,' on which I hope to win the steeplechase on the 29th inst.

"I am pleased to hear that I succeeded, two days before reaching Kericho, in driving a considerable number of cattle towards Major Pope Hennessy, who captured them, which made the total of cows, bulls, and bullocks up to 2,400, and Sotiks killed nearly, if not quite, 100, including one biggish chief. This death occurred on the second day after we got in touch with them, though we did not know it at the time. I think he must have been killed by one of the patrols, as I was lying between the two maxims, and did not see him fall in the bush.

"Our casualties were very few, though death from poisoned arrows was most painful. As an illustration the last Masai killed was shot from about ten paces through the shoulder into the lung. The doctor was close by, and in the extraction of the arrow the barb dragged a portion of lung out of the wounded man's back, and, though strychnine was at once injected, the man died shrieking with agony in under six minutes. And it takes a lot to make a Masai give tongue, as he is a gallant savage.

" We all carried a bootlace as a ligature, in case we were hit on a limb, but of course it was useless for a body-hit, and the poison was nice and fresh, as each Sotik carried a species of small glue-pot, into which he dips the arrow-head before firing.

" On July 27 and 29 the East Africa Turf Club held their annual races, which proved a complete success. I was fortunate enough to win three races off the reel, including the first steeplechase ever run in British East Africa, on a horse called ' The Whale,' the property of Sir Donald Stewart ; and the ovation the gallant little bay received as he romped in showed how that officer was appreciated by those under his command. In this race the Hon. B. Cole, an old 9th Lancer, took rather a nasty toss. His mount, in order to avoid a horse which had fallen in front of him, galloped through a wing, driving a stake into his jaw, from which two bits of bone had to be removed.

" Lady de Crespigny arrived from Mombasa in time to attend the Commissioner's luncheon on the course before the first race of the second day, and to see family history repeated—viz. father and son sporting silk in the same race.

" In the evening the Turf Club held a ball, which was a most brilliant success.

" On the following Monday the King's African Rifles gave a gymkhana, at which one event was the Sotik Cup for the three Somali ponies which went through the expedition. It was almost reduced to a match, as early in the march the Major nearly lost

19

his pony, which fell into a deep cutting with a heavy rush of water that nearly drowned it. The Ascaris buzzed round it like blue-bottle flies, but, though brave men, they are ignorant of handling horses. Rescue came in the form of a Gordon Highlander, a stalwart Ross-shire man, great at tug-of-war at the Strathpeffer meeting, limbs like Donald Dinnie, the great caber-tosser and shot-putter in the 'sixties and 'seventies. With a mighty heave, out came poor little ' Hatrack,' as he was called, like a cork.

" My mount swerving badly two or three times in the straight run in, I got beaten by a nose. However, a match was promptly arranged on the spot, which I won by a length."

The next entry in my diary is dated August 5, and runs as follows :—

" August 5, 1905.

" A wire has just been received from Voi, 220 miles from here, saying that two man-eating lions have created a panic in that neighbourhood, so my son and I are just off to see if we cannot add their jackets to our collection.

" The Sotik affair is practically ancient history. The Masai levies have received their share of the cattle, and the remainder are to be sold in Naivasha towards the end of the month. The war indemnity takes the form of the enemy making a road from the Sotik post to Molo Station. The success of the expedition seems to have established a panic among the Nandi chiefs, and what at one time looked rather like a heavy job is likely now to fizzle out.

" Our trip to Voi was a failure, the lions not being

RHINO SHOT BY SIR CLAUDE CHAMPION DE CRESPIGNY NEAR MELANA RIVER.

properly located, and all the surrounding country was thick bush. Even in the comparatively thin portions of the bush, the knives of the savages had, at times, to be called into requisition. There was a considerable amount of various spoors, but as we saw but little game, it obviously harboured in the daytime in bush, which is impenetrable to an un-armoured pedestrian. My son got a long double snap-shot at two half-grown cubs, and killed a spitting snake. This reptile makes remarkably accurate shots up to five or six yards, going for the eyes. Those hit are blinded for a week—olive oil being about the best antidote. We saw a lioness half a mile from Simba (Swahili for lion) Station, just emerging from a bed of rushes for her evening prowl. At Voi I remained up all night on a chair. About half an hour before daylight a lion roared a quarter of a mile off, my son making almost as much row at my elbow snoring ; and a leopard took a crow, which I had shot on the previous afternoon, out of the compound. There was no moon.

" We saw several rhinoceroses from the train. A few stations from here we were warned that one was viewed close to the railway on the south side, which is preserved, so we arranged for the train to be stopped for us and our gun-bearers, should he have crossed to the north and still be in sight. Unhappily he was grazing opposite mile 319, on the wrong side, and we had no horses. If we had had, we could have got him easily, as one of us could have hidden in the long grass on the north side while the other tickled him up with a Derringer or Mauser pistol, when he would have charged for a certainty.

" This afternoon there is a cricket match on the Gymkhana ground, and a meeting of the Tent Club at the race stand, when those who prefer the pigskin to leather-hunting will forgather. The meet may be a fairly big one, but most will only be onlookers, and only four or five of us carry spears.

" An Ascari in the Sotik expedition had a unique experience. He was a boy in Hicks Pasha's army when it was annihilated, became a Dervish, and fought against us at Omdurman, was recaptured by us, and is now a loyal soldier in the 3rd King's African Rifles."

The following account of the Tent Club Meeting appeared in the *Times of East Africa* :—

" The inaugural meet of the above was at the Grand Stand on the racecourse, adjoining which to the E.N.E. is what is locally known as the Pig-Ground.

" There were present at the meet Lady Champion de Crespigny, Mrs. Stordy, and Mr. and Mrs. Russell Bowker on wheels and mounted, Sir Claude and Captain V. Champion de Crespigny, A.D.C., Messrs. Percival and Griess, with spears, and Mr. and Miss Allen, Mrs. Sanderson, Messrs. Kenyon Slaney, Allen Watson, Buckland (an old Master of the Bombay hounds and veteran pig-sticker) and Goldfinch, without spears. We were not far clear of the racecourse, when several pigs were on foot, unfortunately one grand tusker slipping away across the open near Lady de Crespigny's carriage, unviewed, or from the line he took, he would have led us over the best of galloping ground in the neighbourhood with short grass, so we had to content ourselves with less noble quarry, each selecting his own pig. Our bursts were short, but though we succeeded in turning several pigs, the long grass towards the papyrus fairly beat us.

" ' After a short dart after a cheetah, who was again favoured by the tussocks and high grass, we formed line for a fresh draw—a big boar plunging through the barbed wire and gaining on us by crossing a watercourse, got unsighted after leading us about a mile ; but a fresh pig almost immediately springing up we raced after it, the A.D.C. on the ' Whale,' who was none the worse for his gallant victory on Saturday, getting first spear within yard of an earth.

" ' After scratching away for a quarter of an hour a hind leg was espied, when the A.D.C. promptly took a header into the bowels of the earth, his boots just protruding—these were immediately seized by the Game Ranger, and after a desperate tug for dear life out came ten feet of trooper and wartling. The brindle hound Jack and two other dogs settling some little difference, hurricane fighting over the soldier's body, as he was being extracted, as if they hadn't got the whole of the Athi plains adjoining for an arena.

" ' So ended a pleasant afternoon's ride ; but in a week's time when more grass has been burnt, we may anticipate some ripping gallops.'

" On August 17, the Commissioner's party of five left for a ' Safari ' which had been anticipated for some little time, with no little pleasure, though for Sir Donald himself a considerable amount of duty was blended with it—inspecting stations, their accounts, police, etc., settling boundaries, receiving chiefs with their followers, and numerous and various presents, the latter of which included enough live stock to set up a menagerie.

"The principal chiefs were Karuni, Murad and Kabala Bala, the latter being as fine a specimen of fighting Masai as I have ever clapped eyes upon, a leader who would instil the most implicit confidence in his followers had he the chance of leading a forlorn hope or a second Balaclava charge. To this day they talk of his indomitable courage when, after being left for dead with his skull smashed in, eye kicked out, lower part of ear cut off, he crawled—travelling by night for many nights subsisting on sugar-cane—back to his native kraal.

"A party of friends awaited us at the drive leading up to the 'Homestead,' and waved us 'bon voyage.' Our next check was at the admirably arranged farm of Messieurs Felix and Faure, which showed every indication of a *most* prosperous future, on to our first camp at Kiambu. In the evening we tried for duck, but only got a ducking, as rain came down in torrents.

"Our 'Safari' lasted five weeks, and took us over a great variety of ground. It would be useless to go through it in detail, as much of the country has not been mapped, and the camping-grounds which were logged were mainly local names.

"The *crème de la crème* of the shooting was expected on the trans-Tana plains, and such proved to be the case; but you must not judge of what we did kill by what we might have killed. Our grandchildren have to be thought of, so our licences limit us, among other things, to two rhinos, one bull buffalo, and one bull eland. There are heavy penalties for making

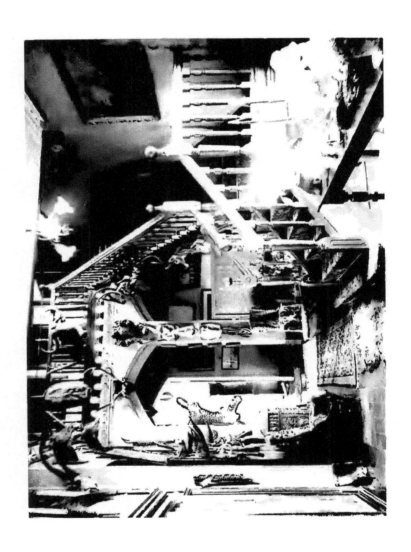

mistakes, some of which are extremely difficult to
avoid, with forfeiture of trophies. In long grass, etc.,
it is at times almost impossible to distinguish the
sexes, especially in the case of single beasts. Should
you come across a herd of elands, there is not much
difficulty in picking out the bulls, as they are so much
bluer in colour.

" The best of Italian sportsmen, the Marquis of
Pizzardi, who joined us for a day or two, had recently
made a mistake in killing a barren cow buffalo, which
he at once reported in the most honourable sportsman-
like manner. He had, of course, to pay his fine, and
there was a good deal of friendly badinage over it, but
he was greatly pleased when the Commissioner said
he might keep the head. If an old Shikari, like him,
makes a *genuine* mistake, how much more liable would
a man of lesser experience ! I have rarely come across
a better sportsman. He left the Italian Cavalry to
kill the man who had killed his brother, and I shall
hope to see him in London, as he has accepted an
invitation for a night at the National Sporting Club.
This, apparently, he thinks may prove somewhat
insipid, as he is particularly anxious to witness an
old-fashioned knuckle-fight.

" Our Askaris have wonderful sight, and love their
masters to fire at something, and as they do not
have to pay the fines, are not very particular at what,
especially as they invariably get as much as they
want of the flesh, of which they can consume huge
quantities. In fact there is a tradition that one described a kongoni, which weighs at least 150 lbs., as an
unsatisfactory sort of a beast, being ' rather too much
for one man to eat, but not enough for two.'

" On one occasion we saw a head poking out of some long grass, which my gun-bearer solemnly affirmed was a bull buffalo, so I took up a position on a slight incline, sending three or four men—we generally had some porters handy to carry in the game—to beat up to me. Soon I could see the high grass waving as some big beast advanced towards me, and then out came, within easy shot, a cow-rhino and calf. Of course, as she did not charge me, I did not fire.

" Close to this spot I shot a bush buck. It lay on the ground apparently dying. When my Askaris went up to cut its throat, it sprang up, and with difficulty staggered into some high grass close by, the three of us plunging in after it, when out rushed three rhinos, one of my Askaris throwing himself into a hollow in the ground to avoid having daylight drilled through him.

" My son and I were each charged twice, and I think that two of the rhinos were as close as they well could be without serious, if not fatal, damage.

" On the first occasion the A.D.C. was riding across an almost dry water bed to join Mr. Slaney and myself, as a lion had just been viewed ahead, when a savage grunt in the long grass just enabled his horse to swerve in time to avoid the charge, the horn missing the rider's leg by two or three feet.

" The rhino having ascended a hill towards some plains, I galloped after it on the hurdle-racer Mary, hoping to make rings round it till the others came up with their rifles, but unfortunately he turned sharp round to the left into some impenetrable jungle, and was lost to us.

" That afternoon we had some remarkably good

guinea-fowl shooting at Elder's Camp, where we met Mr. Swift, a settler, looking none the worse for a really nasty fall which he got in the Nairobi Steeplechase. As I passed him at the fourth fence from home he was lying flat on his face knocked out, and one foot hung up in the stirrup.

"The next time we were charged we were close together, on the line of a wounded buffalo, when a cow and calf, which we had previously passed, moved from the scent of some porters and came top speed bang into our party of ten. Of course we only had soft-nosed bullets in our rifles, which have as a rule about as much effect on a rhino as a peashooter. To within three paces she was coming straight at me, and I was just about to drop my rifle and play the amateur matador, when she swerved slightly to her left, which gave me the chance of a neck shot, of which naturally I was prompt to avail myself, and at two paces from the muzzle of my ·303 she fell stone-dead with her neck broken, the A.D.C. being about the same distance on the other side. Of course her poor little calf blindly charged in her wake, and a fool of an Askari shot it, though Colonel Harrison shouted to him not to fire. This was a thousand pities, as it would have been worth many hundreds of pounds if it could have been reared by hand, which could have probably been done, as Chief Murad had a large herd of cows a few miles off.

"The next occasion was not such a close affair, a rhino having spoilt my shoulder-shot by swinging its head towards me as I pressed the trigger, so my bullet only caused annoyance, and it charged. However, another shot at thirty yards, followed by a solid from my jungle gun at fifteen, and the gallant beast bit the dust.

" If you are wrong for the wind, a rhino's sense of smell is marvellous. On one occasion the A.D.C. and I, when riding alone after eland, saw a rhino lying in the grass on the farther side of a valley. When we were fully a quarter of a mile off it suddenly got our wind, sprang up, and made off. They are almost blind, their eyes being of hardly any service to them beyond a very few yards range.

" The last rhino which I shot must have winded our mixed bag of porters at least half a mile off, which, if you only knew them, would not surprise you ; they are highly pungent.

" Then again, if you are down wind it is surprising how close you can get to them. On one occasion we suddenly came on a cow and a calf, when the A.D.C. crept close up to them with his camera, I standing over him with a rifle in case they charged, and he got quite a good snapshot, before they winded us and bolted in the opposite direction.

" Some time back I mentioned the vitality of a bush buck. All the gazelles possess it to an extraordinary extent. As an example, one day the A.D.C. knocked over a fine impalla, with, so far as one can judge, a beautifully placed bullet just over the shoulder-blade, but it was hardly on the ground before it was up and off. In answer to his shout, ' Try and cut it off,' I, being the better mounted, did my best for fully four miles over rough ground, the blood pouring down both shoulder-blades. As the impalla in no way slackened its pace and I had lost my party, and was riding directly from our camp, I reluctantly reined up. No doubt when the wounded beast once lay down it would get stiff and become food for hyenas, etc. Riding my own heelway, and using a powerful whistle, I eventually met my party. It is no joke getting lost in the jungle without food or water; but it is worse still if you take a toss and lose your horse, which is just as likely to join the first herd of zebra it comes across—and there are plenty of them—for it is improbable that a search party would be sent out till the following morning. A horse did this at Naivasha about five weeks before Nairobi races, and it was a month before he was caught, and uncommonly lean he was, too, about the ribs. Nevertheless, much to our astonishment, judiciously ridden by his owner Mr. Seymour, late 3rd Hussars, he won his race.

" Naturally, there is very little twilight under the equator, so if you mistake your distance from camp it is easy to find yourself let in for a long, rough ride over ground nearly, though not quite, so bad as where we were pig-sticking last year in Morocco. The acumen of the horses in picking their way, hardly ever putting a foot wrong, proves them to be a long way in front, in intelligence, of many so-called Christians.

" Of one rough ride I have a vivid recollection, though it was a daylight one, but the A.D.C. had to do it some hours afterwards in the dark. After a long stalk, he had got a magnificent buffalo with a clean shot through the throat.

" He remained with it while I rode off to the camp, many miles off, for porters, piloted by a Kikuyu guide. After going for about a mile I came across a herd of eland, headed by a real ' monarch of the glen,' which

I fortunately got in one shot. Our lucky star must have been in the ascendant that day, as we got a rhino, a buffalo, and an eland all with single shots, and all with soft-nosed ·303's. I think that eland will prove to be a Tana record, though Mr. Jackson killed one of better measurement near Mount Kilimanjaro, which is to German East Africa what Kenya is to British. We had some splendid views of the latter when in the Nyeri district.

" Kenya was climbed a few years ago, with the greatest difficulty, by some members of the Alpine Club.

" Continuing my ride, I eventually reached camp, having left an Askari with the dead eland, but as it was then long past lunch-time I knew that those who were left out with the game, and those who were despatched to bring it in, could not possibly be back till long after sundown; so as soon as it was dark, I kept a big fire going, and at intervals coloured rockets were sent up. We could just hear the A.D.C. answer them with shots from his revolver. However, all duly arrived after a hard day's work.

" A wart-hog is another gallant beast, which will, at times, carry away an enormous amount of lead, and go for you if wounded. As an example, one afternoon we were on our way to try for hippopotami, three jumped up in long grass and started to race past us, I being at the time eighty yards behind the A.D.C., cut the throat of one who rolled over without a motion, a fluky shot; the A.D.C. wounded a sow, who at once charged the gun-bearer standing to his right; a second shot made an awful mess of her shoulder, but did not stop her; but a third,

A FINE ELAND.

p. 300]

through her head, killed her stone-dead at the gun-bearer's feet.

" We had two charming dogs out with us, known as ' Jack ' and ' Toto,' belonging to Mr. Hyde Baker, a nephew of Sir Samuel of that ilk, the great traveller and game shot. Mr. Baker being on leave in England, they were left in charge of the A.D.C. ' Jack ' has been a great fighter in his day, and has many honourable scars. He has been mauled both by lion and leopard, and a tope once drove its horn in by the back ribs, travelling along the body, and coming out behind the shoulders. Notwithstanding these vicissitudes, such is his strength, that if once he can pin a wart-hog in an earth, and a man can grip his hind legs, out come both dog and pig.

" His various encounters have made him a little less reckless than in his salad days, for I noticed on one occasion, when I had rolled over rather a fine Neumann hartebeeste, two hundred yards from the column, out dashed the dogs, for the word ' discipline ' was not in their vocabulary. The old campaigner allowed his younger and less experienced companion to seize, with the courage of ignorance, the wounded antelope by the throat, while he worried at the other end.

" The amount of game of various species, which we could kill, was practically unlimited, the water-buck being distinctly the grandest ; but, unless we wanted a particular trophy, we waited till we got fairly close to our new camping-ground, as the porters had first to carry their 60-lb. load from camp to camp, and then go back to carry in the venison, of which they invariably received a liberal portion.

"We had no luck with the lions; in fact, not a shot was fired at one. In addition to the one seen by Mr. Slaney, we saw a lioness and cub at the end of our march half a mile from mile-post 400 on the Uganda Railway, but before the mounted men could get up to her she had disappeared in the bush.

"Our big-game bag consisted of 8 rhino, 1 hippo, 3 buffalo, and 4 eland. I was allowed a third rhino, as the one which gratuitously charged us had poor horns, and was only shot in self-defence, and I was lucky to get the hippo, my first bullet catching it above the nostrils, and the second under the eye, which turned it feet upwards at once. If you only mortally wound them, and they sink, they take, sometimes, many hours to rise, and you lose them if on the march. This happened at Meranga, where Sir Donald got his only rhino. My son and I pumped no end of lead into the head of an obviously dying hippo. The next morning the natives reported that there was not one dead; but as we had marched they had probably eaten it, as they fight like wolves over the flesh, or maybe they were afraid to cross to a shallow hidden in an island, for on my return a week later the number of vultures perched on adjoining trees indicated that a carcase was close by.

"Some of our dishes might astonish whomso-ever may be the successor of the great Soyer, of Crimean fame—such as rhino and hippo-tail soup, ostrich-egg omelette, eland and kongoni marrow-bone, etc.

"There can be no mistake about British East Africa being a grand country with a great future, and, if the present game regulations are strictly enforced, for many years to come a sportsman's happy hunting-ground.

" Personally I may consider myself extremely fortunate, for, as a Government officer remarked to me, ' During your five months' stay you have done far more in the way of sport than I have in five years.'

" The pleasure I had derived from the excellent sport obtained during my trip in East Africa was sadly marred by the news of Sir Donald Stewart's death, which we received by cable on the voyage home.

" His death was not only a grievous loss to those who could count him among their personal friends, but a serious blow to British rule in East Africa. It was once said of him, and with perfect truth, that what he did not know of protecting and governing the peoples of Africa was scarcely worth troubling about. He had only been fourteen months in the Protectorate at the time of his death, but he had in that short time acquired a thorough grasp of the requirements of this part of His Majesty's dominions. He was quick to realise that if that country was to become a white man's country, some drastic changes must be introduced. With that conviction fixed in his mind, he lost no time in appointing Commissions to enquire into the working of the Land Laws, the Labour Question, and that of Education.

" His policy with regard to the natives was one in accordance with the belief that a firm and just policy is not only in the interest of good government, but also in the end the more humane and for the benefit of the natives themselves. The expedition against the Sotik was a case in point. He took a keen interest also in the welfare of the settlers, and the development of the agricultural resources of the Protectorate.

" His experience of the African continent was unique in its way, and full of excitement and variety. On the Gold Coast his strong personality and pluck brought him safely through many dangers. On one occasion he and his escort were surrounded by a threatening horde of savages. Luckily, Sir Donald kept his head, and refrained from giving the order to his followers to fire. Had he done so the chances are that he and his escort would have been annihilated to a man. But he didn't, and that particular native rising was put down by a liberal use of Sir Donald's stick.

" He was a chivalrous friend, and the kindest and most courteous of hosts. He was always most thoughtful and considerate for the feelings of others. An incident that occurred before I left Africa will illustrate this. On September 22 I accompanied him on his last ride, when he visited Mr. Percival's to inspect some of his trophies. On his way home he mentioned feeling a bit feverish, and did not turn up to dinner that night. The following night there was to be a dinner-party, a little farewell to my wife and self, with the King's African Rifles band. This he insisted should take place, though he was too ill to attend it, adding that the sound of the band would cheer him up. But for once in a way his orders were disobeyed."

The entry which I see I made in my diary concerning the Nandis, turned out to be absolutely correct, and the expedition started soon after I had left for home. Major Pope Hennessy, who was in command of one of the columns, afterwards purchased Sir Donald Stewart's gallant little horse "The Whale," on which, as will be remembered, I won the Nairobi Steeplechase.

The Nandi rising looked serious at the outset. News of Sir Donald Stewart's death reached the Wa Nandi with all the wonderful speed of native communication, and was made the occasion of a great baraza, at which, according to the account brought by a native, the head Hybon promised his excited people success, and taking a live goat, first cut off the tail, saying, " Such is the injury the English have wrought on us," and then hacked off the head, crying, " So have I done to them—I have slain their great lord."

My fourth son, Vierville, who was with this expedition, had a somewhat exciting adventure with a lioness, while after big game. As he came up to the lioness, his horse, frightened by a sudden roar from the latter, bolted, and the saddle slipping round, my son fell, one of his feet sticking in the stirrup ; and he was dragged a considerable distance. However, his foot came out in the nick of time, just as the lioness sprang at him, and he was able to roll her over about fifteen yards off.

I retain very pleasant recollections of East Africa as a " happy hunting-ground," and would ask nothing better than to take another trip there after big game one of these days. But even the best of things must come to an end, and so, after several glorious months, I duly returned to England and civilisation once more.

20

CHAPTER XII

RACING BY LAND AND AIR

JUST after I got back from East Africa my son
Raul brought off a double victory at the Aldershot meeting in November, 1905, winning the Open
Military Steeplechase with Bay Duchess, ridden by his
elder brother (and a very fine race he rode, too!) and
the Three-year-old Hurdle Race with Warner. The
last was an unexpected victory, as Lady Dunmow
was a prime favourite. A little later, at Warwick,
I rode his horse Prince Talleyrand in the Debdale
Maiden National Hunt Flat Race, finishing second to
Mr. O. H. Jones's Armature.

There was a good deal of discussion about this
time concerning the growing scarcity of "soldier
jockeys." There is no doubt, as I said at the time,
that this is largely due to the fact that in these days
the gentleman rider does not work half hard enough
in riding in his early morning gallops. As the late
Jack Jones once put it, "These soldier officers eat
a big dinner, go to the theatre, with supper to follow,
send their servants with their kit-bags to Sandown, and
then think they can get up and ride races." Personally, as I have remarked before, I have always been a
glutton for hard exercise, as the only prescription for

keeping really fit; and to this I attribute my success
in being able to ride for such a great length of time
without getting knocked up.   The regular use every
morning of clubs and dumb-bells—the latter varying
between two and fifty-six pounds—works wonders in
this respect, and a cold tub before breakfast may be
held indispensable to a man who wants to keep
himself in first-class condition.   But, in addition to
this, I am constantly taking more severe exercise in a
variety of forms.   Cutting furze with a bill-hook,
in the little gorse just outside my house, is capital
exercise ; so is thinning out the branches of various
trees on the place that need attention.   Quite lately
a friend tells me he was staggered at the reply made
to the query, " Is Sir Claude in ? "   " He's up a tree,
sir."   I was hacking away at an old willow, about
the most awkward wood there is to cut, owing to its
sponginess.

Pedestrianism is another means by which I manage
to keep myself " fit " all the year round.   On most
days I do a little mild running, something in the way
of a " jog trot."   Many sportsmen regard walking
with genuine horror ; but for myself, I have always
been very fond of it, whether on a solitary tramp or
with a companion.   A short while ago I took a walk
from my home in Essex up to the Grand Hotel,
London, a distance of forty-five miles, winning thereby a wager of no less than half-a-crown ; whilst
between breakfast and luncheon I trudged over to a
friend's one morning, a distance of twenty-six miles or
so.   Even more recently it was suggested to me that
I should back myself, without any special training,
to walk fifty miles in a day along an ordinary high

road. The reply was that I would certainly do so any day for a moderate stake. The task ought not to be a difficult one, especially in decent weather. Years ago I used to do a great deal of walking in London, rarely—unless greatly pressed for time or encumbered with luggage—resorting to a conveyance. In about a year I walked the best part of two thousand miles of London pavement.

But apart from the question of keeping fit, it seems to me that there is less nowadays of that healthy spirit of rivalry which formerly animated the best "gentleman riders," such as "Bay" Middleton, Wenty Hope-Johnstone, and Captain L. H. Jones.

Says the *Daily Telegraph* of December 5, 1905, in commenting on this subject :

" A wealth of interesting matter could be written around the riding careers of famous amateurs of the past, amongst the most sincerely regretted of whom was Captain Middleton, a man of a type seldom met with nowadays. He was universally liked, was passionately fond of the sport, and rode with a determination and skill born of genuine enthusiasm. If he had a fault as a rider it was that he invariably spurred his mount in the shoulder, being apparently unable to sit his horse without turning his toes out. His name will always be associated with that of Lord of the Harem, upon whom he won races innumerable. The horse was, however, more than once steered to victory by Captain Hope-Johnstone, whose triumphs on Champion are still fresh in the memory. In one season he won no fewer than ten races on the old grey, who became quite an idol with the public, not only on account of his gameness, but also because of the striking figure he cut when galloping in a field of horses. His colour, together with his long, flowing tail, gave rise to the curious impression that he was flying over the fences like a swallow, if such a simile can be formulated. Captain Hope-Johnstone, for a tall man, was a very graceful horseman, and few have had an experience which was so long and varied. He more than once steered five winners in the day ; though Mr. Arthur Yates, now so rotund of person, at Kingsbury, many years ago rode in seven events and won them all. The two gentlemen named once had a close contest for premiership amongst successful jockeys, and two better or more representative specimens of the bonâ fide amateur could not be found. One of the most brilliant jockeys of his time was Captain ' Roddy ' Owen, and it will be readily conceded that a man required to have developed more than than average ability to be able to hold his own with the brothers Beasley, Mr. Arthur Coventry, Mr. G. Lambton, Captain L. H. Jones, and Captain W. B. Morris. In later years it is questionable if he had a superior, either amateur or professional ; and, furthermore, he was an excellent judge of the game, as was evidenced by his choosing to ride Father O'Flynn in the Grand National in the face of several eligible mounts which were offered to him. Mr. Arthur Coventry, the present starter, built up a great reputation, and was equally at home on the flat or over a country, one of his most notable victories being that gained on Bellringer, in the Grand National Hunt Steeplechase at Derby, when Mr. E. P. Wilson was second on Golden Cross and Captain Middleton third on Minotaur. Other well-known amateurs who rode in that race may be mentioned in Mr. W. R. Owen and Mr. C. J. Cunningham.

" A very fine horseman, and one who was prominent for a lengthy period of years, was Captain ' Doggy ' Smith, who rode Game Chicken to victory in the Grand National Hunt Steeplechase in 1864, and was riding in the Grand National at Liverpool so late as 1882. To be precise he piloted Zoedone into third place, behind Seaman and Cyrus, the horse winning the ' blue riband ' twelve months later, in the hands of its owner, Count Kinsky. It was said that Captain Smith would ride anything, and not only was he an admirable steeplechase jockey, but no one went straighter to hounds, and he was on all kinds of strange animals. Captain Bewicke, who appeared in the saddle to within quite recently, stood out by himself, whilst the late lamented Captain Reginald Ward represented the very best kind of amateur rider. He was always inspired by an enthusiastic devotion to steeplechasing for its own sake, as was shown by his plucky purchase of Cathal, and his gallant attempts to win the Grand National on him. The disappearance of such men creates a void which it is not easy to fill, and one can only regret that the glories of steeplechasing are not so pronounced as was the case when those enumerated above were notable figures in the land of sport. Even the universities used to produce riders of ability, and Mr. Harry Custance, most esteemed of old-time jockeys, tells of four undergraduates who regularly came over from Cambridge to take part in the meeting at Peter· borough. These included Mr. J. M. Richardson, who twice won the Grand National on Disturbance and

Reugny respectively. He turned out to be one of the best gentleman jockeys known to history, though few could have prophesied such a lustrous career for him when he rode at the little hunt meeting at Peterborough. The other three undergrads were Mr. Cecil, or 'Parson' Legard, Lord Melgund, now the Earl of Minto, Viceroy of India, who rode as ' Mr. Rolly,' and Lord Aberdour. They travelled from Cambridge in the morning, and were only too glad to get a mount of any kind. There is, I fear, too much of the solid business element about sport between the flags to hope for a revival of the spirit which actuated such men as these ; and without taking a too pessimistic view of the situation, it does not appear as though in the immediate future we shall see many of that stamp of old-fashioned amateur or military riders which was so conspicuous twenty, or even fifteen, years ago."

At the Aldershot meeting in May 1906 occurred the sad fatality to Captain Meyricke. His horse twisted himself at a jump, and colliding with the hind quarters of Lieutenant Sherrard's horse, the two came down together, Captain Meyricke apparently falling on his head. It was the first time in thirty-five years that any serious accident had occurred at this meeting. In this race my eldest son rode the winner.

Kozak gained another victory at Chelmsford in this year, carrying his owner in the Hunters' Steeplechase. He repeated his success a little later in the Datchet Handicap Steeplechase at Windsor ; and also won the Household Brigade Hunters'Challenge Cup.

The following year was a quiet one as far as racing was concerned ; and in 1908 I added one more to my ballooning experiences, being a passenger in Mr. Griffith Brewer's "Lotus," which won the International Race from Hurlingham.

The account of the race may be best told in Mr. Brewer's own words :—

" At last, after a busy day, all the balloons were inflated, and the little auxiliary balloon was attached to the side of ' Lotus,' and, in our turn, we were brought up to the starting mat, and carried to windward in readiness to take our place after the departure of Count de La Vaulx. On weighing up, the Lotus was found to lift quite readily with five bags of ballast, each weighing about 35lbs.

" The winning-post had been chosen at Burchett's Green, three miles beyond Maidenhead ; and as by now the wind had considerably reduced in strength, the question of whether five bags of ballast would be sufficient to carry us a distance of about thirty miles, added another factor to the many governing the race.

" At 3.50 p.m. we let go, and followed the other twenty-one balloons in front of us, on a course west of south-west, crossing the Thames over Putney Bridge, which was black with people ; and then continuing over Barnes Common and Sheen Common, we passed Richmond, and crossed the Thames again over Messum's boathouse. Here we took our first reading, and made an accurate line upon the map, which showed that our course was too much to the south, and it would be necessary to rise into the current noticed earlier in the day, at a height of about

3,000 feet. At the same time it would not do to pass through that current if it proved to be very thin, and so we only threw a little ballast and rose slowly. As we progressed we found that our course first became due west, and west by north-west, and so it became a question of whether we could remain in the current or whether we should be obliged to sink below or rise above it. It was now that the ballast required the closest watching. Every tendency to dip down had to be checked, with sufficient ballast to prevent a descent, but not sufficient to make a quick rise; and in this way we went on, gradually working up to our maximum height of 5,900 feet, at which altitude the course became due west again, showing that we had completely penetrated the intermediate current. Colnbrook was passed at 5.30, and then Slough came in sight in the distance, and it was not till now that we realized we were immediately above Ditton Park, the lovely seat of the donor of the cup which all aeronautical Europe was struggling for. We scooped a little sand down to Lord Montagu for luck, and the Thames, which had appeared to bend towards us from Windsor, slightly turned aside again towards Boveney.

" The race now became exciting, because our line of direction was so good that we hoped to see Burchett's Green, and if we could only work a little more north we should then be able to utilize the lower current, and possibly fall near the actually selected spot. We found, however, that we had made as much northerly progress as was possible; and shortly after crossing the Thames at Maidenhead, we could distinguish the white cross in a field opposite Burchett's Green, still considerably to the north.

" All the balloons we had seen on this journey were away to the south, and nobody seemed to be in sight at all. We did not suspect that the Valkyrie was already on the ground, and only one and a quarter miles south of the winning cross. We therefore came down with moderate speed by opening the valve, knowing that the longer we took to descend, the more out of our course we should be carried by the lower current. The question of whether we landed 200 yards or so farther from the winning cross did not then seem to be of importance, as we appeared to have the race to ourselves, and so I did not descend as I should have done had I known that another competitor had landed, and quickly deflated to obliterate his position. As we neared the ground we saw a crowd of people to our left, but for the moment we did not associate this collected crowd with one of the descents of the balloons, because we thought it was simply a crowd that had collected in the neighbourhood of Burchett's Green waiting for the balloon to come along. A few minutes later our car came to the ground—namely, at 6.56, in a field in the parish of Hurley, which is the parish containing the winningpost. The field which we struck contained a crop of beans, and, not wishing to damage them, we were carried immediately from the beans into a grass field near by, where the deflation was quickly effected."

Last year I again accompanied Mr. Brewer, this time in the " Vivienne," in the International Point to Point race instituted by the Aero Club.

Before starting I expressed a wish that instead of

making Tye Common the goal, Boreham House, with its beautiful lakes, which would be visible for many miles, would be far preferable, and make it easier for those who had a lesser knowledge of the country than myself. I also stated that when we got into a higher altitude than the small pilot balloons were in, when seen leaving Hurlingham, we should get the breeze a bit more from the south, and so get blown north of Billericay. My deductions proved correct.

At the rate we were travelling we could easily have done the extra seven miles, and packed our envelopes, netting, etc., by daylight. At one time we could count ten balloons, not including our own; the year before double the number were visible when half the journey was covered.

When over Pyrgo Park we were within talking distance of the "Valkyrie," which was a good second to the "Lotus" in the previous year, and a good deal of aerial badinage passed between the pilots. Suddenly Mr. Pollock, who had with him Princess Blucher and Mrs. Assheton Harbord, shouted, "We've run out of ballast!" and they at once commenced to descend—in fact we could see them bumping away almost immediately below. Though they landed several miles from the goal they were within measurable distance of winning a prize.

The highest altitude we reached was a fraction over 7,000 feet. Our descent was in a fallow field. We narrowly missed the brickwork over a well; and while rising diagonally over a belt of trees the trail rope fouled them; but shortly afterwards we succeeded in landing comfortably in a grass field about 300 yards from Writtle Park.

In July, last year, I took part in the Hare and Hounds Aerial Race, as a passenger in Baroness Von Hercheren's "L'Espérance," piloted by Mr. Brewer.

This year I have been up twice, both times from Hurlingham in the "St. Louis," piloted by John Dunville, whose wife accompanied us on each occasion. The first was a long distance race, in which we were second, the winner being the Hon. Mrs. Assheton Harbord. We came down at Tattingstone, in Suffolk, where we were most hospitably entertained by Mr. and Mrs. Kerrison. Curiously enough, in the second race, a point-to-point, the positions were exactly reversed, Mrs. Harbord coming in second, and ourselves first. On this occasion we made our descent at Purleigh, six miles from my house.

The present year has seen a complete revolution in the art of aerial navigation, and the recent sensational achievements of M. Paulhan and Mr. Grahame-White have astonished those who, like myself, were inclined to scout the much-talked-of "Conquest of the Air." It only goes to show how unsafe a thing it is to prophesy about anything in this world.

Personally, I hope to do a lot more ballooning yet, and perhaps a little aeroplaning as well. The latter would add a zest to the rest of my sporting experiences, and perhaps provide me with a new sensation —who knows?

But it may be thought that I ought to be getting past the time when a man may expect to enjoy "new sensations." The rather saddening reflection that there may, in the ordinary course of nature, come a time when I shall have to address myself to tamer

pursuits than steeplechasing and other more or less
hazardous forms of sport, has flashed unwelcome
across my mind once or twice of late years.

Still it will be my endeavour, after the example
of not a few good men I have known and heard of,
to see the thing out, and in the world of sport, like
them, to drink " life to the lees."

What the public will think of a man who has not
fully sown his wild oats, though over sixty years of
age, and of a life which has been almost entirely given
up to various sports and adventures in all parts of the
world, is not for me to predict. It may be that the
verdict will be that such a life has been chiefly mis-
spent, for it is an age rather devoted to the carking
cares, the ceaseless anxieties, and the restlessness of
business than to exploit and adventure ; and in the
" getting and spending," in the piling up—as well as in
the losing—of fortunes, that the powers and thoughts
of very many of us are centred. Such things indeed
must be ; a drone myself, so far as the strictly
work-a-day and commercial side of life is concerned,
I fully recognise this. It would not do for us to be
steeplechasers and balloonists all. Yet there are
many who share with me this belief in sport, in its
even more robust and adventuresome side, as
necessary to the development and prowess of the
rising generation of Englishmen; and they, at any
rate, will perhaps regard with leniency some of the
escapades herein set forth with all endeavour to avoid
exaggeration and inaccuracy.

In conclusion, I will admit that the extreme fre-
quency with which the first person singular has come
to the surface throughout these reminiscences has

somewhat discomforted me once or twice. But in a book of this kind it is not possible to altogether avoid conveying the impression of being rather an egoist. It has been a real pleasure to turn from my own doings to those of the host of sportsmen and good fellows whose ways have, from time to time, been my ways. If anything has been related of these comrades likely to give unintentional pain, I trust they may pass an act of oblivion, and I ask them to feel assured that nothing has been set down in malice. For the rest—

> " What is writ,
> Would it were worthier ! "

Printed by Hazell, Watson & Viney, Ld., London and Aylesbury.

Lightning Source UK Ltd.
Milton Keynes UK
UKHW021906270621
386263UK00002B/8